PLEASANT GOOD EVENING — A MEMOIR

My 30 Wild and Turbulent Years of Sportstalk

DAN RUSSELL

Tellwell Talent
www.tellwell.ca

ISBN
978-0-2288-6731-9 (Hardcover)
978-0-2288-6730-2 (Paperback)
978-0-2288-6732-6 (eBook)

DEDICATION

To my son Ben, his sisters Palita and Anna, and their mom Paula.

AUTHOR'S NOTE

It was the wee-est of hours. 4:45 a.m. June 15, 1994.

It was nine hours after the world's most famous trophy had been presented, and nearly seven hours after *Sportstalk* had signed on a few blocks away from the World's Most Famous Arena. Now, after dramatic riot coverage, heart-breaking game analysis, gut-wrenching dressing room interviews, media reaction and marathon phone response, it was time for one last call. After all, despite the Canucks' loss to the New York Rangers, the sun had decided that it was still going to rise over Vancouver.

"*Sportstalk*, go ahead."

"Dan, thanks for taking my call. You won't believe this. I've been hitting redial since the show started, and now after all this time I'm finally on."

Despite deciding in primary school that I wanted to be a broadcaster, not once while growing up did I ever consider I might one day become best known for hosting a sports talk show — let alone becoming a trailblazer while doing so. Not even high-quality radar would've detected that. How could it? Aside from a few short-lived Vancouver market attempts in the '60s and '70s, this radio genre was rarely thought of and never taken seriously. Most importantly, my heart's desire was calling the game while *it was on*, not talking about the game when *it was over*. And certainly not on off nights. Or off seasons.

It was only after a thrilling double-overtime Vancouver Canucks win at Chicago Stadium in 1982, followed two days later by Roger Neilson famously waving a white towel, where I felt something was seriously amiss. No one anywhere on the radio dial was talking about these incredible games when they were over.

Surely I wasn't the only die-hard wanting so much more. Was I?

Two years later, *Sportstalk* was born, and with it — long before email, texts, smartphones and social media — a gathering spot for local fans was established; it became an on-air forum often more impactful than the game broadcast itself. It was the dessert after the main course, serving die-hards and casual fans of all ages.

With its blend of guests, callers, opinion and entertainment, *Sportstalk* kept growing and growing until it had become appointment radio. And it seemed most of British Columbia was buckled in as we travelled home and away in 1994 — on game nights and off nights, weekdays and weekends, often extending well past midnight — during the Canucks' most memorable playoff ever.

As for that caller who tried all night only to get through moments before our sign-off? He made it on the air *after* the Canucks' charter had already landed at YVR.

—— ∞ ——

If I had a nickel for every time someone approached me suggesting that I write a book, well, I would have a whole lot of nickels in my bank account. What those people didn't know is that during my radio career, I was a tenacious keeper of notes — almost to the point of hoarding. I also kept a log detailing every episode of *Sportstalk* — every guest, how many phone calls, what worked, what didn't, and on and on.

I spent August 2013 on vacation and used the opportunity to hammer out the roughest of manuscripts, with only my kids in mind, figuring if I didn't document my life's work they might never really know what their dad had done with his life. I put it away after the summer, went back to doing the show and didn't think much about it. Until, like most everyone else, I needed the perfect project to keep me busy during the COVID-19 pandemic.

Even though few broadcasters have interviewed more book authors than I have, it took going through this process to really appreciate what must happen to turn ideas into words and ultimately into an actual book. That was the fun and the grind. But the most rewarding part was appreciating what we accomplished during our decades-long *Sportstalk* run for the first time.

And while first and foremost I wanted this book for my kids, I also wanted the *Sportstalk* legacy on the record and to give my loyal listeners a behind-the-scenes look at what was really going on before the familiar music played and before I uttered those same three words I used at the beginning of every show.

TABLE OF CONTENTS

CHAPTER ONE

Jesus saves! And Esposito scores on the rebound!

You could be excused for thinking that my thirty years as the host of the trend-setting *Sportstalk* was a fairy tale existence.

Actually, it was… and it wasn't.

By the time my career in radio ended, my business card could have looked like this:

Dan Russell CJOR CKWX CFMI KMPS CKNW CISL

Those letters aren't indicative of university degrees, but they do indicate the speed bumps I may have encountered as I made my way through the Vancouver radio scene.

Anyway, while it all didn't start at a fifty-watt radio station somewhere in BC, I could make the case that it began in the visitors' dressing room at Pacific Coliseum…

———

So there I was at the ripe old age of nineteen, nervously walking into the dressing room of the New York Rangers, an NHL original six team, clutching my first NHL press credential, issued simply because I was the sports director of our campus radio station at the British Columbia Institute of Technology (BCIT). But what started as an incredible experience, further cementing my sports media desires, would soon be going south.

Just a few hours earlier, while wearing the unofficial media uniform — sports jacket, dress shirt and tie, slacks, black shoes — I had arrived at the Pacific Coliseum, picked up my pass and game notes, and enjoyed a free buffet. Then I was escorted high to my press-box seat, one I had so longingly stared at so many times from below since I began going to NHL games in 1970.

I had always been more interested in the coverage of the game than the game itself. The view was incredible. Not just of the ice, but also the press box, as I sat in awe of people whose coverage of the Canucks I had listened to and read for years. John McKeachie and Robb Glazier to my right. Archie McDonald and Tony Gallagher to my left. Big Al Davidson, Bill Good Sr., and Babe Pratt one level below.

I tried to soak it all in. For all I knew this might be a one-off, an experience to tell my children about sometime in the future when we would stare up together from the cheap seats. How would I describe it to my future son? The mature me would say something along the lines of it being my first step in what turned out to be an incredible media journey, one that led me to essentially invent a radio forum and preside over a gathering spot for all these fans around us, and many more around the city and province, in a way no one had ever done. Whereas immature me would have called the whole thing intoxicating, something that left me wanting more. So much more.

At game's end, it was time to visit an NHL dressing room area for the first time. Other than falling in line with all the other media types in the march down several flights of stairs to the basement level, I had absolutely no idea of the post-game protocol. So I simply copied the others and stood outside the visitors' dressing room waiting for Fred Shero, the Rangers' head coach, to emerge. When he did, we swarmed him. I was trapped at the back of the scrum, barely able to hear anything, except when the legendary coach said, "That's it boys; the room's open."

Being farthest from Shero meant I was closest to the dressing room door. That forced me, in tight quarters, to walk in first. Yes, I was the lead dog in this media pack despite having absolutely no idea what to do. All I could do was pretend I'd been there before.

Before arriving in Vancouver, the Rangers had been stumbling, allowing twenty-five goals in their previous five starts. And on this particular night they needed to score late to beat a mediocre Canucks team. In other words, aside from winning, it was less than pretty. That wasn't important to me. What was important was to get some interviews on tape for the next day's BCIT campus radio show.

As I continued my walk into a much quieter dressing room than I had expected — what the heck did I expect? — the first player I saw, in fact one of only a few who made themselves available, was the legendary Phil Esposito.

Many thoughts were running through my young head, including how just thirty seconds earlier I had been that close to Shero, remembering how much I hated him for leading the Philadelphia Flyers, his goon squad, to two Stanley Cups. I especially disliked him for having beaten my Boston Bruins. Also, what the heck, it was pretty clear I despised Shero more than Esposito because Phil now was playing for him! But there was Espo, late '70s-style long hair soaked with sweat, wearing that black turtleneck undershirt he always wore during games, hockey pants still on, skates off, peeling the tape off his hockey socks and chucking the balled-up strips towards a garbage can near the far wall. Even though he had scored the winning goal on this night, he looked less than satisfied and not exactly approachable.

That led me to my first big decision as an accredited NHL reporter. Do I approach big Phil straight on or do I veer off, stand back and defer to other reporters? Many have used that bailout approach over the years: hover, wait for someone else to start the interview, then casually stick in a mic, making sure the flasher call letters are in clear view of TV cameras. Slide in, slide out, seldom ask a question, get paid. Every market has a few of those types.

In a split second I not only made my decision but surprised the former Bruins sniper by sitting down beside him. I really had no idea if I was supposed to make myself at home — but hey, why not?

I then conducted my first of what would be more than twenty-five thousand interviews. After seating myself beside Esposito, my first concern was making sure I hit both the play and record buttons on my cassette machine. Then I plunged ahead and asked if I could "please" talk to him.

"Yup — go ahead," he said.

Whew! That was easy. It wasn't an official question, but the man who once scored an amazing seventy-six goals in one season, had three times scored more than sixty in a season, and was one of Canada's greatest hockey heroes had just spoken to me.

Then came my moment of truth. There was no way of knowing how many questions I would ask sports figures over the next few decades, but for my first one …

"Phil" — I addressed him by his first name even though every bone in my body was thinking I should call him Mr. Esposito — "I know you feel good about winning, but was it difficult playing from behind most of the night and just squeaking out the win?"

Or something along those lines. It wasn't a bad icebreaker, if I do say so myself. But like many a flashy player caught admiring his own pass in open ice, I got hammered! Absolutely levelled by his response.

"You see that's the big trouble with freakin' reporters like you," he started, speaking slowly and glaring straight into my eyes. "Do you think the game is freakin' easy? Well, it's just not. Yeah, we've given up a lot of goals, but everyone knows sometimes that happens," he said, with only slightly less animation than he showed during his famous 1972 Summit Series post-game interview with CTV's Johnny Esaw, about sixty-five feet from where we were now seated. "You guys should be able to figure that out. That's the way hockey goes!"

He continued for about twenty seconds before concluding with this dagger: "You guys are all the same."

Gulp! All the same?

I wanted to say, "But this is my first interview, that was my first-ever question, and you're grouping me with everyone else?"

If only I could have told him how much I had cheered for him. Well, actually for Bobby Orr, but by extension admiring him, Derek

Sanderson, Johnny Bucyk, Wayne Cashman, Ken Hodge, Gerry Cheevers and the rest of the big bad Bs.

If only Phil knew that was the reason I even liked hockey, that I was one of those tens of thousands from my generation turned onto the sport because of Orr and his Bruins.

If only I could've explained to Espo how I, too, nearly flew through the air as Orr did in winning the Stanley Cup on Mother's Day of 1970, or how happy I was two years later when they defeated the Rangers to again lift the Cup.

If only he had known how much I despised the Montreal Canadiens, every Jacques, every Guy and especially the seemingly unbeatable Ken Dryden with his leisurely trademark pose — chin resting on his folded hands atop his stick during stoppages in play — because of Orr and the Bruins.

If only he had known that even after the Canucks came into the NHL, knowing full well I would need a backup, Boston would still be my "co-favourite" team.

If only he had known how much pleading I had to do with my dad before he finally relented and put my favourite bumper sticker on the back of his Buick LeSabre: "Jesus saves! And Esposito scores on the rebound!"

To this day I can't remember what my next question was. I only know that I was able to keep the conversation going.

And going …

CHAPTER TWO

Hanging out with Pete Rose

Before you get the impression that BCIT was home to this bustling campus radio station, I must disclose that in those days, years before the Canadian Radio-television and Telecommunications Commission (CRTC) granted the school a low-frequency signal, we only programmed to the public-address speakers located inside the Student Association Centre (SAC).

Coincidentally, this meant that I started and finished my career broadcasting to folks in the SAC — with the bulk of my audience over the next three decades listening while in bed. But I digress. At BCIT we were "playing radio," which, come to think of it, was an extension of what I'd been doing throughout my childhood.

Before I turned seven, my dad, Ken, who worked for BC Tel but had a love of radio when he was younger, took our family to the Pacific National Exhibition (PNE) where Vancouver radio stations often set up in order to broadcast on location. I remember standing outside CKWX's remote trailer, watching with fascination as this heavy-set disc jockey spun the records. When he turned on his mic and I heard his voice transmitting from the loudspeakers above the trailer, I was captivated. I stared through those windows for so long that he eventually asked me to come inside. I stayed for two hours — bypassing the wooden coaster, octopus and all the other rides my siblings were enjoying. I wish I could remember the name of that disc jockey because he greatly influenced me. Watching him work was like viewing a magic show.

How did he know what to say? How did he cue up that record? Where did those commercials come from? Why did it look so easy?

But it was my dad who had given me the bug when a few months earlier he made sure I got my first radio. To this day, that black Sony 8 transistor AM radio is the best Christmas gift I ever received. Still vivid in my mind is being tucked into bed that Christmas night with Dad saying I could listen to the Vancouver Canucks WHL game as I was falling asleep.

Allow me to pause on that thought for a moment, as I can point to December 25, 1967, as the exact day I fell in love with radio and hockey — in that order. This night marked my introduction to Jim Robson, who was calling this game from Portland on CKWX. Though so young, I still remember wondering why they — the Canucks — were playing on Christmas night. And why was Robson telling me they would return home tomorrow, and that's when he and his family would celebrate Christmas? What? A man on the radio actually calling a hockey game? On Christmas night? And that man saying he'd be with his family tomorrow? This was too much. I was hooked. From that Christmas night in '67 until the early '90s, I listened to, without exaggeration, every single game called by Robson, the radio voice of the WHL/NHL Canucks for more than 40 years.

Soon after that PNE visit, Dad set up a home studio in our basement that allowed me to play radio. This would occur several days a week for years, and over time my home show would evolve in its sophistication. Two turntables for records, a tall stack of vinyl 45s (new ones purchased from Richmond Centre each Saturday), my own microphone (with CKDR call letters), a cassette machine loaded with commercials I had taped off local radio, plus a freshly typed program log that I would initial after each of the (fake) ad spots aired.

Long-time friends of my older siblings say they used to eavesdrop from outside my studio. They never said they were laughing, but I would have been. My only known listener was Mrs. Rice, who lived next door and could hear my show, but only during summer months — not via a magical AM radio skip but when it was too hot for me to keep my windows closed.

I've always considered myself extremely fortunate to have known what I wanted to do at such a young age. My only question was: How would I make it happen?

By Grade 4, I remember hearing about BCIT, even though John T. Errington Elementary didn't exactly employ career counsellors. Grade 5 was exciting because that's when the Canucks entered the NHL, and my friend Tracy Sapera took me to a game against Toronto — the Canucks' second game (first victory) — on Thanksgiving Sunday, October 11, 1970, a day before my tenth birthday. By Grade 6, I was memorizing NHL rosters and the names of arenas and announcers. I had a book with separate pages and logos for each team, plus a bio on every coach, including the Canucks' Hal Laycoe. In Grade 7, Paul Henderson scored hockey's most famous goal to win the 1972 eight-game Summit Series and, like in most schools, we were allowed to watch the final game on a large black-and-white TV set in the gym. However, I bolted across the street to our home early in the third period in order to peacefully watch the amazing end in living colour on our new twenty-six-inch Zenith.

No one could possibly have known then I would one day have original Canucks captain Orland Kurtenbach on *Sportstalk* reminiscing about being the first star in their first win, Laycoe bragging about his half-dozen twenty-goal men that season and Henderson confirming not a day goes by when someone doesn't tell them exactly where they were.

Even though I would one day talk to some of the world's greatest athletes, I did not excel in sports. I played house soccer (Dad was the rep coach and he cut me) and baseball (mostly outfield while batting low in the order). I did win Richmond's U12 tennis table title — yes, before the demographics drastically changed around my home. I didn't play hockey unless you count endless games on the road with my friends.

I did, however, excel at making money, as I always had a job. The first one was also in the media, delivering the *Richmond Review* on Wednesdays and Fridays, and collecting the subscription fees long before local papers gave up and delivered them for free. My next job set the tone for many of my adult years. A local farmer paid me five dollars per stall to clean up after his horses after school. I also caddied at the Richmond Golf Club, sold Dickey Dee ice cream from a bike, umpired kids' baseball and refereed high school girls basketball.

At fourteen, I launched into full entrepreneur/marketing mode by designing small advertising cards that claimed I could cut lawns, wash cars, paint fences, and babysit. I delivered them around my entire neighbourhood. By the time I reached Matthew McNair Secondary, I tailored my high school courses to be BCIT friendly. I also was the creator/editor/writer of *Rumours*, our school newspaper, and often was asked by friends to call whatever game was being played in the gym.

Mostly I was known for my mock horse races, usually in a classroom setting, sometimes on a bus during a field trip. Here I would use the names of ten classmates who entered the starting gate in preparation to run six and a half furlongs. The races always featured one horse (invariably Brad Robinson) breaking slowly. The pack would always be tightly bunched as it went around the clubhouse turn before beginning to separate on the backstretch. And there was always an incredible stretch drive with someone — usually the favourite Terry Rose — edging out Mike Kerr, always by a nose. All of this would take place as each student loudly pounded on their thighs, simulating the sounds of the horses' hooves.

By this time everyone, especially my family, knew how badly I wanted to broadcast. Perhaps too much so, as I recall one night at dinner when Dad told the rest of the family how one of his biggest wishes was for me to get into radio.

"Why?" asked my older brother Brian.

"So we can turn him the hell off," Dad responded playfully.

My advertising card worked, most notably with Eve, a friendly woman from down the street, who asked me to babysit. Her husband,

Bill, was a teacher, so it didn't strike me as odd when one day he asked what I wanted to do when I finished school. I told him I wanted to be a disc jockey or a hockey play-by-play announcer. He then asked if I had ever tried calling hockey games. Only from television, I said. He replied that I better start practising now. It turned out that he was the head coach of the Vancouver Jr. Canucks, who played out of the PNE Forum. After asking me to check with my parents, he invited me to join him so I could practise calling games.

I quickly discovered I sounded terrible! Actually, it was worse than that. Not only was I super green, but also, logistically, I didn't know how to do this with fans in the buildings, fans who I'm sure didn't want to be disturbed from watching any more than I could bear the thought of anyone hearing me. So I parked myself as far away as possible, isolating deep in one end zone. Naturally, this made things extremely hard when play was at the other end. Nevertheless, despite far less than ideal conditions, I forged on and slowly honed my play-by-play skills.

My "audience of one" was the coach, who (if they won) would want to hear some of the game on the drive home. He claimed it helped him recreate the game in his mind, as video as a coaching tool was nearly nonexistent then. The coach? That was Bill Wilms, who years later would be my broadcast partner for hundreds of WHL radio and TV games. A year later, Wilms became head coach of another team in the league, the Kerrisdale Couriers. Naturally, I was — unofficially — part of that deal. This was exciting because the old Kerrisdale Arena offered something much better for me. It had an actual press box that meant, for home games at least, best friend Mike Milholm, my colour man, and I wouldn't have to whisper while sitting among the spectators.

January 2, 1978, was the day I could finally apply to BCIT, and I was there at 9 a.m. My application package included a resume, demo tape, letters of recommendation from employers and teachers, plus a three-page handwritten endorsement from Wilms. Two months later, I was asked to come in for an interview with local broadcaster Terry Garner, best known as the long-serving host (1961-82) of *Reach for the Top*, the CBC quiz show for students. Not only was Garner extremely intimidating, he wasn't nearly as impressed by my package as I was. All I took from him was, "You're too young and we won't be accepting you."

Say what?

This famous broadcast school I'd been dreaming of and working towards since age ten didn't want me? I was heartbroken and stunned. And who was this washed-up old game-show host to dash my broadcast dreams in less than fifteen minutes by telling me I was too young? The fact that he may have been right was beside the point.

With two months before graduation and not knowing what to do next, I began scouting other broadcast schools and discovered that as long as I ponied up the money — much more than BCIT's tuition — they would cheerfully accept me at the Columbia School of Broadcasting or something called the Fraser Radio Academy, which was run by Frank Callaghan, who, to me, possessed the personality of a fire hydrant. That was something I'd learn all too well only three years later when he would become my boss!

As I was seriously considering which of those two I could afford, a letter arrived from BCIT. I figured this would be a form letter thanking me for my interest and inviting me to try again next year. That's why I haphazardly tore open the envelope, barely noticing that it was nothing of the sort.

"Dan Russell has been officially accepted into the BCIT broadcast journalism program; radio elective," it read.

I was stunned again.

Old man Garner became the great/illustrious/fabled Terry Garner of CBC fame. The man who so professionally hosted the greatest quiz show ever, while also overseeing the top broadcast journalism school in all of Canada! Honestly, I don't know what changed. I just knew my first broadcast dream had been achieved, and I was on cloud nine.

Come to think of it, Cloud 9 was the name of the restaurant high above Robson Street in downtown Vancouver where a Pete Rose media gathering took place in February 1980. The greatest hitter in Major League Baseball history was to be a paid guest for the Vancouver Outdoor Show, so, naturally, I believed our non-existent BCIT audience ought to hear me speak with Charlie Hustle. Off I went in my red 1968 Volkswagen Beetle to the iconic revolving restaurant. Upon arrival, I listened to the opening speeches then waited my turn as Rose was made available for one-on-one interviews.

I knew my rightful place in the media pecking order, so I patiently waited. And waited. And waited some more while the established media types conducted their interviews. It felt as if Cloud 9 might revolve around the moon before it would be my turn. Again, I didn't have an issue being last, but when my time came, Rose suddenly said he had to go because he didn't have any more time for interviews. Instead of dejectedly walking away, I naively explained to the man who undoubtedly would be a first-ballot Hall of Famer that I had waited a long time for a chance to speak with him. Rose surprised me by not only apologizing but by saying, "If you want, you can come by the hotel tomorrow afternoon and I'll do your interview then."

I'm sure he had sized me up as a young nothing burger, which I absolutely was. It's why I'm certain the last thing he expected was to get a call from the lobby of the Bayshore the following day just after 1 p.m.

"Hello," he answered.

"Is this Pete Rose?" I asked.

After he confirmed it, I said, "This is Dan Russell calling. I met you yesterday at Cloud 9, and you said I could interview you today."

After about two seconds of silence, which felt much longer, Rose asked, "Where are you?"

"In the lobby," I cheerfully replied.

Again there was a few seconds of silence before Rose said, "Sure, come on up."

What? He's not coming down to the lobby? I thought. *He wants me to come up to interview him in his room?*

After asking his room number, the next thing you know I — along with tag-along classmate Graham Gurniak — was in an elevator heading for the top floor, the same floor billionaire Howard Hughes famously had blocked off during his much-publicized reclusive six-month stay eight years earlier.

We timidly knocked on the door. Rose's manager opened it and welcomed us inside. We walked down a narrow hall towards the main part of the suite and there was the thirty-seven-year-old Rose — already a winner of two World Series titles (with a third to come), a World Series MVP, eventually to be a seventeen-time all-star with three batting championships and the most hits in MLB history — lounging on a large sofa, wearing grey sweats, a baggy T-shirt and white socks.

Rose, extremely friendly, stuck out a hand and said, "Come on in, have a seat." His eyes were glued to the TV coverage of the Lake Placid Olympic Winter Games. "If you're not in a hurry do you mind watching with me?"

Do we mind? Are you kidding?

The next thing we knew he was offering us soft drinks and snacks as we settled in to watch the action from Lake Placid. Surreal doesn't even begin to cover this. The Olympics are on, Pete Rose is lounging in his sweats, he's feeding us and asking our opinion on the various events, and I'm pinching myself. It would be another week before Al Michaels would utter his most famous Olympic line, but in my head I was beating him to the punch, asking myself: "Do you believe in miracles?"

We ended up watching for about an hour before Rose asked if I was ready to interview him. He was as kind and generous on tape as he had been off mic. Years later, Rose made huge news by being assessed a lifetime suspension by MLB for betting on baseball, which, among other things, means he is ineligible for the Hall of Fame (HOF). I have always thought it was a ridiculously harsh penalty because Rose wasn't found guilty of betting when he played, nor did he ever bet against his team as a manager. Others felt otherwise, one being Rod Beaton of *USA Today*, *Sportstalk*'s highly respected baseball expert. Beaton was on the HOF selection committee and I tried countless times, without success, to get him to change his mind. I did feel strongly that Rose should be in the Hall. But, truth be told, I also was trying, in my own small *Sportstalk* way, to pay back Rose for the act of kindness he had shown me years earlier on the top floor of the Bayshore.

CHAPTER THREE

Dreaming the dream

Young and aspiring with narrow horizons. That was fifteen-year-old me, who had eyes on only two positions: hockey play-by-play announcer or disc jockey.

Naturally, it would turn out to be Door No. 3. But well before *Sportstalk*, I wanted to be the next Jim Robson or perhaps the next "Raccoon" Carney.

Not the semi-maniacal screaming "Raccoon" whom I first heard early evenings on CFUN 1410 — effectively noticeable, but nowhere near my comfort zone. More like the friendly Raccoon in the Afternoon on LG73 — and yes, it was big news when he jumped from CFUN (Pepsi) to CKLG (Coke).

Raccoon — given name Ralph Carney Albani — once was kind enough to invite me to watch his show at 1006 Richards Street in a building that had housed some of the biggest Vancouver radio personalities heard from the late '60s through most of the '70s. Watching him in his domain, in full command, especially when teeing up his "Raccoon Tune of the Week," was intoxicating.

The radio habits of kids my age were basic. We constantly bounced between CKLG and CFUN. Our car radio preselect buttons were set up the same. Push hard on the button located on the extreme left and you were on 'LG, with the one on the far right taking you to CFUN. The odd time, when both were in commercials, we might venture over to 1220 to hear what CKDA Victoria was playing. Meantime most parents would likely choose CKNW, CJOR or CKWX.

I preferred 'LG because I loved its announcers. The two big breakfast stars were the edgy "Real" Roy Hennessy at the start of the '70s and "Doc" Harris with his must hear "Harris Report" at decade's end. CKLG also had the incredibly smooth Fred Latremouille; "Jolly" John Tanner, who was fired for telling his listeners he'd seen a license plate that started with the letters FUK; Rick Honey, who would go on to CKNW fame; Darryl B (the B should have stood for Boss Radio); Jim Hault; Don Stevens; Stirling Faux; and Mike McCoy, who in the middle of the night would open up the "love lines," asking female callers, "What are your numbers?"

CKLG in the '70s was bright, tight and never boring. Unlike most anything you hear today, the DJs were active between every song, only had three-hour shifts and were as big a part of the station sound as the music. Same with the catchy jingles: "Everything we do, we do it for you ..." The news aired at twenty minutes before and after each hour. Every weekend was a "Solid Gold Weekend" that included the weekly Top 30 on Saturday mornings. The most anticipated show of the entire year was the Top 100 countdown on New Year's Eve. Trust me, it was a big moment when they finally revealed the year's top song. I listened to it all, taped tons of it and was shaped by it. Plus, it was always so exciting to be introduced to and (without internet lyrics) sing along to the great songs of that era.

Had you asked me in my mid-teens if I would have taken a career as a DJ at 'LG, there wouldn't have been any hesitation. Just as I never thought about how much money André Boudrias or Don Lever were making to play for the Canucks, I honestly never wondered what kind of money those radio guys were making. Nor did I wonder about the kind of management/bean counter/political bullshit that might be going on behind the scenes, all of which I would encounter during my career.

Attending BCIT was terrific. Not just because I got to meet Esposito and Rose but because I got to practise radio. During first year especially, I would often stay for hours after school and return on weekends to practise in an authentic studio that was more advanced than my home version. I also made friends like Scott (Verecchia) Russell, Craig Henderson, Tom Thomas, Heather Murdoch, Elaine Scollan, Graham Gurniak, Rob Robson and Dave Doroghy, and instructors John Ansell, Brian Antonson, Don Hamilton and many others.

Terry Garner had probably been right to be concerned about my age, not just because I was ordering beer with my classmates as an underage at the Burnaby Villa, but because I was the youngest in the class. It felt strange to be in seminars with some classmates who were up to ten years older. Mind you, I'm sure it was weird for them to see me arrive some mornings when I'd been up all night doing an actual graveyard on-air DJ shift at CJOR.

I may have been the youngest, but I also turned out to be a wunderkind of sorts.

Because BCIT was a two-year program, it was common for students to try to get summer radio jobs between years. I definitely wanted one of those and knew where I wanted to be. Our family vacationed annually in the Okanagan and, as I did in Richmond, I would scan all the radio stations at night, often while sitting beside a campfire on the shores of Wood Lake. That is where I discovered CKIQ Kelowna, which was a smaller scale hybrid between CKNW and CKLG. Once when I was about fourteen, I asked my parents to pull over outside CKIQ's station on busy Harvey Avenue. When I went inside and explained that one day I wanted to work there, the friendly receptionist surprisingly offered me a quick tour.

I already realized that essentially all broadcasters of that era needed to start in a smaller market, and I had mapped out in my mind how one day I would do the 'IQ graveyard shift, catch a few hours sleep and then hit the beach in the afternoon. There was a problem though — every other broadcaster in that area seemed to have the same dream. I never did get to work there, but I was unusually thrilled years later when CKIQ became a *Sportstalk* network station.

I would occasionally pop in when I was in the area just to roam the halls and meet the staff.

As was the late first-year BCIT tradition, our class hopped on a double-decker bus for the annual provincial tour of stations. All year long we had heard the legendary stories from previous class trips — the tours, the alcohol-induced frolicking and, yes, some hookups. Perhaps because I was youngest, my class elected me as the top-deck, front-row bartender. We were stoked to go.

The trip took us through Kamloops, Salmon Arm and the Okanagan, then north through the Cariboo, reaching as far as Prince George. Two months earlier I had decided the best way to ensure getting a summer job was not to apply to only a few stations but to all of them — tiny markets like Princeton, small markets like Penticton, medium markets like Prince George, semi-large markets like Victoria, and the biggest market, Vancouver. I dubbed fifty audition cassettes, photocopied fifty resumes, painstakingly found the names of fifty program directors and typed fifty personalized cover letters before stamping and licking (yuck) fifty oversized envelopes. Having never been away from home on my own, I was extremely excited by the prospect of being a DJ in any small town and starting to live independently, if only for two months. To me, the scatter-gun application strategy had to greatly increase my odds.

As hoped, I did hear from two radio stations before our tour began, with both wanting to interview me when our bus came through town. Only three of us had interviews lined up, and I was the only student to have two. It was Dan Russell vs. Scott Russell for a daytime job in 100 Mile House (population: 1,800), and Dan Russell vs. Craig Henderson for an all-night job in Prince George (population: 76,000). As it turned out, yours truly, Mr. Wunderkind went 0 for 2. I was already envious of Henderson because he had worked as an all-night DJ on CKOK Penticton before BCIT. Now I was jealous of both of them.

However, this turned out to be the first of a few times in my life when I learned that the job you sometimes don't get can turn out to be a silver lining. Before boarding the bus for the ten-hour trip from Prince George, I called home and my mom told me CJOR's program director had called with an urgent message — I was to see him as soon as I returned.

So much for living independently.

CHAPTER FOUR

"Available at Woodward's"

Randy Taylor was the thirty-something bespectacled program director at CJOR who would later tell me the only reason he hired me was because I was wearing a sports jacket and tie when I came in for the interview. I don't remember much about the interview, only that it turned out to be the most important one of my career.

Still in my first year at BCIT, I was about to advance to a much greater campus than the one on Willingdon Avenue in Burnaby.

CJOR became my underground campus. Since the early 1940s, it had been located in the basement of the 1913-built Grosvenor Hotel at 840 Howe Street. CJOR is where I really found my calling and ultimately my call-in show. But long before that, I was hired as a board operator with a few other duties for $3.50 an hour. One of those duties was to work the phones for helicopter traffic reporter Linda Lee, calling various police departments and highway, border, tunnel and ferry patrols, then conveying the information to Linda, who thus was able to sound like she was everywhere.

I did that every afternoon after operating an hour of the *Terry Moore Show*, which was hosted by one of my favourite people. Moore was a multi-talented broadcaster/actor who could do it all — even sing opera. As a host, Moore was a Jack of all trades. He could interview anyone, but he was also an authority on household hints. As a kid I remember hearing him on CKWX when his listeners jammed the phones asking him — not some expert guest — the best way to remove mayonnaise from corduroy pants, fix paint cracks in a ceiling, and deal with rodents in an attic. He even shared different cooking recipes. A precursor to syndicated home improvement radio expert Shell Busey?

Once during my first week on the job, Terry left the studio late in a commercial break. I didn't know why at the time, but he was testing me to make sure I didn't panic. I didn't.

Of all the things I did in broadcasting, board operating may have been my greatest skill. I'm not kidding and I'm not bragging because no one aspires to be a board operator, but I was damn good at it. I was organized, always ahead of the game, tightly played commercials, expertly screened calls, set up the incredibly archaic CJOR delay system and had strong chemistry with the hosts, which I would learn years later was extremely important.

In a move that rightfully irritated Terry, the program director had legislated that twice per hour the talk flow would be interrupted by a hit song.

"We'll get back to the BC premier in just a moment, but first here's Poco with 'Crazy Love' on CJOR 600."

Just one of so many decisions I'd see from program directors during my career that made me shake my head.

During this era, CJOR's lineup included Monty McFarlane in the morning, John Reynolds' hard-hitting political talk show, Moore, John Wilson, the famous *Hot Line* with Pat Burns, and weekend programming that included three hours of gospel music with Wilf Ray and a pair of deeply religious shows every Sunday hosted by Bernice Gerard, a Pentecostal minister.

I may have been a good operator, but my confidence nearly cost me early one Sunday evening in 1978. I was operating Ray's show while listening to a Canucks game from Chicago. Volume-wise in master control, I'd say the hockey broadcast was at 80 percent and the Ray show at about 20 percent. I also had my feet up on the console, leaning back while eating a snack. That's when this man, equally short in height and hair, walked in. You know that feeling when you recognize someone but for a couple of seconds can't place them? Well, within those two seconds he had walked closer and extended a hand.

"Hello, I'm Jim Pattison."

Never in my life had I snapped so quickly to attention. In one swoop it was feet off console, food put away, hockey game turned off, CJOR program turned up and me nervously replying, "I know, and it's nice to meet you."

The multi-billionaire owner of the station was there to see his good friend Wilf. However, Pattison wasn't aware that Ray uncharacteristically had taped his show that night. When Pattison bid me farewell, I honestly thought the radio station might bid me the same after he reported back on my less than professional demeanour. I did have a couple of sleepless nights, but it wasn't ever mentioned.

Years after successfully running Expo 86, the richest man in Vancouver appeared on my show predicting how well Vancouver would do as an Olympic city. My P's and Q's were just fine on that night.

I'm not sure how this piece of radio station programming brilliance came about, but someone surmised that CJOR's geriatric listener base ought to be treated to eight hours of uninterrupted disco music every Saturday night. And it was my responsibility, along with host Phil Roberts, to make this pulsating sound come to life on an AM signal. Roberts' voice tracked the show, leaving me with a giant stack of vinyl records, his cold intros and anecdotes on a reel-to-reel tape, along with firm instructions to not screw things up. We mostly played extended versions of hit disco songs. For example, Rod Stewart's "Do You Think I'm Sexy" was usually a four-and-a-half-minute song, but on Disco Saturday Night our version was nearly nine minutes.

Other songs lasted as long as fifteen minutes.

Gary's Gang, Gloria Gaynor, Donna Summer, the Village People and dozens more — we lined them up each Saturday and played them, repetitive lyrics and all. And I was careful because I knew Roberts was listening at home.

My disco shift ran to midnight when I gave way to Dave Doroghy, who had to maintain momentum until his all-night show began at

2 a.m. Dave is a much nicer guy than I am but a far worse board operator, something that was best illustrated during a midnight disco transition when he got busy chatting and didn't notice that he was playing the 45 rpm extended version of "Freak Out" at 33.

"Awwwwwwww frrrreeeeeeeeeek ouuuuut" is how Chic's smash hit song sounded on CJOR, which is what Roberts was doing at home while frantically calling our emergency line. (Every control room has a special number with its own special ring. It's never good news when it rings.) Doroghy picked up, but before he could even say hello, we both heard Phil screaming on the speaker phone.

"FUCK DAN! WHAT THE FUCK ARE YOU DOING? THIS SONG IS NOT PLAYING AT THE RIGHT FUCKING SPEED! COME ON! GET YOUR HEAD OUT OF YOUR ASS!"

As I said, Dorg is a much nicer guy, which might explain why he wasn't about to correct Phil, even though Roberts should have known I was no longer operating. Instead, Dave threw me even deeper below Howe Street when he adjusted his voice to a higher pitch and said, "I'm really sorry Phil, it won't happen again."

Before Roberts could respond, Dave hung up.

I remember the maze of CJOR's dungeon-like layout as if I was there yesterday.

Walking into the hotel off Howe Street, you took a few steps past the lobby bar, then down some dimly-lit stairs. Once at the bottom, if you turned left you were in a men's washroom for bar patrons. To the right was the station's front door, which had all the charm of a place where you might get your dentures fixed or your taxes done. In no way did it scream radio station.

Three steps inside those doors and past three mismatched waiting room chairs, you were already at the entrance to the main studio that housed so many talk giants during its heyday. One door to the left was Master Control featuring a long list of eccentric Al Erdman engineering quirks that somehow seemed to always work. Down the hall was the main production studio — okay, the only production studio — which was home to Al Jordan, a man so influential to me that my middle child, Anna, carries Jordan as her middle name.

Next to that was a closet studio where one of my jobs was to edit four-minute hit songs into 150-second versions because CJOR was either playing ten-minute disco songs on Saturdays or two-minute hit songs for Monty's heavily advertised weekday breakfast show.

Heading in the other direction took you to the pint-sized CJOR newsroom, which probably measured 10x12 feet. It may have been tiny, but some terrific broadcast journalists worked in there like Maury Hesketh, Frank Stanford, Tom Mark, Kim Calloway, Dave Hankinson, Hal Rodd and Richard Dettman. They all strongly competed against CKNW's vaunted newscasts. It was exciting watching the competition, especially when they had a big story that Warren Barker's team didn't.

Off air, Stanford was a bundle of energy who, wearing a bright Hawaiian shirt, would arrive each morning around 4:30 with a Pepsi in one hand and a cigarette in the other. A smooth and unflappable communicator, Stanford truly understood the craftsmanship of one-to-one broadcasting. Once while on air, he spilled hot coffee on his lap, turned off the mic, yelled "FUCK!" so loud the entire station heard it, turned the mic back on and calmly said, "In other news ..."

Calloway was of the same ilk. Effortlessly smooth on the anchor desk, even better in the field, which figured because years earlier he had been on location for the Martin Luther King and Robert Kennedy assassinations.

Moving a few steps past the undisputed grungiest coffee room in radio station history and now deep in the dungeon was the sports department, which was headed by the well-organized Garry Raible, who also prided himself on competing strongly against the "Top Dog" (CKNW) down the dial.

Number two in the department was Ian Michaud, the most eccentric man with whom I ever worked. Best known as the voice of the Vancouver Whitecaps during their North American Soccer League (NASL) glory days, Ian was infamous off the air for five things that seemingly mattered most in his life: Germany's Borussia Monchengladbach soccer club, famous English author/humourist

P.G. Wodehouse, banjo-playing legend Earl Scruggs, bowling star Dick Weber, and opera. Michaud didn't drive me nuts with those things, but his love of rain sure did, especially the night we were returning in a driving rainstorm after a Whitecaps broadcast in Seattle. We were in Ian's late model Jaguar with his sunroof fully open! And yes, with opera music blaring through the full-range, high-quality speakers.

Though I worked with him for years, Ian didn't share much about himself. I knew he had done hockey play-by-play in Kamloops. He told me he got the Whitecaps gig because he was the only one at CJOR with that kind of experience. Never mind that he hadn't called soccer. Who had? But to this day I've never heard anyone better, especially when you consider the sport barely lends itself to radio. He also was kind to me, and he even tolerated — without complaint — when they occasionally threw me into the booth to serve as his inexperienced NASL analyst when Raible wasn't available.

Somehow money wasn't an issue to Ian, so much so that CJOR's accounting department often begged him to cash his cheques (no direct deposit then), which he often kept for several months before depositing. Bob Lenarduzzi once told me when the 86ers had financial problems, Michaud would on occasion loan the club money to help make payroll.

Red-headed Rob Ironside was the number three member of the sports team, working weekends and beat reporting.

I tried to figure a way to join their club, but first I had to figure out a way to get on the air. It was one thing to be a strong operator working for cheap, but this major-market station was in no hurry to have a greenhorn on its airwaves.

That was the absolute right call, even if I didn't think so.

How can I illustrate just how CJOR felt about this? While operating the talk shows, it was common for a live tag to be read on behalf of the sponsor at the end of their commercial. Example: A spot would air for a company selling a new fishing reel, and when it was over the board operator was supposed to turn on their mic and say something like: "Available at Woodward's."

Three words. What could be so wrong with letting me announce three freakin' words? Plenty, it seemed, because they wouldn't let me and I was getting livid.

Those in charge would examine the commercial log when I was operating and, when they saw spots that needed live tags, they would ask a house announcer to pre-record them.

"Sale ends Saturday," Bob Dawson might record.

It got to the point where I would study the logs as soon as I arrived just to see if they'd forgotten to record one. The odd time I'd notice one scheduled several hours into my shift and hope no one would rush in at the last minute with a recorded version. When they didn't, I'd turn on the mic and go for it. Unlike the lack of quality control often exposed today, our PD would notice, state his unhappiness and pay closer attention during my next shift.

As my frustration grew, the one who most often heard my whining was production manager Al Jordan, who, late each afternoon, would come into Master Control with a tall stack of commercial carts he had produced to file them for future airings.

"If you want to come to my studio after your shift, I can work with you," Jordan once blurted.

Though I didn't know it at the time, it unquestionably was the greatest radio offer I ever received. Almost immediately I began working with the best broadcast teacher anyone could dream of, someone who took a genuine liking to me because (as he told me years later) he loved my passion.

In the '60s, Jordan was Happy Pappy and one of the locally famous Good Guys on CFUN alongside Brian Forst, Fred Latremouille, Tom Peacock, Red Robinson and Ed Karl. Al also had been Vancouver's first DJ for teenagers — *Theme for Teens* — and had helped bring along Robinson.

Jordan would become as fine a commercial voice as has ever been heard — anywhere! Seriously. Anywhere. He really was that good. Often called "Vancouver's perfect pitch" by local ad agencies, his voice was heard on radio and TV stations around North America.

When *Sportstalk* debuted a few years later, I was incredibly honoured when Al agreed to be our announcer and introduce me every night. I was especially thrilled when he brilliantly narrated our tenth anniversary special.

"You're listening to *Sportstalk*. Weeee open the lines. Youuuu open the mind. Here again is Dan Russell."

It always gave me goosebumps. Still does, in fact.

Everyone was struck by his incredible pipes, but many were unaware that they were his second-best tool. Knowing how to use them so effectively to lift words off the page was his true talent. That's what he tried to teach me.

Jordan insisted I come to his classroom every day where we would begin with his unique warmup. Similar to an athlete stretching before playing, we would do that with our lips and tongues. Al would demonstrate by flapping and loosening his lips and making peculiar sounds. He'd also hold his lips together as if he were playing a trumpet. Then we would each recite vowels — with big versions, mouth wide-open.

"AYYYYYYYYY, EEEEEEEEEEEEEEEEEEE, EYEEEEEEEE, OHHHH, YOUUUU."

All designed to loosen the mouth. Years after he taught me that stretch, I'd do this prior to each show as the *Sportstalk* theme was playing, "A, E, I, O, U."

In those sessions, Jordan would give me commercial copy to read and make me go over it and over it — on his own time after his shift — to see if I could lift some of the words off the page.

Thanks to my U of Jordan sessions I was getting better, though I'm pretty sure the only reason I was soon reading live tags was because Al went to the PD and said, "Give the kid a chance." It didn't matter to me. I was actually on the radio a couple of times an hour with proclamations like "All sales are final!" After getting that taste in my mouth, it wasn't long before I was craving more.

A few weeks after being green-lit to read tags, I asked program director Bob Mackin if he would consider allowing me to do an occasional overnight disc-jockey shift. Mackin — or Buff as Ian Michaud would call him, alluding more to his bald head than his heavy stature — was a knowledgeable programmer and a successful sales rep. Gruff on the outside, soft on the inside, he laughed at my request. But only momentarily. After a few weeks of begging, along came a Saturday night when Doroghy couldn't work. Mackin asked me to operate the Whitecaps game then an abbreviated disco show before carrying on hosting the all-night show.

On July 29, 1979, at exactly 2:05 a.m. — right after the announcer said, "More news when it happens" — I pushed the cart machine button in Master Control that started The Beach Boys song "Good Timin'." And with that, my not-so-memorable DJ career was launched! Like all Beach Boys songs this one lasted two minutes, twelve seconds before it was time for me to speak. All these years later, I'd like to apologize to any of the nine listeners who might've heard me in the wee hours of that morning.

Also, I'd be lying if I told you there was any other reason they let me on the air other than my enthusiasm and work ethic. Years later, in fact, GM Harvey Gold called me "the hardest-working person in the radio station."

It wasn't historic, but it was real. From fictional bedroom studio to 10,000 watts of major-market airwaves. I was actually doing it!

For many years after Al left CJOR, he and I would talk once or twice a week for two or three hours at a time. I so much looked forward to those calls. My own father wasn't someone I could talk at length with about the business or even share life's problems. But I could with Al. If we missed each other, he'd leave messages which were sometimes better than a live call. He would leave such encouraging words and I would keep replaying them just to hear his beautiful voice.

When we became friends, Al was divorced and had become, by his own admission, something of a recluse living on East 6th in a one-bedroom apartment that I occasionally visited. I knew how much he loved his three kids Randy, Brook and Laura. I also knew every October 12 I'd receive a warm birthday greeting, as I shared the same birth date as Laura. I prefer to think he would have remembered anyway.

Until he died in 2009, no one taught me more and no one believed in me more than Happy Pappy, the great Al Jordan.

CHAPTER FIVE

Skipping at night

Who would have thought a transistor radio, that Christmas gift in 1967, and the phenomenon known as the "AM radio skip" could have such an impact on one person's life? The transistor introduced me to Jim Robson, the skip to Larry King. They inspired me and I idolized them. Greatly. It isn't that I didn't have respect for so many others, but Robson and King were my broadcast heroes. When I started listening to Robson, I couldn't stop.

First, it was cool to hear Canucks games from buildings I had never heard of — like the Salt Palace (home of the Salt Lake City Golden Eagles) and the San Diego Sports Arena (home of the Gulls). But as the years rolled on and my Jim Robson Ironman streak continued, my obsession became trying to figure out what made him so good at his chosen profession. I later learned that listeners in most local markets think their guy is the best. They are wrong.

For instance, because Edmonton Oilers fans heard Rod Phillips scream so many "happy goals," they believed he — not just the team — also must be great. They even put Rod's banner in the rafters. But had the Oilers' first two decades been like Vancouver's, it's doubtful such an honour would've been bestowed. Fans of the Pittsburgh Penguins loved Mike Lange but, while "scratch my back with a hacksaw" is funny, it is apropos of nothing. When the short-lived Atlanta Thrashers scored, Scott Ferrall, their announcer with a bizarrely scratchy voice, would start screaming: "And I need a freshie, I need a freshie!"

The purist in me wasn't interested in being remembered for the cutesy stuff. I preferred the textbook stuff. Maybe that's one of the best things about Robson's body of work — he never had a shtick.

The days of local listeners having special bonds with their radio announcer are mostly gone. But for decades the announcer-listener relationship was huge, especially with baseball, hockey and basketball, each with their long schedules. In terms of consistent, accurate and the (seemingly) effortless art of calling games, the cream of the crop in those three sports was Vin Scully (Dodgers), Jim Robson (Canucks) and Chick Hearn (Lakers). Those teams' fan bases were beyond spoiled.

Robson made it such a joy to close your eyes and follow the puck all over the ice, and it seldom got from one end to the other without passing through the neutral zone. Only a purist would pick up on that, along with his tremendous ability to self-edit on the fly, his near perfect word economy and his incredible feel for the game. Jim's craftsmanship and knowledge was the result of calling so many games in so many sports, but his brilliance — it was the same with the other radio greats — was thoroughly understanding this most intimate of mediums. He knew that even though thousands were tuned in, he was talking to each on a one-to-one basis.

Radio sports is the ultimate theatre of the mind, and when presented by the masters there's nothing like it.

"At this time we'd like to pass along a special hello to hospital patients and shut-ins, those of you who can't get to hockey games."

"The Canucks are wearing their home whites with blue and green trim defending the north goal to our right."

"The weather today in Pittsburgh was unseasonably warm ..."

"A hard shot deflects into the crowd — ohhh, I hope that didn't hit anybody."

Had I studied the Bible as closely as I studied Robson, I would be a theologian. I knew his strengths. His near perfect description. His inflections and a build-up that never cried wolf. And especially his ability to stay a step ahead of the play so that the soundtrack of the crowd was always in synch with his voice. His anticipation seldom let him down. Other broadcasters often sound frantic just trying to keep up, but Robson seemed to dare the game to go faster because he knew all the short cuts.

Then there was his fairness, which nowadays isn't only rare but no longer even encouraged. Yes, we assumed he wanted Vancouver to win, but that was the extent of it. Much different from today's often blatant cheerleading approach. Robson was fair to both teams, which was a by-product of radio stations hiring the talent; today it's the home teams who are doling out their headsets to house guys. Long before there was a gondola named after Robson, he called games with two teams on the ice.

For example, when the other team scored, Jim didn't sound as if he had suffered a paper cut. If the Canucks were playing poorly, he let you know. Same if the game was ragged or play was sloppy. He wouldn't trash the sport, but he never insulted his listeners' intelligence.

Robson's most famous Canucks goal call was in the 1994 Stanley Cup playoffs. "Greg Adams! Greg Adams! Adams — Adams gets the winner, fourteen seconds into the second overtime. The Vancouver Canucks are going to the Stanley Cup Final!" He once said on my show that he wished he'd had something better to say. Yes, being humble also was part of his charm. That goal call was so tasty in its simplicity. But lost in all the noise was how brilliantly descriptive Robson was in the few seconds before the bedlam.

Play had just started in the second overtime, and even though Toronto had won the faceoff, the Maple Leafs quickly turned it over. As the Canucks moved into the offensive zone every word out of Robson's mouth was descriptive.

"Trevor Linden with the puck turning on the left boards."

Then it was Linden making a smart pass to the line and Dave Babych's long shot that Robson got away as quickly as Babych did because Robson seemed to sense that he needed to. But what makes this call so subtly great — so damn Robsonesque — is that he doesn't simply say "Babych's shot was stopped." Rather, in the moment, he tells us how Leafs' goalie Felix Potvin "... had trouble with it." And he says it with such an urgent inflection that, as a listener, you felt almost unbearable anticipation. You felt your breath stop as you waited to hear what would happen. That's when, on the rebound, Robson says: "Adams shoots, scores!" Robson was that descriptive long before the climax and before the PNE exploded with noise.

The fact that Robson didn't like his Adams call was typical and not offered as false modesty. Knowing his work as well as I did, having interviewed him countless times, having golfed and played racquetball with him, having dined with him, having been on the NHL road with him, and having visited with him and his wife Bea on the Gulf Islands and at their Vancouver home, I am convinced that he never realized how good he was.

The radio skip — used to describe the atmospheric conditions that allow AM radio signals to travel long distances and made possible because the regulatory broadcast bodies in Canada and the United States require many stations to reduce their power at night — allowed me to tune in to faraway stations and bring them into my bedroom. Long before anyone had heard of the internet, it was a thrill to eavesdrop on faraway stations. For example, I'd listen to talk powerhouse KGO 810 out of San Francisco. Ronn Owens ran a conversational, thought-provoking show starting at 10 p.m., taking calls from the East Bay, Contra Costa, Marin County, Oakland and other Bay Area suburbs.

I listened to polarizing overnight host Ray Taliaferro, as well as funky Al "Jazzbo" Collins on weekends, who started his show with "Blues in Hoss' Flat" by Count Basie and was infatuated with train horns. On occasion, I would listen to Art Finley. (Years later, I was Finley's board operator at CJOR and knowing my fondness for KGO he once arranged for Collins to record a personalized birthday greeting which I still have.) At the end of each KGO newscast, the announcer would give the forecast followed by the various temperatures around the Bay Area. always concluding with: "And on your radio ... it's 81."

On KNBR 680, I could hear San Francisco Giants games from chilly Candlestick Park. During several of our phone conversations, Al Jordan and I would compare "skipping" notes, and I always remember him being tickled on those nights the KABC 790 signal skipped and we could hear a couple of innings of the Dodgers with his favourite announcer, Scully.

My absolute favourite, though, was KFI 570, the flagship station for the NBA Lakers and NHL Kings. This was the first time I had heard basketball on radio, and I was blown away with Chick Hearn's ability to stay on top of action that went end to end so much more quickly than hockey. Hearn was legendary not because he was the first to use "slam dunk" and "air ball," but because of his distinct staccato, a rapid-fire call and an amazing streak of having called 3,338 consecutive games.

Meantime, hearing the voice of the Los Angeles Kings was extra special to me because "Jiggs" McDonald was only the second person I had heard call a hockey game. Jiggs was told to use that name rather than his previous on-air name (Ken) by team owner Jack Kent Cooke, who also insisted McDonald use nicknames for certain players — Juha "Whitey" Widing, Eddie "The Jet" Joyal, Bill "Cowboy" Flett and Réal "Frenchy" Lemieux. It's doubtful that the first and last of those would get past today's censors. Oh, and the Kings' home rink, the Los Angeles Forum, had to be the "Fabulous Forum."

The sponsor tags also intrigued me.

"Kings hockey is brought to you by your Southern California Datsun Dealer — and by the Atlantic Richfield Company, home of your local Arco Dealer."

Even on the clearest of nights, the KFI signal would frustratingly fade in and out, but when I heard static I often would stay with it, waiting and hoping for it to skip back. I was in radio and hockey heaven with two teams and two announcers. If you thought that made me a little off, wait until you hear the nerdiest part of all this. When the Kings and Lakers played on the same night, basketball would air live with the hockey game following on tape delay. I loved this because by 11 p.m., the radio skip usually was much clearer, sometimes making KFI sound like a semi-local station. Now I was able to hear tape-delay Kings games from eastern venues, something I wouldn't have been able to do had they aired live.

But mostly I liked Fridays because that was the main home-game night for the Lakers and Canucks, which meant that on the few occasions when Vancouver hosted LA on a Friday, I could hear the same game — twice! As usual, I would listen closely to Robson live, but then I couldn't wait until 11 p.m. to hear a visiting radio announcer to find out how he described the big parts of the game that I knew were coming, especially the goal calls. This was when I discovered how the same game can actually be described with different slants. Again, I know this was nerdy, but this was my early love affair with radio.

I was lucky to have the LA Kings, but was most blessed to have discovered Larry King, the overnight talk-show workhorse heard from midnight to 5 a.m., reaching upwards of six million listeners per night on about two hundred Mutual Radio Network stations. I really loved King's format — one hour of straight interview with a guest, two hours of calls to that same guest, then two hours of "Open Phone America." King brilliantly weaved his way through all of that, and just as I had done with Robson, I made it a mission to figure out how he did it.

Jumping out was his highly effective though simple interview technique, which I broke down into four areas, especially once I was on a talk-show path. First, King asked short, thought-provoking questions, none open-ended because he knew if the question was short the answers were often refreshingly thoughtful.

Example: If Larry was interviewing the head of a police force, he might ask, "What makes a good police officer?"

Many other interviewers seem to want to show off or hear their own voices.

Example: "It's obvious police officers should uphold the rule of law, but don't you think they should be fair-minded, have compassion and communicate well? Maybe even be a good negotiator?" In that case, the expert guest is often left with: "Yes, I'd say that's right."

Secondly, King listened to the answer and logically followed up, allowing the interview to flow. When you listen to any interviewer closely, you can quickly tell if they understand this.

For a short time, newspaper writer Tony Gallagher went head-to-head with *Sportstalk*. One day, he confessed to me that when he first started he would be so busy worrying about the next question off a prepared list that he wasn't even hearing how the guest was responding.

"Russ," Gallagher told me in his high-pitched voice, "Mike Keenan could've told me he murdered five people on the way to the studio and I would've next asked why his power play was struggling."

Thirdly, King felt no reason to insert himself into his interviews, refusing to use the word "I" in any question because he rightfully felt the opinion of the interviewer is mostly irrelevant.

And lastly, King worked off few notes because he wanted to be at the same level as his listener, learning from his guest at the same time, allowing him to react in real time more authentically.

King's favourite question was one word: "Why?"

It's a perfect follow-up question that most broadcasters seldom use. (Even non-broadcasters should try that question with a friend and see how it enriches the conversation.) No one I've heard was more sincerely curious than Larry. It's why he could interview anyone from any walk of life and bring out the best in them.

In his final two hours each night, King fielded unscreened calls on any topic. A caller from Denver might talk about Ronald Reagan's tax bill and the next caller from Milwaukee might ask about the Brewers' bullpen. The quality I admired most in King was his not being afraid to respond to a caller with "I don't know." It's sad how many insecure hosts there are who are unable to display this kind of humility. In today's common two-host world, you might hear a caller ask a question, followed by a pause, followed by one of the hosts killing time while you know the other is frantically searching the internet for an answer. Emulating King served me well because I discovered that if I didn't know something, some of my listeners would. This would prompt a few to call in and help when they may not have otherwise been inclined to go on the air. It's one way I made *Sportstalk* feel like our show, not mine.

As an added bonus, Larry was a huge hockey fan, often arriving at his Washington, DC, studios directly from a Capitals game. He loved all sports — he once was a radio analyst for the Miami Dolphins — but he was a baseball purist. When the Seattle Mariners heard that one of Larry's biggest broadcast regrets was never having called a Major League Baseball game, Dave Niehaus, the M's great broadcaster, offered King the chance to fulfil his lifelong dream by calling three innings the next time Seattle played at nearby Baltimore. Naturally, I had to hear that, too, but I knew the radio signal of the late afternoon game wouldn't reach Vancouver, so I decided to drive south that day.

First, I had to explain to the border agent why I was entering the USA. After his eyebrows went down and he granted me entrance, I drove south of Bellingham until the signal was clear and I could hear King call baseball. If only all the I-5 commuters had known why I'd pulled over to the side of the highway.

How much did *Sportstalk* eventually pattern King? More than anyone ever knew.

For example:

— King didn't call it open line, it was "open-phones," so we did too.
— Larry created nicknames for some callers, as we later would.
— He didn't take a newsbreak, rather he paused for news on the hour. So, we paused as well. Though we didn't pay homage to great American radio storyteller (famous for his pauses) Paul Harvey, as King often did,
— After every commercial break, King's show played the start of a pop song as his announcer, Fred Lowry, reintroduced Larry. Al Jordan reintroduced me the same way.
— Larry would begin some hours referencing his fictional studio audience located one floor below, and every night we referenced our fictional *Sportstalk* orchestra.

— King did an annual Christmas show, so *Sportstalk* had to as well.

No one made the connection. Then again, the odds that any of my Vancouver listeners knew a Larry King radio show even existed, let alone had stayed up all night studying its format, had to be extremely slim. So as much as I idolized Robson, it was King who was more impactful, presenting a talk-show road map that served me well for decades.

"You're listening to the Larry King show. Call 703-685-2177. That's 703-685-2177. Let the connection ring, we'll answer when it's your turn. Once again, here's Peabody Award-winner Larry King."

Not sure why, but King's show intro is still ingrained in me.

Between the LA Kings and Larry King, between Robson and "Jiggs," and between KGO and KFI, it's a wonder I got any sleep as a kid. Yet I always made it to school and never skipped out.

CHAPTER SIX

"Why would you want to give up *Sportstalk?*"

I could argue that getting that transistor radio was a double-edged sword. Yes, it opened my mind to career possibilities, but it also caused me to dream big. Perhaps in an unhealthy way. As I've since concluded, concentrating all my energy on capturing one of only thirty big league positions may have been setting myself up for a big fall. Also, what would happen if I became unquestionably qualified but, for a variety of reasons, didn't land the big fish? That's what happened to me, and it's not something I counted on.

I'm not saying I have huge regrets. My love of radio provided me with so many professional rewards, but it also resulted in a lifelong itch that I wasn't fully able to scratch. As I've made clear, calling NHL games in any city was the only job I wanted, which, as a starting point, is flawed. I was fixated on getting there for all my formative years. Every job I took on, paid or otherwise, was designed to improve my sound and strengthen my chances. Board operating, sportscasts, disc jockey, junior hockey broadcasting, Seattle WHL radio — even *Sportstalk* — was something I looked at as providing a boatload of "on-air hours" that eventually would lead to an NHL broadcast booth.

Every bone in my body was dedicated to earning one of these positions. Getting there would be a long process, one designed to weed out the non-committed, so I figured that success would be based solely on merit.

That was a mistake on my part.

The first time I met Jim Robson, I was thirteen and had approached him in the lower press box at Pacific Coliseum, the same location from where I would be so thrilled to call many Western Hockey League games, as he was getting ready for a *Hockey Night in Canada* telecast. I chatted with Mr. Robson for a few minutes and shared that it was my dream to do what he does one day. He just smiled. Then he signed a Jim Robson Enterprises business card that I still have. He also told me the Thermos on the desk contained hot tea to soothe his voice (as if he thought this kid suspected something stronger), and he showed me the egg-timer he used as a reminder to give the score.

The next time I met him was two years later when I was working as a busboy in the upper dining room at the Quilchena Golf and Country Club in Richmond. Robson had played in a charity event and was relaxing as the banquet was winding down. Once again, I struck up the courage to approach him to say how much I admired him and again share my dream. To this day I can see him sitting in a big soft chair outside the dining room, holding a glass of red wine.

"Well, young man, you're going to have to stand in line," he said.

Years later, once I joined CJOR and was at the rink daily, Jim got to know me better. I enjoyed that very much and also felt getting close to him wouldn't hurt my long-term chances of positioning myself.

After starting *Sportstalk* in the mid-'80s, I continued doing play-by-play on community TV (for free), including games involving the WHL New Westminster Bruins and a number of Junior A clubs. I also practised calling "mock" NHL games from the Pacific Coliseum. On those nights, I'd take my bulky cassette machine, climb to the catwalk and carefully navigate over many creaky and sometimes loose wooden steps high above the ice surface before finally going down a steep ladder to settle into one of the corner spotlight booths. This set-up was far from ideal but not just because of the frightening walk. I had to sit high above one corner of the ice, there wasn't a headset mic, and without a table I had to balance the lineup card on my lap. Still, I ventured up there many times for an audience of none, knowing it'd help me improve. I would often record Robson's broadcast for comparison purposes. I recall once being happy about a particular breakaway I had called, but was then deflated when I heard how much sooner Robson had the puck on the player's stick.

Soon I struck up the courage to ask Jim if he'd critique my work. Not only did he agree but he invited me to his house. Once we settled into his family room, Robson asked, "How critical do you want me to be?"

"Give me the strongest critique you can," I replied.

Something strange came over me as we were about to begin. It wasn't that I believed a great sounding tape would lead me to a job, but I was convinced a terrible one would do me in. I also was thinking how strange it was for this man I worshipped to be about to listen to me call a game. When he hit play, it became even more awkward. I was looking at him, but his eyes never glanced my way. He stared at the other side of the room or the speaker itself, just as kids of his era did growing up listening to radio plays like the *Green Hornet* in pre-TV days.

It was excruciating. I tried to pick up on his body language — anything for a clue — but he hadn't written any notes yet. About three minutes in I thought it was a good sign that he hadn't stopped the tape yet. Just as I thought that was a positive — bang! — he paused it.

"This would've been a good place for you to have given the score," he said.

The cheeky part of me wanted to tell him there wasn't room in the spotlight booth for an egg-timer.

He quickly hit play again, and darned if I didn't immediately give the score. I didn't show any expression, but I did a cartwheel inside my mind. After about eight minutes he stopped the tape again and said he'd heard enough, which meant I had to brace myself. It's doubtful any *American Idol* contestant would have been more anxious to hear their result, which is why I can still remember, word for word, what Jim said.

"Honestly Dan, I was ready to give you some pointers, but there's nothing there I can critique. I could follow the puck, you identified all the players, your flow was fine and you had good inflections."

If he said anything more I either didn't remember or didn't care because I had been given a private seal of approval from hockey's greatest play caller.

Not much happened immediately after that, except Robson kept masterfully calling games for many more years and I kept gaining more *Sportstalk* traction. On occasion, I would discuss play-by-play with Jim, knowing that eventually he would come to the end of his road. Yet each time I brought it up, his response seemed to get less encouraging. His dream-crushing go-to reply always seemed to be, "Why would you want to give up your talk show to do play-by-play?" I never gained the Robson play-by-play support I so desperately craved, but he highly respected what my *Sportstalk* career had become, often telling me how much he enjoyed the show.

At the end of the WHL season in 2007, I had called about eight hundred junior games and was enjoying them even with the knowledge that my NHL dream was likely over. Two weeks earlier I had experienced my career play-by-play highlight when I called the epic WHL final between the Vancouver Giants and Medicine Hat Tigers, one that culminated in a Game 7 that went to double overtime. It was one of the greatest — and most viewed — games in league history. Jim told me he had watched many of the games and mentioned how impressed he was by the calibre of play and the TV production. But there wasn't a word about the work into which I had poured my heart and soul. It saddened me because that series was my Stanley Cup Final, and the dramatic game-winning goal — scored by the Tigers' Brennan Bosch in the fog on a steamy night in the old Medicine Hat Arena — was my Bob Nystrom OT Cup winner.

Just as a player knows how well they played, I knew I had done some of my best work in that series, which is why I thought Robson might have mentioned something — my accuracy, excitement level, goal calls, identifying players in the thick fog, working in amongst the spectators, anything. Had he picked just one I would have been pleased. As you probably can guess, he didn't.

"Dan," he said, "I still don't know why you would want to do play-by-play when *Sportstalk* is so successful."

If I could go back, would I pursue my NHL dream the same way? No, I wouldn't, even though in my heart of hearts I believe I had as much talent for calling games as I did in hosting *Sportstalk*. My regret isn't failing to land a full time NHL position but rather foolishly believing that ability mattered over all else. I held up my end of the bargain in terms of paying dues, improving my sound and building credibility. It still hurts not to have fulfilled my dream.

However, I have found a way to come to grips with this subject. Forgive my brashness, but to find my inner peace, I decided I would rather have been a good WHL broadcaster who didn't get to the big leagues, rather than someone like John Shorthouse — who eventually did solidly grow into the role — but who was handed a big-league job despite not having paid any dues. He didn't commit his glaring learning mistakes at a lower level in much smaller, sometimes foggy, arenas. But I'm the only one to blame. It was unhealthy for me to have put all my broadcast dreams in one basket.

CHAPTER SEVEN

Lonely CISL nights

One of my favourite CJOR gigs was operating the Vancouver Whitecaps during their historic 1979 run to the NASL Soccer Bowl. That was me behind the control board getting Ian Michaud and Garry Raible on the air, playing the commercials, screening callers for the post-game call-in portion and producing our coverage of the unexpectedly large victory parade.

Around that same time I also operated *The Rafe Mair Show*. Aside from Patti, Rafe's wife at the time, sitting on my side of the glass every day giving Rafe the batty eyes, the thing I remember most is getting to make a special call on our private line on Friday mornings. For weeks before and during the start of Terry Fox's Marathon of Hope, it was my job to call him wherever he was. We would chat for a few minutes as he caught his breath before going on with Rafe. It wasn't something out of the ordinary at the time, but in hindsight it was an incredible honour, something my kids like to tell their friends about on occasion.

It felt like a national kick in the gut when Terry was forced to end his run in Thunder Bay, Ontario. He died a few months later. I'm still amazed as to Terry's modest goal of raising one dollar from every Canadian. All these years later, his run has raised almost a billion dollars for cancer research.

On *Sportstalk*, I often expressed my disappointment with our various levels of government for not doing more to honour Fox's worldwide legacy. How is it possible that BC Place Stadium wasn't named — or renamed — after him? One night, on an anniversary of his death, I strongly suggested his name be attached to the airport. Terry Fox International at YVR still seems quite logical to me.

As my time at BCIT was nearing an end, I knew I'd soon be leaving CJOR in search of a full time on-air position. I was more than prepared to work outside of Vancouver, which used to be part of the deal. You would make your on-air mistakes in a small town, then if you showed improvement you moved up in market size. Sadly, the days when budding broadcasters travelled that path to hone their craft are essentially gone. As a result, the on-air product — if anyone still cares — has been hurt with too many amateurish-sounding broadcasters making their mistakes in Vancouver rather than Vanderhoof.

Before I could pack my bags, the CRTC granted a unique radio licence to a small station in our big city. If that sounds strange, it was. But that's what happened to create CISL, the call letters playing off the name Sea Island, which, along with Lulu Island, is where Richmond is located. This was my first foray into a world where a would-be broadcast ownership group promised the CRTC everything it wanted to hear in order to get a licence. This group convinced the commission that CISL would be all about serving Richmond with local news, sports and community events. At the time I didn't care about the licence. My only thought was: Who better to work at CISL? I was graduating from BCIT, had experience at CJOR and, most importantly, was born and raised in Richmond.

Shortly after I applied, Ian Alexander, CISL's first program director, asked me to come in for what I thought was an interview. Instead, he immediately stuck me in a studio to do an audition on the spot (the only time that ever happened to me). Two days later, Ian called to congratulate me on becoming the first all-night disc jockey in the station's history. My first full time on-air shift would be midnight to 6 a.m. for $700 a month, before taxes.

CISL 940 — just a tad to the left of the big boys (CKNW 980) — officially signed on at midnight on May 1, 1980, with yours truly having the honours. What a thrill it was to broadcast my own show just four kilometres from my old bedroom studio. Just like I did at home, CISL played vinyl records, making it feel like real radio. And, unlike today, we had some freedom as to what we could play. The only all-night sponsors were the Bucaneer Pub at the Steveston Hotel, Cronos Pizza, and Rod's Building Supplies. Their spots played over and over until I couldn't stand them anymore.

One downside, however, was loneliness. No one else was in the station, and CISL's newly-developed and mostly vacant business park, called Ironwood, was scary in its isolation. Worse yet, master control was located at the front of the one-level building, completely visible to anyone who passed by or, heaven forbid, placed their face against the glass.

A few times a week I'd have visitors from the Richmond RCMP on their nightly patrols. At first they would drive by and wave. Then they started scaring the crap out of me by approaching the studio without headlights, waiting until I turned away towards the microphone and, just as I started talking, turning on their blue and red lights, sometimes even their siren. I began inviting them in for coffee and, yes, they often brought doughnuts. They enjoyed watching a radio show in person. We had some great visits which invariably would end when they received a call.

The constable I became closest to was Tom Agar, who, late in the summer, informed me he was having knee surgery and would be temporarily relegated to desk duty while rehabbing. A few weeks later, on September 19, 1980, Agar got up from his desk to offer routine assistance to a man who had rushed into the detachment. Unbeknownst to Agar, this man, later identified as Steven Leclair, had just shot five people (three of whom died) at a beer parlour in Vancouver. He had hijacked a taxi to take him to the Richmond RCMP, and as Agar got up from his seat and limped over to help him, Leclair shot and killed him.

I was shocked. Agar was the first police offer I ever knew. Only five years older than me, he left behind his pregnant wife and their eleven-month-old child. As is customary when a member dies in the line of duty, officers came from all over to pay their respects. The Agar funeral, at the large St. Joseph the Worker Parish on Williams Road, was so crowded that I could only listen to the service on speakers from the church parking lot.

The mandate of the station changed a few months into the CISL operation when they hired Arnie Celsie to be the morning man and program director. He was my boss and the biggest jerk I had come across.

Celsie came from Oshawa, so right away I was suspicious of this outsider controlling our Richmond-oriented station. I never saw eye to eye with Arnie, especially when he added one more hour to my shift and one more day to my week. Worse yet, he insisted that I was to drag myself out of bed on my only day off and report to him by 11 a.m. for an air-check review (used by all programmers to go over announcer strengths and weaknesses — not unlike sports coaches reviewing game footage with players). However, Celsie didn't show the first three times. He didn't tell me why, nor did he apologize. How does that old saying go? Fool me once, shame on you; fool me three times and you're a prick?

Complicating things further was Arnie's love for Glenn Crouter, the son of long-time CFRB Toronto morning man Wally Crouter, who somehow was running CISL's sports department. Glenn possessed what some of us in the station called the Crouter Hat Trick: Clueless when it came to organizing. Inept in terms of writing (or even being able to type, as many of his 'casts were scribbled in pen). And, most of all, he sounded like a rank amateur. On the plus side, he seemed to be a hit with the ladies. I was frustrated and envious because, even though I was doing a few sports shifts, I would have preferred doing that full time versus overnight DJ work. But Celsie kept holding me back. I was later told it was because I was making Crouter look bad.

One day Celsie told me I was no longer allowed to attend Richmond Sockeyes games, as I'd done since the team was born in 1972. He said Crouter didn't like all the attention I received from so many of the fans who knew me.

Finally, after being stood up too many times for air-check meetings, thwarted in my quest to do more sports and banned from attending games, I found a small measure of revenge. As part of a *Breakfast with Celsie* promotion, the station announced it would be delivering three hundred breakfast baskets to random homes. These gift baskets comprised orange juice, bacon, bread, danishes and other goodies, in addition to Celsie show promo coupons and stickers. Naturally, Celsie tasked me with delivering them, claiming it was because I knew Richmond better than anyone else. So, having just finished an all-night shift, another junior employee and I loaded the CISL van and headed out.

I don't know if it was the sight of all this breakfast food, but after dropping off a couple dozen baskets, we were too hungry not to stop at McDonald's for an Egg McMuffin. I'm not sure if we were tired or just fed up with Arnie's bullshit, but before resuming our deliveries, I started wondering who would know if people didn't actually get the gifts. The next thing I knew we were dividing the remaining baskets and our delighted families found themselves knee-deep in bacon, bread and juice for months.

"How did everyone react?" Celsie asked when we returned to the station.

"You wouldn't believe how happy the people were who got them," I said.

Because *Breakfast with Celsie* was far from a hit, Arnie was forced to endure a blow to his ego when he was replaced by an aging Monty McFarlane of CJOR fame, who came to CISL to conclude his long career.

CISL wasn't the first station to deceive the CRTC, but it didn't make it any less smelly. The game became clear within a year. First, get the licence, then start breaking the Promise of Performance in order to slide in and compete as a Lower Mainland station in a lucrative major market. I still recall the day the staff was told we could no longer refer to Richmond while on the air. Had I not lived there my entire life, I probably wouldn't have cared.

Fortunately, I had a lifeline.

CHAPTER EIGHT

No false gods, no fucking match

Frustrated and not seeing a meaningful future at CISL, I reached out to my former station, and was delighted when they asked me to return.

"Thanks for listening to the all-night show. This is the last song I'll ever play for you on CISL 940."

Indeed it was "The Last Song" by Edward Bear. It was cheeky, but only to me, as I couldn't wait to get back to the team of pros at CJOR.

My new job was to operate from 6 a.m. to noon and to assist Frank Callaghan, the program director, with hiring, training, scheduling and operator payroll sheets — all in all a cool position for someone my age.

Art Finley, who had returned to our market after a stint at KGO San Francisco, was anchoring a fast-paced news-wheel format during breakfast time, followed by Rafe (never without Patti) Mair interviewing political newsmakers. The station would be relocating soon, but for now we were using ancient equipment that included a contraption that put the station into a six-second delay that is far too bizarre to explain. Providing you set it up flawlessly, it worked well. And it had to, especially when Pat Burns was on the air.

When I worked with Burns, as I often did, I knew I was working with one of the giants — the man who invented call-in talk radio in Canada.

"Good evening to all of you Hot-Liners as once again we go forward with another few hours of argument, discussion and debate on any topic under the sun. This is the program with no false gods, no sacred cows. The program dares you to think. Wants you to think. And then having thought, speak out."

That's how the raspy-voiced Burns began every night, often followed by a political attack editorial, maybe a couple of other tidbits and then the phone board.

"Burns Hot Line, go ahead."

If it was a female caller, after she said "Hi Pat," Burns usually followed with "Hello Doll," using a much lower, slower, flirting voice.

Burns owned the airwaves in the early '60s, hosting an incredibly popular and provocative show. When he was suddenly fired in 1965 due to numerous complaints to the Board of Broadcast governors and an apparent threat not to renew CJOR's licence, a mass protest in support of Burns was staged downtown at the Queen Elizabeth Theatre, causing a traffic standstill for several blocks. Soon after, Burns took his show to his birthplace of Montreal where he was heard on CKGM during the Front de libération du Quebec (FLQ) October Crisis of 1970.

I used to sit with Burns for hours and ask him to recall old radio stories. Always dressed in a jacket and tie and usually holding a cigarette, Pat would answer any question I asked. However, the day I asked him about what it was like to be on the air in Montreal during the FLQ Crisis, he didn't say a word. Instead, he got up and began rummaging through his big green filing cabinet. Moments later, he pulled out an old French language tabloid newspaper with his picture filling the entire front page. His face was framed in the telescopic sight of a rifle, and the headline read something like "Front de libération du Québec ennemi" (FLQ enemy). The picture was chilling. When I asked him how scared he was, he told me local police had urged him to get a licence to carry a handgun, which he did.

There were times when I was operating when I wished I had had the same licence because Burns purposely wouldn't take commercial breaks. Not because he was on a roll, but so he could save up enough minutes to dart up the stairs to the Grosvenor bar for a couple of quick shots. This was one of the reasons Burns rode a bus to work and why I'd often drive him home to his old low-rise penthouse apartment on Cambie at around 14th Avenue. The other reason was that Burns often forgot where he parked his car, sometimes going weeks without locating it.

Burns' battle with booze led to some sad moments. Once, I saw him stagger in just after lunchtime with a couple of cuts on his face. During these drinking periods Pat would usually go right into his tiny office, sleep and hope to be sober by the 6:30 p.m. start of his show. He was actually pretty good at being able to time that, but not always. As a result, there were occasions when there were no false gods and no Pat Burns. Sometimes he would start with a slight slur but snap out of it before most listeners would notice. However, one particular night during a break, while fumbling to light a cigarette, he accidentally opened his microphone instead of hitting the talk-back intercom button.

"Does anyone have a fucking match?" he said, with heavy emphasis on the F-word.

He may not have had one, but we got lit — as in every phone at the station lit up.

"Tell Pat I don't have a fuckin' match, but I do have a fuckin' lighter!" said one caller.

When Burns was razor sharp, there was no one like him. Sometimes I was mesmerized watching him, especially when he was in an argument with a caller and was hitting the bleep button. What our audience didn't know was that there were times when it was Burns swearing at the caller and bleeping himself!

When I wasn't visiting with Burns, all my spare moments were spent hanging around Garry Raible's sports department. I badly wanted to get my foot in the door, so I would volunteer to do anything. Raible was kind in return. His gift to me was his teaching, just as Jim Robson had taught him years earlier when Garry did his BCIT practicum at CKWX. Mostly this included learning tight writing, editing and how to select the right audio clips. Long before I was ready to work on the desk, Raible had me on the beat covering professional and amateur events.

Call me crazy, but one of the biggest thrills I've had was when I received my first full time NHL press pass. It turned boyhood dreams into reality and gave me the sense that I belonged in the sports media. I used the pass and all the perks that came with it to cover every game. I must have brought the Canucks luck, too, because that was the year they reached their first Stanley Cup Final.

Though I was only covering the home playoff games against the Flames, Kings, Blackhawks and Islanders, it was the road games, specifically two dramatic ones in Chicago, that got me thinking there was something missing from our radio market.

The first of two games at Chicago Stadium featured Jim Nill's double OT winner, ending what was then the longest Canucks game in history. The next game gave hockey fans an even longer-lasting memory when Vancouver coach Roger Neilson waved a white towel in protest over Bob Myers' officiating.

As a viewer/young reporter I recall being so stoked after those games that, for whatever reason, I jumped in my car, wanting to absorb it all. But when I turned on the radio, CKNW was airing Jack Cullen's *Owl Prowl*. There wasn't any place on the dial where someone was talking about Nill's thrilling winner or the birth of towel power. I can't say a light came on at that moment, but I knew I couldn't be the only one who wanted some sort of gathering spot for fans after games like those two.

As my CJOR sports role expanded, I began reading sportscasts for no money on weekends. This was a tremendous investment as I was gaining experience and slowly starting to build a profile.

Not getting paid didn't matter because I was good at making money elsewhere. I was the editor of the Vancouver Canadians' game program/media guide, a contributing writer for the Canucks' program, filed NHL and CFL reports to various wire services, and made side money from CKO to organize their airings of the Pacific Coast League (PCL) baseball broadcasts. That was a good deal because I could also hire friends Brook Ward and Dan Nordstrand to operate the Canadians games. Brook has always jokingly referred to me as "Marv," as in Marvin Miller, the famed head of the Major League Baseball Players Association. For some reason, Brook thought I always made Marv-type deals.

The Canadians also asked if I would compile their stats after every home game, which was no easy task considering there weren't any computers to speak of. I did it all by hand, learning quickly how to calculate batting averages, ERA, on-base percentage, etc. It was labour-intensive, but I'd do it late at night while listening to Larry King. When the C's asked how much I wanted to be paid, I suggested they could take me to their games in Hawaii in lieu of cash. "Marv" negotiated airfare, hotel, car rental, plus a one-week extension in Honolulu after the series had concluded.

Brook joined me — via Ward Air, naturally — on these trips because, while everyone likes Hawaii, no one loves it more than Brook. We had great days at the beach and even greater nights drinking beer at massive Aloha Stadium, before joining some of the players for some early-20s shenanigans near the International Market Place. Who knew Brook would become the voice of the C's years later, although, unfortunately for him, it was after Hawaii left the PCL. I always felt that baseball broadcasting was his calling, what with his great feel for the game, gift of gab and wonderful voice. At that time, Al Elconin, who would later spend many years at the MLB level (using the name Al Conin), was the Vancouver announcer. When the broadcasts went from CKO to CJOR the next year, I worked alongside him.

By 1983, I had been promoted to the afternoon drive sports guy. Once I finished my 5:35 p.m. 'cast on game days, I would quickly drive from our 8th and Hemlock studios to Nat Bailey Stadium for my 6:15 p.m. 'cast that would air during batting practice. It was a good idea that offered listeners the ambience of the stadium to promote our upcoming game broadcast.

After finishing the supper sportscast I would go down to the field to track down an interview for the pregame show, which likely was as close to the game broadcasts as seasoned-pro Elconin wanted me. I'd sit beside Elconin and take in how easy he made things sound, at least until around the fourth inning when the free hamburgers and hot dogs arrived. Yes, it was good to be in the media. Afterwards, I hosted the post-game show from the C's dugout with a bagful of Gillette products to give our special guest, who could be a player from either team. (Without exaggeration, those low-paid minor leaguers were appreciative of getting free razor blades and shaving cream.)

The biggest hosting highlight that year was interviewing legendary comedian Bob Hope, who was the emcee for a three-inning old-timers' game before a C's game at BC Place Stadium. Over forty thousand people showed up to watch the likes of Hank Aaron, Juan Marichal, Whitey Ford and Roger Maris.

The C's struggled mightily in '83, which led to one post-game show when the shit hit the fan. Even though they were the worst team in the PCL, Vancouver did win on this particular night, holding on despite allowing a rare inside-the-park home run. On the play in question, Vancouver centre fielder Dion James missed catching a flyball and collided with the outfield wall, causing the ball to rattle around the fence. The hitter-turned-baserunner kept going until he had touched them all.

You can go to a lot of games and never see an inside-the-park homer, so when I was interviewing outfielder Steve Michaels one of the things I said was, "You guys nearly found a new way to lose tonight." I probably thought my turn of phrase was clever, especially given how many games they had lost. At the same time, I assumed everyone was happy because of the win; I never considered the question might hit a nerve.

Unbeknownst to me, field manager Dick Phillips was listening in the clubhouse, and when he heard my pithy question to Michaels, well, he went apeshit.

"What the fuck were you talking about?" Phillips started in on me a few minutes later as I unsuspectedly approached him. "A young man's life nearly came to an end," he said in something of an overstatement, "and you're saying we found a new fucking way to lose a game?"

Dion didn't die. He didn't even go to the hospital. But I didn't know what to say. Phillips, a lifelong baseball man I grew to like and worked with two years later as editor of the club's magazine, really gave it to me. And it didn't stop there. The next morning CJOR management received calls from C's GM Jack Quinn picking up where Phillips left off. Even though Raible told me it would blow over, I was worried given the owner of the team and the radio station was the same person. James did miss a couple of games, but was far from having his life come to an end. Looking back, it was a valuable sports media lesson and I was an easy target. I was young and didn't grasp the pressure Phillips was feeling. Indeed, he was fired as field manager a few weeks later.

In January of 1984, months before the birth of *Sportstalk*, I broke my first huge story when head coach Roger Neilson was fired by the Canucks. It was strange that I got the story, given that CJOR was not the rights holder and that Raible happened to be on the road with the team that morning. But he wasn't the one who told me. I got the anonymous tip from Canucks PR man Norm Jewison, who, for some reason, chose/trusted me to break the bombshell news. The funniest part of the story was that before I broke it, Jim Robson was having an early breakfast with Roger in an Edmonton hotel. Neilson kept telling Jim he had been fired but Robson wouldn't believe him, so he didn't call it back to his station.

"Captain Video" didn't take long to find work. He was quickly hired by the Kings and, wouldn't you know it, his first game was against the Canucks.

I'm not sure how we had the budget, but CJOR sent me to LA to cover this strange but interesting storyline. This was my first big-league assignment, and after an early flight I went straight from LAX to the Forum, arriving in time to watch the Canucks game-day skate. Roger was watching his old team from the stands alongside a couple of other reporters. I approached the future Hall of Famer for an interview, and he was as kind and accommodating as could be.

When I wished him luck, Neilson said with his familiar sheepish smile, "I sure hope I go to the right bench."

The Kings won that night, but only won a few more after that, and Roger was fired again at the end of the season. Career coach that he was, two weeks later he latched on as Edmonton's video coach and the Oilers went on to win their first Stanley Cup. In a span of five months, he Neilson been fired in Vancouver and LA, and then been part of a championship.

Later in 1984 I was asked to accompany the Canucks on their new private plane — *Air Canuck* — for two games, also in Los Angeles. This was in an era where most pro teams travelled commercial, but citing a large travel disadvantage the Canucks had invested in their own plane. It was my first time travelling with the team, and I was nervous, shy and only spoke when spoken to. The games, dare I say, didn't quite go their way. Vancouver was pounded 12-1 and 6-3. Though luxurious, the trip home was quiet. When the plane touched down just after 2 a.m., I grabbed my bag and walked past coach Harry Neale, who was still seated. He hadn't said a word to me in three days.

"That's the last fucking time you're allowed to come," he said, winking in the direction of Jim Robson.

CHAPTER NINE

The cable guy

Just like an NHL sniper who shot hundreds of pucks every day as a boy or the NBA player who practised free throws forever, I put the same effort into being an accomplished broadcaster. While I'm eternally appreciative of those who helped and influenced me, I had an unrelenting work ethic that led to any success I enjoyed. I'm not saying others didn't work hard, but I never came across a broadcaster who outworked me.

In other words, I was far from a natural.

Case in point: my fifteen-plus years of volunteering to broadcast games for community television. I didn't know it at the time, but while I was doing those mock Pacific Junior A League Couriers games with Mike Milholm from the Kerrisdale Arena in 1978, plans were afloat to televise a few on what then was known as Cable 10 Community TV. The year prior, Peter Rodgers, the Kerrisdale public-address announcer, had called a couple of games using a style reminiscent of Danny Gallivan. But now he graciously allowed me to call them, with him as my colour man, marking the first time my play-by-play was actually broadcast.

In those days, the games were tape-delayed and repeated several times over the course of a week. I was always pleasantly surprised when someone told me they'd actually seen one.

Not long after that, I learned I could volunteer for other community channels throughout the Lower Mainland and Fraser

Valley, and over the next few years my dance card filled up. A routine week often looked like this:

— Couriers game from Kerrisdale Arena on Thursday;
— Nor Wes Caps game from (frigid) North Van Rec Centre on Friday;
— Abbotsford Flyers game from MSA Arena on Saturday;
— New Westminster Royals game from Queen's Park Arena on Sunday.

Incidentally, my four favourite players from those teams were Steve Mulholland, Bill Holowaty, Craig Redmond and Cliff Ronning, respectively.

Because Wednesdays were free, I also hosted *Sports Watch*, a half-hour in-studio show focused on amateurs, originating from North Vancouver every week.

In 1981, I became the play-by-play broadcaster for Cable TV's coverage of the BC High School Boys Basketball Championship. Little did I know that I'd be in that chair for fourteen years, doing two games on Championship Saturday every March. I worked alongside Jay Triano, Gord Kurenoff, Bill Wilms, Brook Ward and others, always from a jam-packed PNE Agrodome.

I called many memorable games, but two of them especially stand out. The first is the 1992 final when Steve Nash led his St. Michaels University School team from Saanich to a 76-48 victory over Pitt Meadows. Nash, the tournament MVP, finished with thirty-one points, eleven rebounds, eight assists and four steals. Despite his performance, I promise there wasn't a soul in that stinky old barn who would have predicted we were watching a future two-time NBA MVP and Hall of Famer. As it turned out, my call that night was the only time Nash led his team to a championship.

Ten years prior was the most emotional game, in any sport, of my career. Two North Shore teams — the Argyle Pipers and West Vancouver Highlanders — faced each other. The term "gut-wrenching" is often used to describe close games, but this one was incredibly "heart-wrenching" as we watched Brian Upson, the popular long-time West Vancouver coach struggle to stand on the sidelines. Upson had stomach cancer, was bedridden except for games, and wore a jacket that seemed at least two sizes too big.

Down one with fifteen seconds left, Highlanders' standout Paul Kitchener hit two free throws, giving Upson's team a one-point lead. With the noise deafening, the Pipers hurried up the floor and got the ball into the hands of their star, Mark Marter, with about three seconds left. Marter put up a buzzer-beating attempt that hit the backboard, then the front rim, and then — as if the basketball gods were paying attention — stayed out. Upson's Highlanders had upset the Pipers 49-48. The smile on his face is still etched in my mind. He died two weeks later.

Back then I called any sport cable TV was showing, including the BC Summer Games in Delta, Senior Little League baseball in Whalley, Major Men's fast pitch at Queen's Park Stadium, and Western Lacrosse Association games that meant ferry trips and hotel stays in downtown Nanaimo. In those early years I met some fine people who worked behind the scenes on our community TV shows, like Paul Brettell, Roland Stockli, Drew Kirby and David McCall. They always seemed to call me when they needed a broadcaster.

My hope was to parlay this experience into a WHL radio job. Without a team in the Vancouver area I applied elsewhere, starting with the Billings Bighorns in Montana. That sounded exciting to me, especially when GM Les Calder seemed hopeful. But a few days later he called back to say he wasn't able to obtain the paperwork that would allow me to work in the United States.

As fate would have it, the Bighorns relocated to Nanaimo a year later and I applied to become the voice of the Islanders. My hopes were even higher this time because I had been told by someone at CKEG, the station that was to air the games, that the job was mine. But CKEG's deal fell through and the broadcast rights went to CHUB, which had a staffer to do the games.

I felt cursed. Then, lo and behold, the franchise was on the move again a year later. The Calgary Buffaloes/Billings Bighorns/

Nanaimo Islanders fell into my lap as the New Westminster Bruins. With the second incarnation of the Bruins (1983-88), I was asked to call their (tape-delayed) TV games out of tiny Queen's Park Arena. The games generated lots of interest and perhaps served as a pre-TSN look at the ferocious hockey appetite in Vancouver.

One highly-anticipated game featured Cam Neely coming in with the Portland Winter Hawks a few months after having been a first-round NHL draft pick of the Vancouver Canucks. A large crowd was on hand but saw only one Neely shift, as he cut one hand to the bone in a spirited first-period fight with Shawn Green.

For whatever reason, I can also vividly remember a 1-1 goaltending clinic staged between Brandon's Ron Hextall and Pokey Reddick of the Bruins.

Then there was the night when Kamloops' coach Ken Hitchcock, upset after his team allowed ten goals, had the bus driver stop at the foot of the Pattullo Bridge and made his players walk across to meet the bus on the other side. That was on a Saturday at 11 p.m. No, that wouldn't be tolerated now either.

Hitchcock, though, was one of my favourites. I was thrilled for him when he went on to have such tremendous pro success because in order to get his shot and ultimately win more than eight hundred NHL games, he had to lose and incredible amount of weight. Hitch usually wore a dirty blue windbreaker behind the Kamloops bench; he was the lone coach I saw who didn't wear a jacket and tie. At that time, he weighed upwards of 450 pounds, and the merciless New West fans often had a field day with their taunts. That included sending boxes of pizza and doughnuts to the Kamloops dressing room in some intermissions. (Hitch told me he ate them.)

He also coined the phrase Best-of-Forever, alluding to the silly best-of-nines the league then used during its playoffs. Of course, they may have been better than the double round robins they had tried in previous seasons. Most of Hitch's series seemed to end 5-0, but the best best-of-nine I saw was between New Westminster and Portland in 1984. The Bruins led 4-3 in games (good enough to advance most years), but Portland won Game 8 to force a deciding game at a jam-packed Queen's Park. Scalpers did a brisk business that night. I did the in-house PA for Game 9 — the only time *I* filled in for Brook Ward — in which Cliff Ronning's apparent late third period game-winning goal, off the back bar and out, was disallowed. The officials missed it and there wasn't video replay. Ray Podloski won the game and series for Portland with an overtime goal.

On *Sportstalk* twenty-five years later, Ronning still frustratingly insisted his shot was in. He wasn't wrong.

CHAPTER TEN

The birth of *Sportstalk*

The origin of what would be Canada's longest-running sports talk show was as simple as it was complicated. Above all, *Sportstalk* was a fluke.

The simple part was my love of radio and sports, but it also helped that I was a guest every Monday on *Little Berner in the Night*, a CJOR man-about-town program with ample talk about Vancouver's entertainment scene. In late 1983, I was asked to be a Monday guest after finishing my 11 p.m. sportscasts. Host David Berner, a local actor/writer/broadcaster, and I were surprised at how many lights flashed on the phone board. However, there wasn't any way of knowing these hour-long guest appearances would form the basis of a *Sportstalk* pilot.

The complicated part began when CJOR GM Harvey Gold summoned Berner to a meeting in the spring of '84.

"You're pink mist," he said to Berner.

Pink mist? That was a new one to me. And it sounded harsh — but I guess that's what would happen if your pink slip blew up in your face. Wondering what they would do with the time slot, I formally proposed hosting a sports show that picked up what Berner and I had been doing. I gave it to Gold but never heard a thing, so I assumed it was DOA.

I knew the station had bigger issues than late night, like their ongoing battle with Rafe Mair, the temperamental morning host who was about to get pink misted himself. Mair's ratings had slipped, but his high maintenance had intensified, and his wife's (Patti) ever-present interference often nauseated management. (Years later I was told by an impeccable source, who might have been the executive producer of all talk at CKNW, that Patti would go into the men's washroom before Rafe's morning business to make sure the toilet seat was clean and that there was enough toilet paper.)

The complicated part, as it concerns the birth of *Sportstalk*, was when Gold replaced Mair with Dave Barrett, a former BC premier, and Mair went to CKNW in the only time slot it had available, one that started at midnight. There was so much bad blood that Gold wanted to upstage Mair by airing a repeat of the Barrett show just as Rafe was starting. This meant the two former political rivals — one leaning right, the other left — went head-to-head on the all-night show. One was live while the other was in bed.

To make this happen, though, Gold needed a one-hour buffer to fill the gap between the end of *The Hot Line* with Pat Burns and Barrett's midnight repeat. He solved this problem by stopping into the sports cubicle on a Friday afternoon to tell me he had decided to insert a sports show featuring calls and interviews.

"And we've chosen you to be the host," he said.

Wish I'd thought of that is what I wanted to say. Instead, I told him I was grateful for the opportunity.

"Great ... you start Monday," Gold said.

I didn't have to ask if he meant in three days because I had already been around radio long enough to know that often constituted long-range planning. The next day — my twenty-fourth birthday — I showed Gold a list of possible names for my new show. I forget what they were, but he rejected all of them.

"It's going to be *Sportstalk* because it's so self-explanatory," he said.

He was right.

Soon after, I met with R. J. McNichol, the new production manager, to pick out a theme song because all shows had one. Like most stations, CJOR subscribed to a market-exclusive service that supplied music beds used for commercials. After listening to a couple of dozen I settled on the theme song that was used for *Sportstalk's* entire run.

"CJOR 600 presents *Sportstalk* with Dan Russell. *Sportstalk*: an in-depth review of today's sports, plus a chance for you to voice your opinion. The phone number is 731-9192 [no area code required then]. That's 731-9192. Now, here's your host, Dan Russell."

Neither the music nor intro would change over the next three decades. It was voiced by three men: Al Jordan, Jim Conrad or John Ashbridge.

After that I had to think about our first guest. Who would it be? Raible and I decided on the Canucks' new head coach. With one call — yes, it was far easier booking guests back then — Bill LaForge was confirmed.

As Monday neared, I didn't have any expectations. I just knew that ready or not — and I wasn't — *Sportstalk* would launch shortly after 11 p.m. on October 15, 1984. Raible insisted on sitting in that first night, which caused me much anxiety. My mouth turned into a desert as the 11 p.m. news ended, and by the time the *Sportstalk* theme music played through my headphones, I was parched.

"Here's your host, Dan Russell," the announcer said.

After a slight pause while I put my heart back in my chest, I spoke pretty much the same words I would use at the start of every show for the next thirty years:

"And a pleasant, uhh, good evening … welcome to our first of what we hope is many editions of *Sportstalk*."

Okay, I thought, *those words actually came out. Just barely. My mouth did work. Not well, but we're on the air!*

However, there wasn't a chance my anxiety would subside because when I looked up, Raible, sitting three feet away, was staring at me without expression. It was why I didn't want him in studio. He could have looked at his papers and doodled or, better yet, come in after I got underway. Later that would become my rule for all guests because I learned — perhaps that night — if you don't start strong, it often sets the tone for the rest of the night. Raible's unnerving stare through his thick Coke-bottle glasses caused me to abort most of my intro and the editorial I had planned. Instead, I skipped ahead to a blurb outlining what I hoped this new show would be.

"Open-line sports programs are very popular in a lot of cities, but, uh, a little bit untried in Vancouver. We are hoping *Sportstalk* will be a success. The reason we think it will be a success is it ah, ah, is being held at a time which I think is very conducive to sports open-line shows. ...."

I had more to say, but with Raible's staring, there was no use. I aborted that as well. To this day, any time I hear that tape, I cringe. Undoubtedly, I was a greenhorn. But I also know I was better than what came out that night. Raible's a good guy who did many things to help me. But, for reasons only he might know, he became a little distant after *Sportstalk* began.

LaForge, the Canucks' rookie coach, was our first guest, but he arguably launched our show four days later when disbelieving and stunned fans jammed the phone board after Vancouver surrendered a club record thirteen goals in Philadelphia, after which LaForge said he saw "positive signs." Two weeks later, the Canucks gave up ten goals at home versus Los Angeles, leaving LaForge with one win in ten games while being outscored 74-33 and leaving me with a full phone board every night. LaForge was fired ten games later, ending his NHL coaching career.

Our second-night guest was Tony Muser, the manager of baseball's Vancouver Canadians, whom I got to know well by being at the ballpark every day. Muser was a personable man who had played and would go on to manage in the Bigs. Two months prior, I had been around the batting cage waiting to do an interview while Muser was throwing BP. He surprised me by yelling, "Dan, grab a bat and take a few swings." Anyone who knows me could have told him it wouldn't be pretty. Of course, he knew that as well. After making clear he was serious, I tentatively entered the batter's box. His first two pitches were quite a bit outside, designed for me to extend myself in reaching for them, which I did to no avail. The third pitch was slower and not as far outside, and I sent a feeble grounder to first base.

Now he had set me up. I thought Muser might want me to get an actual hit with a much easier pitch; instead, he sent a fastball two feet over my head. It scared the crap out of me and sent me to the dirt. I can still hear Tony's triumphant laugh. Needless to say, I was one and done. So having a familiar guest — perhaps more importantly not having Raible staring at me — led to a more comfortable show. I still was green, but I was more comfortable.

On the third night, I ventured into the unknown by devoting the entire show to open-phones. No guest. Just me flying naked and hoping to generate calls. Remember, unlike shows today, *Sportstalk* operated without a co-host. Either the phone rang, or …. To my surprise all the lines lit up, and midnight arrived quicker than it had the first two nights. Ironically enough, until smartphones arrived a full board was the norm. That's why I was brave enough to occasionally try setting aside full hours for only first-time callers or women.

Of course, Canucks' game nights were *Sportstalk*'s bread and butter, just as I thought they would be after Jim Nill's 1982 double-OT goal in Chicago. Within a few months, CJOR added thirty more minutes to the show, which allowed me to turn it into a mini-*Larry King Show* format, scheduling a guest for the first hour and open-phones for the last half hour. Traction, in the form of ratings, was building to the point where we were extended again, from 10:30 p.m. to 12:30 a.m. I wasn't sure why they started at the bottom of an hour, but before I could find out it was extended twice more, first from 10 p.m. to 12:30 a.m., and then to three hours — 10 p.m. to 1 a.m.

From the beginning, *Sportstalk* was often on the road. Canucks' training camp in one of various provincial locales was a given. At one point, I had attended twenty straight. We also did our show from many BC Lions' camps on Vancouver Island or in the Okanagan.

Because of my association with the Canadians, I attended spring training in Scottsdale, Arizona, and Bradenton, Florida — where I ate grits for the first time at a place called The Dugout Diner. I went to almost all the MLB camps and spent the days packaging interviews for our show, which I usually did from some inexpensive motel room, starting at 2 a.m. ET when in Florida.

A huge highlight, in March of 1987, was visiting Dodger Town at Vero Beach, Florida, a former US naval base that served the Dodgers from 1948 through 2008. It was a huge self-contained facility featuring countless batting cages, pitching mounds and practice diamonds, along with their game park, Holman Stadium, Hall of Fame walk arches, street lamps that looked like bats, and each road named after a Dodgers great — Sandy Koufax Lane, Duke Snider Street, Jackie Robinson Avenue, etc.

It's entirely possible I was too much in awe because as I was roaming around conducting interviews, I found myself in the Holman Stadium outfield when I suddenly noticed — and could certainly hear — a rather small man with a rather large belly yelling and waving his arms in my direction.

"Get off the field," screamed the most famous Dodgers manager in history. "Yes, you … young man. Get off the fucking field!"

I wasn't sure how I was in the way, but Tommy Lasorda wanted me to vacate in a hurry as he was beginning another drill.

I was able to shake off that unnerving moment a couple of hours later when the great Vin Scully graciously accepted my interview request. We spoke for about ten minutes from the roof of the stadium, just outside his broadcast booth. Then, just as he was finishing a thoughtful answer, he segued with that famous Scully voice by saying, "… and Dan, the inning is over and I'm going to have to go back to work. Thanks for the opportunity and hello to all the good people in Vancouver." Talking to Scully was like talking to broadcast royalty, and it led to baseball size goosebumps.

The Canucks may have had another non-playoff year in 1988, but we knew our listeners really had interest in one of hockey's all-time greatest rivalries being staged one province over. It was another Battle of Alberta, and I wanted *Sportstalk* to be there. Understandably, CJOR wasn't as excited (re: budget), so I offered to drive, which I did thanks to one of my endorsement sponsors, Barnet Toyota, which let me use a shiny new blue two-door Celica. Producer John

Martin offered to share the driving, which was fine until we got near Chilliwack and he informed me he didn't know how to drive a stick shift.

"What? You didn't tell me that!" I complained, though I didn't realize how much of an issue this was going to be.

Everyone was predicting a long series, and the only bad scenario for us would be an Oilers sweep, leading to a drive from hell. The other scenarios were okay. Over in five meant we could leave from Calgary and break up our trip back by covering a WHL playoff game in Kamloops. If completed in six games, it would give the Celica all weekend to meander back. Game 7 would have meant a classic series and worth the ten-hour drive back.

Naturally, it was a sweep. Game 4 was played on a Monday in Edmonton. After signing off at 1 a.m. MT, we went back to our hotel to grab our things before starting the thirteen-hour drive with only one driver capable of changing gears. Having not slept since the previous night, my eyes were already heavy by the time we rolled into Jasper (about three and a half hours outside of Edmonton). You can imagine how much fun it was to watch Martin in the fetal position on the passenger side sleeping peacefully.

I finally pulled over around 7 a.m. for a Rocky Mountain nap. I was less pissed about the Calgary loss than I was with them being unable to come up with at least one win. (Further salt was rubbed into that wound a year later when the Flames willed their way to sixteen playoff victories.) We limped back to Vancouver around 5 p.m. and went right to the station to put together the Tuesday night edition of *Sportstalk*. Yes, I may have been short with some callers that night.

Three months after that Oilers sweep, *Sportstalk* broke its biggest story — arguably the biggest in Canadian sports history, the previously unthinkable trading of Wayne Gretzky. Gretzky was traded on a Tuesday, and we broke the story the previous night. I had one source for this story, a listener I had never met who never provided me with his identity or phone number. It was risky, but I had talked to him several times, starting a few days prior, always trying to gauge how credible he might be. Initially, I didn't believe it. But he kept calling me, offering me more details, and I kept peppering him with questions to gauge if this was legit.

In the early evening of August 8, he called again, telling me the deal was going to happen. I still didn't want to go to air with it, but I told him I'd convey the strong rumour, which I did off the top of our show. He called back during the next newsbreak, this time providing me names he had heard were going to be in the trade. He was absolutely certain it was going to happen. As the weather forecast was being read, I was trying to assess it all as I feverishly wrote down the names.

Moments later, I went with my gut and went to air.

"This trade is going to happen and it may be announced tomorrow," I said.

Someone from The Canadian Press was monitoring the show and immediately put out a bulletin. Shortly after, a radio station in Hull, Quebec, also reported what we had. Bilingual tipster perhaps? Regardless, that's when I breathed a sigh of relief, confident we'd gotten it right and had been first.

Gretzky's trade to LA was announced the next afternoon, and I came into the station extra early to hook up a live audio feed from Edmonton. It was the news conference the entire country wanted to hear, the one in which Gretzky broke down in tears. Just as the news conference was beginning, I got into an argument with the assistant program director, who claimed we couldn't carry it now.

"Why not?" I yelled.

"Because we have to break for the two o'clock news," was the response.

"This is the two o'clock fucking news!" I might have yelled.

CHAPTER ELEVEN

Thanks for having me on, Dan

Show me any successful venture and I'll find you a turning point.

Sportstalk is no exception.

Ours occurred on June 3, 1987, the day Vancouver Canucks' general manager Pat Quinn hired Brian Burke to be his director of hockey operations. That night we sent the *Sportstalk* limo to the Burnaby Villa to deliver us the man who would become our greatest guest.

I'm not kidding about the limo. For a few years we had a "contra deal" with a limo company to fetch our guests and transport them to and from our studio. That is until a BC Lions player (whom I won't name) gathered a couple of his buddies and took our limo for an extra-long post-show joyride through Stanley Park, ran up a huge long-distance cell phone bill, and neither paid nor tipped the driver. Sadly, that was the end of our great limo deal.

Burke may have liked his nice ride, but he was blown away by the forum we offered and the phone response. Before sending him back in the limo, I said something along the lines of, "It'd sure be cool if you could come on regularly."

"I'll come on every week," he quickly said.

"Really?" I said, not yet knowing how much Burke was going to adore media attention.

I wasn't convinced he meant every week. But he did. And it was ground-breaking. Every week of the year, no matter where he was, he wouldn't miss. He could be on a Hawaiian vacation with his wife, a ski trip with his kids, fishing with his pals or wherever his hockey business took him. He never missed. Wednesday nights meant the "Weekly Canucks Update with Brian Burke," and it wasn't long before that became appointment radio. According to Burke, it was the first time any executive from a major sports team had done a weekly call-in radio show. Smart, outspoken, funny, quick, passionate and loyal. As a host you look for a couple of those traits in a potential guest. Burke checked all six boxes.

"Thanks for having me on, Dan" was the comforting way he began and ended every show.

On occasion, when Burke was somewhere in Europe, we'd have to wake him because of the time difference. While he was on the air, producer Scott Woodgate would call back the hotel and order breakfast to his room. It was always amusing to hear Burke stop talking on air in mid-thought to tell us someone was knocking on the door.

"If this is breakfast again, I'm going to ring Woodgate's neck," he'd say with fake anger.

It was good radio fun to hear Burke put down the phone, prompting me to do a play-by-play of him opening the door, predicting he'd stiff the room service waiter of a tip, hearing him mumble as he brought his breakfast tray back to the phone, and then asking him to describe to our listeners what Woodgate had ordered. Burke always played along so well. He was a natural for our medium, and it totally endeared him to our growing number of listeners. He loved those kinds of moments as much as we did. Also, he never asked us to pay the room service charge.

"What started off as a professional relationship turned very quickly into a very close personal relationship," Burke recalled years later. "I think he's a tremendous radio personality, and I consider Dan to be one of my closest and best friends."

Too close as it would turn out. But not yet.

Burke didn't invent our show, no matter how many times I reminded him of that. However, he greatly accelerated our growth.

I was in my mid-twenties and beginning to enjoy what *Sportstalk* was becoming. Burke offered tremendous access, including allowing me to hang out at his office and overhear some of his hockey calls. He also helped secure guests from around the NHL and was always suggesting ways to further boost the show's impact.

Unquestionably the first phase of our relationship was a win-win, even though I was occasionally uncomfortable when he would overstep his bounds, not so much by guest suggestions, but when he tried to alter my opinions. Our relationship being what it was, I'd usually tell him something along the lines of, "Why don't you concern yourself with your last-place hockey club and let me worry about the content of my first-place show." Burke's usual response would be something like "Fuck you."

Make no mistake — Burke loved *Sportstalk*'s bully pulpit where he was able to spread the word according to the Canucks or himself (most often that word was the same), but there were times when Quinn would get angry over something Burke had said. For example, there was the time when Burke created this national headline: "Burke threatens to fight own defenceman Doug Lidster." Well, that's how it was reported. But to put it in proper context, Burke was frustrated with Lidster's contract negotiations and how Lidster talked about his options in the media. That's when Burke said, "If I'm his teammate, we probably have a fight the next day in practice."

Even though the media chose to omit "If I'm his teammate" and "probably," I was okay with this as it again raised *Sportstalk*'s profile by a couple of notches.

Occasionally, Burke might call and tell me that I wouldn't look bad if I were to say such and such on the air. I knew that was Burke code for "You can take that one to the bank." However, there was one scoop I regretted. It happened on a Wednesday when Burke was initially scheduled to join us in the 10 p.m. hour. On this night he was working late and warned us he might have to come on at 11. It turned out he was working on Richard Brodeur's contract and, given the goaltender's popularity, we had been covering developments for days, and that included talking with Brodeur's agent.

While waiting for Burke and conducting open-phones, I asked Woodgate to try the agent one more time to see if there might be an update. Sure enough. King Richard had signed minutes before our call. So we went to air with the scoop at 10:45. By this time Burke was on his way to the station and couldn't believe his ears. This was his story. He wanted to break the news on his radio forum, and the last thing he wanted was for the agent to look heroic. Too late. We had inadvertently upstaged Burke. I should have known he would be that sensitive, but I didn't. Until he arrived at our studios.

As the eleven o'clock news began, he had a few choice words for Woodgate. Then he made his way into the studio where he immediately laid into me.

"Why the *fuck* would you let that *asshole* break the story?" is how he started. I mentally noted the emphasis on the word "fuck," but a much heavier and stretched-out emphasis on "asshole."

And it got worse from there, lasting through the entire six-minute newsbreak. Every time I said I didn't realize it was that sensitive, he'd start in again. Never before was hearing the *Sportstalk* reintro theme music so welcoming. I could see the steam pouring out of Burke's ears as I was setting up the hour, tossing in some scores and ragging the puck a little, all the while hoping he might calm down before introducing him.

"Time now for our weekly Canucks update with Brian Burke," I started as usual.

"Thanks for having me on, Dan," Burke said as per normal.

The interview went from there, beginning with the Brodeur signing we'd just upstaged him on. Burke answered my line of questioning, though less than enthusiastically. To his professional credit, he was fine on the air, albeit short with me, but gracious with the callers.

As we approached another time I dreaded, our first commercial break, I wondered if he would lay into me all over again. What will I say if he does? How's this going to play out?

"We'll be back with more of our weekly Canucks update after these messages," I said, throwing the show to a commercial break.

Ever wonder how long five 30-second commercials, a station ID and a show reintro really feels like? I actually calculated in that moment that it added up to 175 excruciatingly long seconds in which not one solitary word was spoken. Burke wouldn't even look at me, and I knew it would be best not to say anything to him. When the break was over, the listeners hadn't any idea how much tension there was in the studio.

This was repeated three more times that hour, and after he said, "Thanks for having me on, Dan," he darted from his chair, quickly grabbed his coat and was out the door before I could sign off the show.

Had we just had our last "Canucks Update"? I didn't know until six days later when Patti Timms, his administrative assistant, called to ask what hour he would be on that night. This episode reinforced how much Burke craved the *Sportstalk* platform.

This first phase of my relationship with Burke took part in an era when most of the old NHL buildings were in operation, and I once remarked to him that it was a dream of mine to visit all of them, especially Boston Garden. Within days, he was helping me and Woodgate plan a trip to see the buildings in Toronto, Boston, New York City, Philadelphia and Montreal.

Our first stop during this 1991 trip was Maple Leaf Gardens where we saw the forever rivals, Montreal vs. Toronto. To this day I can't describe the feeling except to say it was like morphing a piece of my living room furniture (our TV that brought us *Hockey Night in Canada* every Saturday) into real life.

Boston Garden — my personal Great Wall of China — was our second stop, where we watched the Bruins and Pittsburgh in a rink that didn't look much bigger in person than Queen's Park Arena in New Westminster. Not only did we see the Bruins, but Burke insisted we stay the next day for the start of the famed Beanpot tournament, which was kicking off with two games featuring teams from Boston College, Boston University, Harvard and Northeastern.

Six more hours at the Great Wall? This was heaven. I checked out every nook and cranny, wondering what it would've been like to witness Bobby Orr soaring through the air to win the 1970 Stanley Cup, watch Phil Esposito smash the NHL single season goals record, see Gerry Cheevers' famous stitches mask in person or applaud ringmaster Don Cherry's blue-collar teams.

By the time I'd felt the incredible buzz of Madison Square Garden and met up with Burke for a drive to the Philadelphia Spectrum, my mind was made up. This was something our listeners should have a chance to experience. After getting Burke's assurance of help, we began planning the *Sportstalk* Roadtrip of a Lifetime (RTOL) for our listeners. I couldn't wait to scour the next season's schedule. After mapping out what I knew my listeners would like, I worked with Burke and Timms to secure the most important ingredient — game tickets — and to obtain the Canucks' team rates for hotels and buses.

For two weeks I promoted RTOL, instructing our listeners that in order for them to join us to watch the Canucks play in some of the world's most historic arenas, they had to call on a specific date at 3 p.m. to secure the trip. The first year we had forty trips for sale. I knew people would love the idea but had no idea if they would be willing to pony up the money. Early in the afternoon on our designated selling day, I went to the station anxious to see how many would call. I was shocked to discover all of the spots had sold in just twelve minutes! Had anyone ever sold that many trips that quickly? Even my daytime CKNW co-workers watching the phone action were blown away.

All four of these trips were absolute hoots, and Burke usually ended up serving as an unofficial tour guide. We both got a big kick out of seeing the looks in people's eyes knowing we'd made dreams come true.

One personal thrill was doing *Sportstalk* from the Boston Gardens' press box. Because of the late hour — 1:00 to 3:00 a.m. ET — we had my all-time favourite NHL rink entirely to ourselves, which was so amazing ... until the night watchman, who had no idea we were up top, came into the main arena bowl and shut off all the lights.

Mike Milholm was with Woodgate and I that night. Yes, the same Milholm who served as my Kerrisdale Couriers mock colour man, my co-commissioner for the RHL hockey pool (among the longest running in Canada), fictional *Sportstalk* band leader Ken Ballaooofy, RTOL entertainment co-ordinator and my best friend since high school. It was about 2:45 when the Garden went black — not even the exit lights were illuminated. Shades of the Stanley Cup Final six years earlier? It was one thing to be accused of often being in the dark by guests like Burke, but now it was completely accurate. The only dim lighting we had came from our console equipment and the front screen of our cell phones (smartphones with flashlights hadn't yet been invented).

The difficult part wasn't broadcasting. It was packing the equipment, carefully making our way down a ladder, gingerly feeling our way one step at a time between rows of seats and navigating through the concourses. When we finally descended all the way to the security desk, the old man guarding the place, the one who had killed the lights, was fast asleep. We exited into the North Station and a snowy Boston night without him even being aware we had been in the historic Garden.

Another time, while headquartered in Toronto, we took the group to see the Canucks play the Red Wings. After getting into Detroit, each bus captain (yes, we named one for each bus) was responsible for purchasing (from this sketchy area we happened upon) a full-size garbage can, plenty of ice and twenty dozen beer in preparation for our return.

Then, near the start of our four-hour return trip, everyone stayed nervously quiet when the Canada Customs agent hopped on and asked a few questions, each of us hoping he wouldn't head to the back of the bus and discover our stash. When the agent got off and the doors shut, it stayed eerily quiet for about thirty seconds before the bus erupted in loud celebration. The Detroit garbage cans seemed to have brought the inner Bob Probert out in all of us.

On this joyful ride back to Toronto, I called to the show (Brook Ward was hosting) and conducted our first ever RTOL roving mic, interviewing various guests using my best Bill Hughes style in tribute to all the years he famously hosted the real *Roving Mic* on CKNW. A few guests in I approached my good friend and sponsor Doug Lum. As soon as I introduced him, the entire bus — on cue — loudly began singing a song they had practised all trip, done to the tune of the famous '50s song "Sh Boom Sh Boom."

"Doug Lum, Doug Lum – deeannnnaannanna. Doug Lum Doug Lum ..."

Well, you get the idea.

We had one particular lowlight which occurred as we attempted to watch two games in one day — an afternoon affair in Philadelphia and a night game on Long Island featuring the Canucks. Because of a tight schedule and the approximate three-hour drive (depending on traffic), the entire bus voted overwhelmingly to leave the first game after two periods so we could get to see the entire Canucks game. Well, as the saying goes, "There's one in every crowd." In this case, it was a pair. Whomever they were, they decided they didn't want to leave the first game early. This resulted in our entire busload of *Sportstalk* listeners sitting in the Spectrum's parking lot listening to the third period of the Flyers game and not getting a head start on post-game traffic, never mind making it a guarantee we'd see the entire Canucks game. You can imagine the greeting those two received after they finally boarded. That jeering intensified when we arrived at the Canucks/Islanders game *after* the first period had finished.

Among other moments, our road trippers once saw an incredible shower of hats when Cam Neely scored a Boston Garden hat-trick; Vancouver's last game at Chicago Stadium; a goosebumpy Bruins/ Habs game at the Forum; and Pavel Bure becoming the first fifty-goal scorer in team history only to have his apparent historic goal in Winnipeg called back by (newly created) video replay. We even saw an NBA game — after dining on New England lobster — on the Celtics' famous parquet floor.

Sadly, the combination of a weak Canadian dollar and the death of most of those old buildings spelled the end to *Sportstalk*'s fun journeys.

When one of our sponsors, Fogg N' Suds, asked if we would consider broadcasting a few times a year from their restaurant, I was hesitant. Yes, I had advanced considerably since Garry Raible stared me down on opening night, but I was still fussy about anyone watching our show — let alone a couple of hundred people. But the Fogg was one of my personal endorsement clients, and the folks there made me feel like a (semi) big shot when they said I could eat for free (with guests) any day I wished. Management even mounted a plaque — "Dan Russell's table" — in one of their prime booths.

That relationship, combined with Burke being all over this idea, soon led to "*Sportstalk* from the Fogg." Our listeners, er, drank it up, not only because they got to see Burke and I spar in person, but they also saw special guests like Bobby Orr, Gordie Howe, Johnny Bucyk, Eddie Shack, Mike Milbury, Pavel Bure and Trevor Linden.

The great Orr appeared twice at the Fogg in what must be labelled more as events than shows. Tickets were precious and were sold on a first-come, first-served basis. Our show started at 10 p.m. The first night Orr appeared, the restaurant was jammed at five! Attendees were fuelled by the hours-long consumption of suds and the anticipation of getting within arm's length of this hockey icon, and the ovation Orr received when he arrived a few minutes before airtime was deafening.

Inside, I was giddy. Of all the guests I had, No. 4's appearance was absolutely the most special. Over the years, I learned there are times when our sports heroes aren't what you expect when you meet them in person. Orr was better. He was a perfect gentleman — accommodating and playing well with the audience — and he was mostly forthright with answers, the exception being any question that involved Al Eagleson, his disgraced former agent. When his hour was over, Orr graciously signed autographs before departing. He was total class, and I felt damn proud to have provided a chance for these listeners to get that close to hockey greatness.

One year later, Bobby returned to the Fogg, this time alongside Howe, who told our audience he had only one criticism of Orr.

"In all probability, Bobby's the finest player to ever put the blades on," Howe said. "I can't knock him except to say when he was very young I was afraid to hit him because I might get sprayed by the pimples."

Burke also invited us to do remotes from the isolated Langara Fishing Lodge in the majestic Queen Charlottes (now Haida Gwaii). That was his favourite R and R spot, perhaps because there wasn't any cell phone coverage. Guests from there included NHL general managers Pat Quinn, Harry Sinden, Glen Sather and Dave Nonis.

Personally, I loved the night, only a few weeks removed from the '94 playoff run, when we put Quinn and Burke on air together, something that rarely occurred.

Quinn: "This is marvellous. We've had a great two days, lots of fun. Harry Sinden and I happen to be in the fast boat. In the slow boat there's Slats [Sather] and [San Jose Sharks' owner] George Gund. That boat is slow. The people fishing in it are slow. Slow getting to fish. Slow talk. Lot of slow things. But a lot of fast things are happening in our boat."

Russell: "How would you describe the Brian Burke boat?"

Quinn: "Oh [laughing], that's that big barge they brought in!"

Russell: "Tell me, Brian, who caught a bigger fish today? You or Pat?"

Burke: "Well, Pat caught a bigger fish; I released several that were bigger than his."

Quinn: "Involuntary releases is what they're called!"

Burke: "You know, I'm fishing with Dave Nonis and we don't have a guide, nor a great big fancy boat like Pat and Harry."

Quinn: "Who was the third man in your boat today?"

Burke: "Well, we had a guide today."

Quinn: "Oh, woah! You had a guide today, did you? What did you mean, do you have a guide or not?"

Burke: "No, the first day we didn't, but today I think we got Helen Keller's twin brother the way this guy works. It's too bad the white cane doesn't work on the water 'cause we didn't find any fish."

Russell: "So who caught a bigger fish today?"

Burke: "I already answered that question. Why would you want to ask it again? Pat kept a bigger fish than I did today. I released other fish that were bigger than the fish he kept."

Russell: "The reports we got, and we were covering this story very closely, was that none of your fish were as big as the one he landed."

Burke: "Your report is incorrect, as I found in the five years I was on your show, occurred frequently."

Russell: "How big was your fish, Pat?"

Quinn: "Thirty-two-plus pounds. And believe me, the reports I have from sources within the boat said Burke was saying, 'I have to have a fish bigger than Quinn's or I'm going to kill somebody.' So this little story that 'I released, I released,' that's just a drug-induced fantasy."

Russell: "Well, isn't that nice, Brian? Somebody called you drug-induced for once."

Burke: "Yeah, real nice. I happen to think it's an awful thing to say about somebody. I would never do that."

Peter Pocklington was on one of the trips as well. I couldn't care less that he arrogantly refused our invitation to appear on the show, but I disliked how he pompously pissed off the staff with his special orders, including an insistence of a certain vintage of wine they were forced to fly out to find.

On the opposite side of that spectrum was meeting an actual real-life hero, Ken Taylor, the Canadian diplomat who famously negotiated the release of hostages in Tehran on behalf of the American government in 1979. Unassuming as he was, it seemed strange to be idly chatting and putting on my marine gear next to him.

Fishing time sure didn't mix well with *Sportstalk* time, as we made our way to our boats before five each morning. The trip was exclusive and luxurious, but I actually didn't like fishing, though that didn't stop me from somehow joining the "Tyee Club" when I somehow landed a thirty-three-pound chinook.

During one of those trips, Burke also began a different kind of fishing, which in this case involved enquiring about one of our co-workers, Jennifer Mather, whom he had met once when in studio. Long story short, Burke asked Woodgate and me to see if she might be interested. We did and she was.

Soon after, Jenny started receiving flowers at the station seemingly every week. Ultimately, this previously untried *Sportstalk* cupid method actually led to marriage, though, written in our fine print matchmaking contract, we never guaranteed long-term happiness.

In those days there really was no end to what Burke might do to help our show and/or perhaps settle scores. For example, because of his dislike for Tony Gallagher, he convinced Rod Beaton to leave Gallagher's new radio show and join us. Burke had met Rod when Beaton was the first hockey writer for the newspaper *USA TODAY* in 1982. Beaton loved his puck, but his bosses knew he had an encyclopedic baseball mind and switched him to the MLB beat a few years later.

Beaton gave *Sportstalk* the greatest baseball guest our market has ever had and, just like Burke, he joined us every week from wherever he happened to be. Rod's knowledge was second to none. Without exaggeration he not only accurately knew every player in the majors, but I'd safely say more than 90 percent of the players at the minor-league levels, the top amateurs, plus all the draft eligibles. His instant recall was amazing. You just couldn't stump him. Plus, he had such incredible enthusiasm with a voice that nearly jumped through the radio speaker. One comment I heard over and over was: "I'm not a fan of baseball, but I never miss Rod Beaton." The best compliment any guest could receive.

Soon after we met, I became close friends with Rod. I stayed at his home in DC, went to an Orioles' game with him at Camden Yards in Baltimore when it was the first MLB "retro stadium," and he toured me past the Lincoln Memorial, the National Mall and the White House. Rod also came to Vancouver a few times often staying at our green house.

Beaton loved Vancouver and once seriously considered a *Globe and Mail* offer so he could live in BC. He loved the Salmon House in West Vancouver, getting Asian cooking lessons from my wife and, for some reason, the awful tasting durian ice cream we always had to get at La Casa Gelato on Venables Street.

Rod had an absolute zest for life. He loved his wife, Maria, his boys, Kyle and Cody, great food, travel, baseball, hockey and so much more. Beaton was infectious. Whenever we elected to pre-tape our segment, I'd ring him at home. Once he knew who it was, he'd suddenly be proudly yelling to his family, "Hey, everyone, Dan Russell is on the line!"

It's what made what happened next so cruelly sad.

Around 2008, Beaton was diagnosed with Parkinson's disease. No one who knew him could believe it. The man with the filing-cabinet memory and the best gift of the gab was going to lose both? Once the shock subsided, I knew the day would soon come when we would lose Rod as a guest. But not yet. He loved doing *Sportstalk* so much.

As it was, *USA TODAY* was scaling him back, supporting him, but limiting him in what he could do. So much was being taken away from him that I just didn't have the heart to cut him from our show. It was a terrible dilemma because when he came on, he sounded off. He definitely wasn't the same effervescent Rod we were used to. He was trying so hard, but he talked slower, sometimes forgot the question and was slurring words.

Worse yet, we started getting emails from his loyal fans wondering if Rod was drunk. Even then, I still didn't have the heart to cut Rod, so I came up with a plan to postpone the inevitable. I would do away with his live appearances and pre-tape him each week so we could edit the interview to make him sound better. When I called to tape, Rod still announced to the family, "Dan Russell's on the phone," and for a while it worked fairly well. Recording and then going through every minute to clean up his pauses, forgetfulness and slurring was far more labour-intensive at my end, but I wanted to do this because it gave Rod a sense of purpose.

However, the news just kept getting worse. His Parkinson's had either been mis-diagnosed or elevated to Lewy body dementia, a progressive neurological disorder that eventually causes death from poor nutrition, swallowing difficulties and immobility. His wife, Maria, deserves a gold medal. She and the boys did everything they could to care for him, but eventually he became too much to handle. The disease so drastically changed him. He would alternate between being isolated, sometimes angry and potentially violent. The outbursts forced Maria to make the difficult decision to put Rod into a long-term hospital, and over the next couple of years our encyclopedic Rod came to no longer recognize her or their sons.

He was fifty-nine when he passed away, but the real Rod had died years earlier when that infectious spark was stripped from him. Being a friend of Rod Beaton's was a great joy in my life, and it was made possible because of my relationship with Brian Burke.

CHAPTER TWELVE

Used to be a ballpark

Though I eventually got used to changing stations, the first time it occurred it came with a thud … for two reasons.

First, we were on a roll. Towards the end of the '80s *Sportstalk* had found its stride filling a marketplace void, and the ratings were growing with every book. Second, and even more shocking, was that CJOR, which had served Vancouver for sixty-two years, would cease to exist. All-talk was changing to all-rock. With that, the iconic call letters would be retired. Those call letters, which some people claimed (though it never was confirmed) stood for Christ Jesus Our Redeemer, would become CHRX.

We had heard whispers about a possible format change, but no one took them seriously. I was out of town when station GM George Madden summoned the entire staff to a banquet room at the Burnaby Villa and confirmed what was happening. Then he told everyone to go to the back of the room to find their name on an envelope and open it to see if they still had a job.

Most did not.

Over forty professionals lost their jobs that day. A few years later, perhaps after it was proven *Sportstalk* could thrive on a music station, Joe Leary, then the CHRX music director, told me they had made a mistake in not keeping my show. He was right, considering *Sportstalk* skewed the lowest demo on the station. We were attracting exactly what CHRX was hoping for in their target demo: a large chunk of males between eighteen and thirty-five.

Upon hearing the news, I cut my vacation short and drove back to host the final few shows. Shortly after I got to my Richmond townhouse, the phone rang. It was Madden wanting to set up a meeting to deliver the news I already knew. Three hours later we met at the Hyatt Hotel in Richmond. He was holding a letter that contained the cause of termination and the terms of my severance. I was pleasantly surprised. Madden was giving me a year's salary. I wasn't making tons, but it would be the biggest cheque I had ever received up front. And I was already fielding calls from parties that might be interested in my services, meaning if all went well I was going to be paid by two stations.

However, within a few days Madden got wind that other stations were showing interest, and he wanted a do-over. He had misjudged the strength and marketability of *Sportstalk*, which is why he called me back to say he had made a mistake. He now claimed the offer of one-year's severance pay was to be paid monthly and would stop if I found employment elsewhere. I hung up the phone, stewed about it and then sought legal advice for the first time in my life.

My lawyer suggested I call Madden to remind him that we already had a deal based on what he had told me at the Hyatt. He hadn't said anything about severance stopping if I was hired elsewhere, and I reminded him we shook on it. Madden didn't argue. He only said he was trying to correct a mistake, not considering he might be incriminating himself if I happened to be recording the conversation. Once I gave the tape to my new lawyer, the initial deal was back in place. This time, Madden asked me to sign a waiver promising I wouldn't divulge the terms of the settlement.

Arriving at CJOR for the last time on September 2, 1988, was a strange experience. *Sportstalk* would be the final program it would air. The daytime shows had bid their farewells earlier in the day, and now it was my duty to close down six decades of this radio station. Its incredible history included the likes of Jack Webster, Pat Burns, Ed Murphy, Jim Nielsen, John Reynolds, Terry Moore, Chuck Cooke, Al Jordan, Monty McFarlane, Rafe Mair, Dave Barrett, Fanny Kiefer, Barrie Clark, Art Finley, Jack Short, Bob Mackin, Jerry Landa, Denny

Boyd, John Wilson, Ian Michaud, Garry Raible, Wayne Cox, Dave Abbott, Red Robinson, Brian Forst and countless others.

The final voice CJOR would air would be yours truly.

I did the final show having already heard strong overtures from other stations. I knew we'd likely have a new landing spot, but the listeners didn't. Some who called surmised as much, but all I would say was, "Hopefully *Sportstalk* will continue." There was lots of emotion that night, on and off the air, especially on our phone board. One sampling went like this:

"For five years we've been listening to you, and I'm really sorry to hear you are leaving the station. Unfortunately, I have an eleven-year-old who's just been introduced to your program and enjoyed it so much he's practically in tears. If you don't mind, he'd like to say goodbye."

She put him on, and while he was indeed sad, he was just as proud to tell me that because it was summer he was allowed to stay up past eleven every night to listen.

Moments after his call, it was time to bid farewell. I knew the ideal song with which I wanted to end, but it was pre-internet so I needed help finding it. Desperate and running short on time, I thought the only one who might have it would be Dave McCormick, the former CKNW DJ and long-time host of CFMI's popular *Discomentary*. Somehow, I got "Big Daddy" on the phone. He said he had it and that I could pick it up at his house in South Vancouver. Thanks to Dave, we chose a perfect Frank Sinatra heartfelt tribute for the final moments of CJOR. A song that expressed the sadness at the loss of a baseball team and its home. "There Used to be a Ballpark."

When the song ended, we faded into the familiar *Sportstalk* theme, which marked CJOR's final breaths at the stroke of midnight. One second later, the birth of Classic Rock CHRX began with Bob Seger's "Old Time Rock and Roll." CHRX did okay for a couple of years but quickly faded, as did most AM music stations.

Sportstalk, on the other hand, was on the move, and our growing audience was coming with us.

CHAPTER THIRTEEN

CKNW vs CKWX

Losing the CJOR job led directly to a personal aphorism I would share with colleagues in future years — you never make any real money in radio unless it's your phone that rings.

I was fortunate that there was lots of activity before and after the firing. I had four offers, so I knew *Sportstalk* would live on unless I gave serious consideration to the fourth one: to become general manager of the WHL's Tri-City Americans.

Owner Ron Dixon was serious. At least that's what he kept telling me. A resident of Delta, Dixon had relocated his New Westminster Bruins to Kennewick in eastern Washington State. I'd known Dixon for five years, and I specifically remember receiving two phone calls from him.

It wasn't quite a Paul Henderson/Neil Armstrong "I knew where I was" moment, but the first call was the first one I ever received from a cell phone. Ron got miffed because he had something to discuss and I couldn't stop laughing at the thought of someone driving while talking on a phone.

Soon after we started getting cell calls on *Sportstalk*, and because they were paying airtime we bumped them to the front of the queue. Then, as I brought them on the air, we asked them to confirm their special status by honking their horn. Callers really enjoyed this. Some gave a little toot, some a louder blast, and I'd occasionally try to guess what make their car was. Plus, it sounded good. Another theatre of the mind image we tried to deliver. The best horns came from the truckers in their big rigs, until I heard one long blast from the conductor on a CP Rail train and another from the captain of a BC Ferries vessel.

Quality horns blew us away!

The other call from Dixon I remember came around four o'clock one Saturday afternoon. He wanted me to watch his team play an exhibition game that night in Portland.

"It's a little late for that," I told him.

"Meet me at the South Terminal in one hour," Dixon said.

He didn't have to ask twice. An hour later, Ron, his wife Joan and I were aboard a six-seat private jet enjoying a couple of soft drinks and a few snacks. Ron insisted on playing rummy as we flew in style to watch his Tri-City Americans.

Ron had a car waiting for us in Portland to whisk us to Memorial Coliseum where his team lost big. We left at the final horn and went directly to the airport. Only this time, he instructed the pilot to drop him off in Kennewick before Joan and I flew back to Vancouver.

The start of the 1988-89 WHL regular season was only a couple of weeks away and Dixon was desperate to name a GM. I kept telling him he had no business offering me that kind of job, which I came to learn was precisely the point. The new arena in Kennewick wasn't finished, and without a suitable rink nearby the Americans were going to play their first eighteen games — 25 percent of their schedule — on the road. Dixon called every couple of days and each time tried harder to sell me. I laughed, telling him I was sure he would fire me before I got to my first home game.

The second offer came from Jim Johnston, the program director at CFOX, who would later become one of the best bosses I would work for. But not yet.

"If you don't have anything else going in the way of offers, we'd love to have you do your show once a week on Sunday nights," he said.

It was a kind gesture, one that would also help his FM station comply with CRTC programming requirements but, given the two other offers, the FOX wasn't going to rock for *Sportstalk*.

Which brings us to the finalists: CKNW vs. CKWX.

Greg Douglas was pursuing me hard in his role as 'WX sports director while 'NW GM Ron Bremner called the day after CJOR died to tell me Doug Rutherford, his program director, would arrange a meeting.

I first got to know Douglas during two Vancouver Canadians spring-training junkets in Arizona where late-night beers led to late-night songs. I swear Greg liked me best for my surprisingly strong rendition of Frank Sinatra's "New York, New York."

Douglas, GM Tom Peacock and PD Ted Farr not only wanted our show locally but also to bolster their fledgling Satellite Radio Network. Being heard outside of Vancouver was intriguing, but most importantly they were prepared to give me my ten to midnight time slot. Douglas tried hard to sell me, inviting me every afternoon to his West 6th Avenue townhouse for drinks, knowing full well that when CKNW showed interest in a local broadcaster it usually won out. Naturally, I really wanted to know what 'NW had in mind, but when I got to Rutherford's office I didn't like what I heard or how he delivered it.

In a precursor to the bullshit I would experience in future years, Rutherford didn't have a concrete offer. He couldn't even specify when *Sportstalk* would air. He only wanted to play keep away. I kept pressing him before he finally said, "We'd probably put you in early evenings, maybe around 6:30 p.m. to 8:00 p.m., or thereabouts."

Probably? Maybe? Thereabouts?

I knew nine to midnight on CKNW was sacred ground with Jack Cullen having hosted *The Owl Prowl* since the 1940s, so why was I even there?

"Do you know how many people would like to be sitting in this office talking to me right now?" Rutherford said.

Every bone in my body was screaming at me to blast him, but I tried to make light of it instead.

"I'm not sitting here because of the smell of my cologne," I said with half a chuckle.

Even though I hated the arrogance, I also knew it would be difficult to say no to CKNW, especially given my play-by-play aspirations. But should I give up the future of *Sportstalk* just to get my foot in the door at the hockey station?

Meanwhile, those afternoon visits to see Douglas also took the form of counselling sessions, especially when he was a few drinks in. The day before I was to make my decision, a well-lubricated Douglas begged me to take his offer but a moment later predicted I'd give in to 'NW. To Greg's surprise — and, in many ways, to mine — I chose 'WX. I knew that keeping what I had built up was the right decision even if it turned out to be a death knell for my play-by-play dream.

So we set up the *Sportstalk* shop only a few blocks from the CJOR studios, moving from 8th and Hemlock to 8th and Ash. The studios were new and management was nice. I actually was in awe of Peacock, not just because my family woke up listening to him in the late '60s when he did the morning show on 'WX, but because he was the Canucks' PA announcer.

"Vancouver's first goal scored by number four, Barry Wilkins," Peacock famously announced the night the NHL came to Vancouver in 1970.

The eloquent Danny Gallivan came on *Sportstalk* soon after I joined 'WX, facilitated by my friend Wayne McKay, a Van City VP and generous friend of our show. Perhaps the last of the highly-literate play-by-play broadcasters, Gallivan relished sitting in our studio, sharing stories from his days calling Montreal Canadiens games, including sixteen of their Stanley Cup titles, for *Hockey Night in Canada*.

I remember Gallivan being assigned a Canucks game on a Saturday night a few years earlier. As it happened, Vancouver also played the night before and, as luck would have it, Danny was assigned the press-box seat right beside me. As Gallivan settled in, he made some small talk before asking if I'd mind if he practised in preparation for the next day's game. Imagine that! Here was a man who had done hundreds and hundreds of games wanting to make sure he was sharp for the next one. Not only did he do personal play-by-play for me, but he took his pen out and held it as though it was a microphone. It was like Elton John performing a concert in my living room. Somehow, I suppressed the urge to do colour. He used his other hand to cup his ear, as he had since first calling games in the mid-forties. Even after the invention of headset microphones, *HNIC* always provided Danny with a dead hand mic to hold during games.

That night on *Sportstalk*, he waxed poetically about many topics, including a detailed description of the origin of his famous "cannonading drive" catchphrase. As he concluded, Gallivan admitted he was hurt at having received numerous complaints from people telling him cannonading wasn't a word.

"I knew right away that you would have to be very charitable and look diligently to find justification to use the word 'cannonading,'" he said in true Gallivan lexicon. "Then, three or four days later I got a letter from a pseudo-English professor. Very terse. To the point. He said, 'How dare you? There is no such word.' I wrote him back and said, 'How dare you — there is now!'"

Dick Irvin, Danny's long-time partner, was also on a few times and once recounted Gallivan's final night in the spring of 1984. After the Canadiens' charter landed following their last playoff game, Irvin said to Gallivan, "See you next year."

"No, you won't" was the reply that Irvin assumed was end-of-season fatigue.

But Gallivan wasn't kidding. He didn't return.

Incidentally and without exaggeration, one of my greatest broadcast thrills was a night at the Montreal Forum when Irvin asked me to be his radio intermission guest. It was, as Irvin's partner might have said, a scintillating moment for me.

As per usual on Canucks home nights, I'd watch nearly two periods of the game before high-tailing it to the station in time for our 10 p.m. start. On December 16, 1988, producer Scott Woodgate and I stopped near the lower press box at Pacific Coliseum to get our coats when we noticed that legendary Hall of Famer "Babe" Pratt was the only person in the room. He appeared to have fallen asleep on one of the comfy chairs in the media lounge. We quietly scurried past him and continued towards the exit. As we were going down, we noticed three white-shirted paramedics, one carrying an oxygen tank, quickly going up the stairs. I didn't even consider that it had anything to do with Pratt. I just thought the Canucks game was so boring that the Babe was having a nap.

It wasn't until we hit the air that we learned those paramedics were on their way to treat Pratt and take him to hospital. Douglas, the first Vancouver Canucks NHL media relations manager, had known Pratt since 1970, and he quickly made his way to our studios and tracked down Dr. Dave Harris, the team doctor.

"Can you give us an update?" I asked, shortly after our show began.

"I'm afraid I have bad news," Dr. Harris said. "I just spoke with VGH and Babe was pronounced dead on arrival. When he left the Coliseum we didn't think there was much hope for him. We had seven paramedics at one time working to resuscitate him. Unfortunately, we were not successful. I just talked to the hospital thirty seconds ago. They just informed us he passed away."

After more than a couple of seconds of silence, a disbelieving Douglas said, "The Babe is gone? Man ... I've spent so much time with him. He could hold court like no one."

One of the great storytellers had suffered a heart attack and was likely dead when we thought he was sleeping.

We also had Tom Scallen, the Canucks' original owner, on the show to break a long silence regarding his fall from grace. This was years after he was convicted of stealing three million from Northwest Sports Enterprises Ltd., the company that owned the Canucks, and using the money to pay off debts to his parent company, Medicor. Scallen served nine months at the British Columbia Penitentiary in New Westminster before being released on appeal. He received a pardon from the Canadian government in 1982. He told us he had witnessed a stabbing during his first day in the penitentiary and was in despair while behind bars, but overall was treated well by the other inmates.

"The guys in the joint, if I may use the language, were great hockey fans," he said. "And they gave me many kindnesses, a lot of which were based on an admiration for having brought hockey to BC because they all listened to the games. We were the shut-ins! I can remember laying there with the headphones on listening to Canucks games myself."

Pleasant hello, circa 1961!

My parents Pat and Ken Russell in 1962. Dad spent his entire working career at BC Tel, while Mom was with the Royal Bank. I got my organization skills from Mom and my sense of humour from Dad.

The baby of the family in 1962, looking spiffy with sister Cathy and brother Brian.

With my dad in 1965 at Birch Bay State Park. My parents took us camping almost every weekend from April through September.

At age nineteen I hosted *Sports Watch*, a weekly amateur sports show originating from North Vancouver, produced by Furio Sorrentino (left) and Lesley Payne.

When the WHL's New Westminster Bruins returned in 1983 I called all their TV games until they relocated to Kennewick, Washington, five seasons later. *(Western 4 Sports)*

I got to spend some time with Pete Rose, MLB's all-time hits leader, in February 1980. That's *Vancouver Sun* columnist Jim Kearney in the forefront.

Thanks to Garry Raible, I was able to get my foot in
the CJOR sports department door in 1981.

I produced and hosted Vancouver Canadians baseball games. One
of the perks was traveling to Aloha Stadium in Honolulu in 1983.

Sportstalk made its debut on October 15, 1984.

From the master talk studio at 8th & Hemlock in 1986, a few years after
CJOR vacated the Grosvenor Hotel basement at 840 Howe Street.

Soon after I had bragged about receiving a baseball cap from the evening shift workers at Duke Point Sawmill in Nanaimo, listeners sent in almost 500 more. *(Greg Osadchuk / Province)*

Pat Burns, the most impactful talk show host in Vancouver history, possessed an encyclopedic mind, including tremendous sports knowledge. His show was the perfect lead-in for *Sportstalk*.

When CJOR folded in 1988 I immediately received four offers, and to the surprise of even myself I chose Real Country WX over the Top Dog, CKNW.

Original Vancouver Canucks owner Tom Scallen in 1989, years after serving time at the BC Penitentiary.

In our early days, pre-email, Sportstalk received many letters, including this one in 1989 that stopped me in my tracks. The following year the writer was convicted of first-degree murder.

Gordie Howe appeared several times on *Sportstalk*, even after John McKeachie once told me Mr. Hockey had died.

Broadcast legend Danny Gallivan in 1989 was behind the mic for sixteen Montreal championships and also for the first Canucks game on CKNW in 1970. (Wayne McKay)

Talk shows on FM in 1990 were unheard of. But after agreeing to my timeslot request, I made the jump from CKWX to CFMI. The Rock 101 days, including our highly popular nights from the Fogg N' Suds, were my favourites.

With *Sportstalk*'s all-time greatest guest in 1992. Brian Burke was smart, outspoken, funny, quick, and passionate. His appearances were "appointment radio."

Bobby Orr made his first of three *Sportstalk* appearances twenty years after writing me. On this Fogg N' Suds night in 1990 ticket-holders arrived five hours before No. 4.

Jim Robson was my second all-time favourite guest, and I pinched myself with each appearance, including this 1992 Fogg night.

Road Trip of a Lifetime was a resounding success. Those lucky listeners experienced buildings like the Montreal Forum, Boston Garden, Chicago Stadium, Maple Leaf Gardens, Madison Square Garden and the Philadelphia Spectrum.

We also saw the Canucks play at Landover, Maryland, just a few hours after my brother, Brian, and I sat in front of George H. Bush's home.

Rod Beaton was an outstanding guest and great friend. He showed me many DC landmarks and also took me to a Baltimore Orioles game when I visited him in 1993.

All photos from author's collection, unless noted.

The first Canucks playoff *Sportstalk* ever covered was their second-most memorable series with Calgary in 1989. It began with Vancouver's Paul Reinhart scoring an overtime winner against his old team in Game 1 and ended ten days later with Joel Otto kicking in the series winner in Game 7 overtime. The decider was Mike Vernon's greatest game, a goaltending performance for the ages, against Kirk McLean who exacted his revenge in the same building five years later.

I'm not sure how I was able to convince management to let me stay — it was probably the Gretzky factor — but after the Canucks were eliminated we did our show in the Saddledome following the first two games of the Flames' next round against Los Angeles. That allowed me to witness the Flames scoring a goal with trainer Jim "Bearcat" Murray tending to a shaken up Vernon in his goal crease. Somehow it counted!

I also caught Calgary in Round 3 of that Stanley Cup year after we'd taken our show on a Brian Burke-suggested trip to Milwaukee's Bradley Center to see the Canucks' farm team. It was a trip during which I saw Bo Jackson appear in the coldest (3°C) and windiest baseball game I ever attended. I also conducted a long, reminiscing interview with original Canucks GM Bud Poile, who by then was the International Hockey League commissioner.

From there I drove ninety minutes to the actual Windy City for one of the highlights of my life: my first visit to Chicago Stadium. Since listening to Bob Cole do the final game of the 1969-70 season on CBC Radio — the culmination of the NHL's craziest final day — I yearned to someday see and hear the Stadium in person. The season finale in 1970 was a game in which Montreal needed a point in the standings or to score five goals in order to capture the final playoff spot.

Trailing 5-2 halfway through the final period, the Habs kept pulling goalie Rogie Vachon and the 'Hawks, to the delight of their raucous fans, kept filling the empty net with the horn blasting after every goal, until they reached ten. I couldn't believe my ears. I fell in love with this rink before my eyes had even seen it, as it wasn't until a year later that I saw a TV game from Chicago.

Because we only saw games from Canada, it was beyond belief when the seemingly alien world of American arenas was beamed into our living rooms with the advent of Sunday TV games. These games were almost always between two US teams, games that until then we had only read about in the summaries on newspaper agate pages.

Once I started *Sportstalk*, I always loved asking current and former players to talk about playing in the Stadium, with its staircases from the dressing rooms, the fabled 3,663-pipe organ, the goosebumps Wayne Messmer's national anthem created, the incredibly loud goal horn (which scared the crap out of me when it was tested an hour before warmup) and the unique nasally/monotone PA sound of Harvey Wittenberg. From years of listening to games from Chicago, I remembered it seemed to take forever for a goal call to be announced, as if a runner had to take the scoring play from the penalty box to an upper PA booth before we'd finally hear Wittenberg announce: "Blackhawk goal scored by number nine, Bobby Hull. Assist to number twenty-one, Stan Mikita, and to number fifteen, Eric Nesterenko, at 4:28."

Darcy Rota, a former Blackhawks player, became one of my favourite interviews and always enthralled me with his stories about the rink's location in one of the most dangerous neighbourhoods in America. Rota told me that when he was a rookie he had to park across the street from the fenced in lot the veterans used. When he arrived, someone would invariably say, "Five dollars to watch your car tonight," which was code for "It'll still be here after you play." Eventually, Darcy was able to park in the compound right beside uniquely named Gate 3½, a tiny side door that provided an entrance for the players and media.

The night I went there, I arrived early so I could explore every nook and cranny. I climbed to the top in order to see the incredible view from the nosebleeds, sat in various seats and imagined where Jim Nill was when he scored in double OT. I went down to the bench to recreate Roger Neilson's famous white-towel-waving episode and then to the basement where I visited both dressing rooms. Like an excited kid on Christmas morning, I walked up both sets of stairs to the ice surface, always an incredible TV shot, imagining what it'd be like for a player to pop up after twenty-two steps and be greeted by that ear-splitting roar of the crowd.

Twice while I was in Burbank, California, I attended *The Tonight Show with Johnny Carson* and was blown away by how small his studio looked compared to TV. Same thing with Chicago Stadium. It wasn't near as large as it was intimidating.

Because of the dangerous neighbourhood, then-Calgary newspaper writer Ben Kuzma suggested I might want to leave through the main door a few minutes early because taxi drivers listened to the game from The Loop, the downtown district about three miles away, and as the game neared an end they would swoop in to see if someone hailed them. Sure enough, when Hakan Loob scored the 4-2 goal with eight minutes remaining, I vacated the endzone press box, made my way to the main entrance, exited — and didn't see a thing. Barely a car, let alone a taxi. But I did see a group across the street that looked less than friendly. I waited close to the arena door for about ten minutes hoping for a cab that never came. Soon eighteen thousand fans were exiting, but they all had rides home whereas I didn't.

Not knowing what to do, I went back inside and used my media pass to go to the dressing room area. I hung around for much of the post-game activity, hoping I could find someone to help me. When that didn't work, I began wandering outside Gate 3½ to see if I might find a taxi there. That's when Flames coach Terry Crisp asked where I was going. When I told him, he said, "To hell you are. Get on our bus, we'll take you back." And so, six wins shy of their first Stanley Cup, I was able to hitch a ride to safety with Crisp, Lanny, Theo and the rest of the eventual champs.

CHAPTER FOURTEEN

A home on the FM dial

I had been on CKWX for three months when, surprisingly, I received another call from CKNW. It started with some small talk and ended with a request to reconsider. I said CKWX was fine and I had signed a one-year contract, so I wasn't in a position to reconsider. Just as importantly, my non-negotiable time slot still wasn't available with them.

Four months later, another call. Same thing. Small talk followed by, "Have you given any more thought about coming over to us?" I gave the same answer, declining CKNW for a third time.

Four more months went by before they called again. This one came in September while I was covering the Canucks' training camp in Parksville on Vancouver Island. This time there wasn't any small talk. Doug Rutherford, the program director, said he had something new to run by me and if I agreed to listen he would fly over that afternoon. For reasons I was never clear about, when I'd agreed to join CKWX, GM Tom Peacock only felt comfortable offering me a one-year contract. At the time, I wasn't concerned, but as time wore on I was bothered that no one initiated discussions about the future. Five hours after we hung up, Rutherford arrived outside the aptly named Oceanside Arena where the Canucks had finished practising for the day. We walked over to an adjacent park and sat on a bench.

This time he was far different. The patronizing side of Rutherford had disappeared, at least for the time being. He was charming and showed respect. He said he and GM Ron Bremner had been talking a lot about me and had come up with a new strategy concerning *Sportstalk*.

"As you know, CKNW doesn't have the time slot for you," he began. "But what would you say if we offered you a chance to do *Sportstalk* on (Classic Rock) CFMI?"

What?

Not a chance in the world had I seen that coming. I'm sure I probably stared into the ocean for several seconds while digesting what I had just heard.

"My involvement was instigated by Ron Bremner, who had listened to [Dan] often, and also because a couple of his teenage sons were very big Dan Russell fans," Rutherford recalled years later. "Ron and I kept monitoring it and kept thinking about it before he asked me to go over to Canucks' camp to see if [Dan would] be interested in joining CFMI, which was quite a departure for both his show, obviously, and for FM radio in the Vancouver market because it hadn't been done before."

Classic Rock CFMI was willing to stop the music every night at 10 p.m. and insert a talk show? I didn't know of any FM program director who would embrace that, including Rick Shannon, who, for the longest time, refused to even allow *Sportstalk* promos to air in other day parts. This was textbook out-of-the-box thinking. A regular weekday talk show hadn't been done on Vancouver's FM dial. Remember this was 1989, long before satellite radio, Spotify, YouTube or any other sources where you could find music with high-quality sound. You either bought a CD player or you listened to FM. Also, and this was a huge consideration for me, unless you were driving a new vehicle, chances are you didn't have an FM band as a standard option.

"Wow, I have to give you guys full marks for this one," I told Rutherford, glancing away from the ocean but still in semi-shock.

I told him I was intrigued but needed to think about it. I did, long and hard for several days while jotting down the pros and cons, as I did with all major decisions. Was CKNW still playing keep away or did they think this was a great move for the market? I pondered many things. The thought of *Sportstalk* on an FM rock station felt weird, but on the pro side of the ledger, CFMI's audience was exactly in *Sportstalk*'s demographic wheelhouse — males aged eighteen to thirty-four or eighteen to forty-five. Then I would recall how CKWX had given me a chance to keep the show's momentum in late evenings, but I could also see some cracks, as illustrated by non-existent talks on a contract renewal. Could I trust 'WX to be a long-term home for *Sportstalk*?

I also admired CKNW's persistence. Even though Rutherford had initially ticked me off, I needed to remember that 'NW did offer me some kind of employment when CJOR folded. And when I became that rare local broadcaster who actually turned them down, they didn't ignore me, they kept pursuing me — three times in one year. Truth be told, that was what tipped my decision: a belief that if I kept saying no, I might never hear from the station again. Besides, 'NW had clearly listened to what was the most important thing to me: time slot.

A few days later, I called Bremner to tell him I was willing to put a deal together, and he invited me to go see him in New Westminster. The first thing he told me was how it was his two teenage sons, regular listeners on CJOR and CKWX, who kept telling him how much they loved the show. Soon we began talking about a contract, but at this point I hadn't sought legal advice. That would come a few days later after Bremner and I hammered out part of the basis of an agreement.

With the possibility of moving into the same building as the hockey station, I found it necessary to keep Brian Burke in the loop. After asking how the process was going, he said, "You ought to have a lawyer."

Not only did I think that was good advice, but Burke, a lawyer himself, also provided me with the name of the man he had in mind, Roger Bourbonnais, a former Edmonton Oil Kings star who had played for Father David Bauer at UBC and for Canada in the Olympics. Bourbonnais not only had a trained legal mind but possessed incredible patience. I would call him countless times over the years to vent over some broken radio station promise, and within a couple of minutes he would have calmed me down, mostly by assuring me that I wasn't crazy. I lost track of how many times Roger labelled CKNW's decision-making style as crisis management, but I definitely had the feeling he was used to working with people on a far different level, and not just financially.

Roger took me on, as he had a couple of NHL coaches, more for a change of pace as the majority of his legal work centred around banking, lending and real estate. Roger not only handled my contract negotiations but also real-estate transactions, estate planning and more up until he retired in 2019. I often told my inner circle that his legal bills were the best money I spent during my career. I wonder how many people can say that about their lawyer.

Roger came into this first negotiation after many of the terms had been decided, but there was one ratings clause he negotiated that I would cash in on for years to come. Radio ratings are measured in several different ways. In those days, stations heavily emphasized their quarter-hour averages. Before I signed on, CFMI was averaging fewer than six thousand listeners per quarter hour between 10 p.m. and midnight. Before finalizing my base salary, Bremner offered a bonus of one dollar for every listener above six thousand. That meant if the next Bureau of Broadcast Measurement (BBM) rating showed an average of ten thousand listeners, the station would pay me a bonus of $4,000. The way Bremner was structuring it, if I then increased it to twelve thousand listeners in the next ratings survey, they'd pay another $2,000 to mark the difference between ten thousand and twelve thousand listeners. We didn't have a problem with the first part of that premise, but Roger, thinking CFMI would only be paying once but still selling those larger numbers to advertisers for the length of the contract, suggested whatever I made in bonuses during Year 1 must then be rolled into my base salary for the subsequent years in the deal. Using hypothetical numbers, this meant if the base salary was $50,000 and there was $10,000 in bonuses in Year 1, there would be a bonus cheque for $10,000 and the Year 2 base salary would climb to $60,000. Bremner agreed, probably not imagining I would increase CFMI's listenership from six thousand to more than eighteen thousand, which meant I earned a lot in bonuses and much more in my base salary for years to come.

Next came the unpleasant task of telling CKWX, which clearly had been asleep at the switch, that I was leaving. Honestly, I was so busy with my 'NW negotiation that I hadn't given any thought as to what 'WX would do after I told them. In the absence of any conversations about a renewal, I naively assumed they would go back to playing country music. They took the news even harder than I thought when they suddenly realized they were going to lose their sizeable late evening ratings.

At first, Peacock tried to block me from signing with 'NW and told me they were going to keep paying me. I'm sure they knew they didn't have a leg to stand on and were just trying to buy time — crisis management — while figuring out their next move. When they finally relented and I stopped in to pick up my exit papers, the overconfident network co-ordinator Taanta Gupta told me, "We're going to go up against you and we will beat you."

She was half right. They initially plugged my time slot with Greg Douglas and famous newspaper columnist Jim Taylor, still calling the show *Sportstalk* even though I'd had the presence of mind to remove all copies of our theme music from the station.

Sportstalk 2.0 lasted only a few days before CKWX came to lightning-quick terms with *The Province* columnist Tony Gallagher to go head-to-head with me. Gallagher was an extremely effective writer and an excellent guest, but hosting wasn't his forte. To this day I wonder why so many radio executives have such a low opinion of their own industry that they continuously hire people for big money who have absolutely no broadcast experience.

This would be the first time we had competition — *Sportstalk* breaking new ground on FM, *Gallagher on Sport* debuting on 'WX. Everyone told me competition was good. Some counselled me not to listen to Gallagher and only worry about myself. I not only disagreed but always recorded his show. After getting back to my Richmond home, often around 2 a.m., I would go for a long walk to listen to his program and assess how we did against him.

Gallagher improved over time, though his dry sense of humour didn't lend itself to this medium. Due to connections he had made while on the NHL beat, he did have some great guests, which brought up a good question. Would a listener prefer hearing a big name being interviewed by an unseasoned host or a seasoned host who knows how to structure all parts of a show? The latter scenario won out when CKWX gave up the fight two years later.

Gallagher was our first victim, but he wouldn't be the last.

For his part, Douglas never got over my leaving. He even admitted years later, "We were devastated when we lost him." I'm sorry Greg took my departure as a betrayal because I always liked him. I'm even sorrier that it led to his not talking to me since it happened.

CHAPTER FIFTEEN

What's your position on this?

It should have felt great to be the only show in town again, but we soon ran into much bigger competition than Gallagher, who had been down the dial. Now the biggest threat to our future came from down the hall — from people within.

It wasn't Rick Shannon's fault, but when I was brought in to CFMI he was a program director who knew little about talk radio and less about sports. That's why we didn't see any reason not to allow CKNW program director Doug Rutherford to oversee our show when we cut our first deal. For some reason, that led to sports director J. P. McConnell falsely believing that *Sportstalk* should fall under his umbrella. Unnecessarily gruff on the outside, McConnell really did have a soft side but, unfortunately for me, it took far too many years to find it.

One of the many upsides of working at night was avoiding most of the daytime politics that played out at CKNW. As an added bonus, *Sportstalk* originated from the lightly-staffed Expo grounds studios across from BC Place Stadium, not the crowded main station in New Westminster. However, before debuting on CFMI, we needed to set up the technical logistics, which meant spending the better part of a day in New West. Until then, the only time I'd been at the 8th and McBride headquarters was when I had entered through a private side door that led to general manager Ron Bremner's private bathroom and then into his office. Why? Because Bremner didn't want anyone in the station to know he was negotiating with me.

But now the shackles were off so, while waiting to meet with the chief engineer, I was free to wander around the station that I had loyally listened to for years. The building had been a Safeway store until it became CKNW's headquarters in 1969. As I roamed, I was trying to imagine how that could be. However, before I came to grips with that, I found myself in the sports department located just off the newsroom. I really wish I had found the produce department instead because not two seconds after I walked in, McConnell was yelling at me in front of everyone. And he wasn't welcoming me to my new home. Nope. What I was experiencing — it wouldn't be the last time — was a good old-fashioned power trip, as J.P. tried to set the tone for how things were going to be for *Sportstalk* in its new home.

At first I smiled, nodded and tried to change the subject. But then he started up again, only this time much louder. I realized, especially with half the newsroom reporters staring at us, that I should stand my ground. That's when I let him know as kindly and as firmly as I could, but loud enough for most to hear, that I didn't report to him. Little did I know how much or for how long this would bother him. But I found out about a year later when a bunch of us from the radio station gathered at the North Shore home of talk-show host Philip Till, a former BBC and NBC reporter I had gotten to know by working alongside him each night.

On a number of occasions prior to this gathering, Philip had generously invited my producer, Scott Woodgate, and me to his house for dinner. The Tills were of French heritage, which meant four-hour multi-course meals and drinks — fine red wine, always followed by Jameson whiskey, neat. Those nights often lasted until after three in the morning and even longer on the nights when Philip loudly played music from his favourite, Luciano Pavarotti.

Till's best mate and broadcast partner, Jon McComb, was usually there, too, and we all loved hearing Till's war stories from when he was in Beirut as NBC Radio/TV's chief foreign correspondent. On the night of Till's much larger radio station party, I arrived well after the others and first stopped for some small chat in the living room. Out of the corner of one eye, I noticed J.P. among a handful of others who had congregated in the kitchen. McConnell had a glass of red wine in one hand and it was safe to say it wasn't his first. A couple of minutes later, I went towards the kitchen island to grab a drink, and that's when the two of us got into it. McConnell started it by randomly blurting, "I am your boss, you report to me, and that is in your contract," so everyone nearby could hear. He then added, "Oh, and by the way, your contract is sitting on the front seat of my car. Which is unlocked."

I don't ever remember being that ticked. But after chirpping back with choice words of my own, two of the now uncomfortable partygoers stepped in and wisely guided me back to the living room. Though we avoided each other the rest of the night, I stewed about it for the remainder of the weekend. I waited until Monday to phone Rutherford, the person I was supposed to be reporting to but who wasn't at the Till party. Rutherford asked me to drive into the station so we could meet in person, but our face-to-face conversation offered nothing of substance. He didn't necessarily take McConnell's side, but it was clear he wasn't going to reprimand him either.

I drove off wondering what I had gotten myself into, especially since Bremner, the general manager and driving force behind me signing there, had left 'NW to become the station manager at BCTV. Rutherford hadn't officially replaced Bremner, but he sure acted like he had. The new general manager was Rod Gunn.

The next in-house fight happened in 1991 and was among my biggest. It involved our massively growing post-game Canucks coverage on CFMI versus the staleness of CKNW's *Overtime Show*. *Sportstalk* was faster paced, quicker to the punch and far more exciting and biting (when required) than anything 'NW was serving up. And it drove Rutherford, the hockey station's PD (his first priority), batshit crazy.

The best way I can explain this is what I often told my inner circle: "Management loves it when CKNW and CFMI are number one and number two in the market. But you better not dare fuck up that order."

We were fucking up that order, and Rutherford, in what was such a clear conflict of interest (as my boss he should have recused himself), was going to attempt to curtail (sabotage?) *Sportstalk*.

The first sign occurred one night late in the regular season when Woodgate and I were driving back from Pacific Coliseum to our Expo studio. I received a call from Rutherford (no, I didn't honk), which was unusual because he often went weeks without touching base. On this night, though, he was on a mission. He called to say he no longer wanted *Sportstalk*'s in-rink correspondent (Steve Snelgrove) feeding us post-game interviews. Despite knowing full well my contract allowed me editorial freedom, Rutherford said our show should only be about taking calls on those nights.

"Besides, CKNW's the rights holder," he added, "so we should be the ones providing reaction from the dressing rooms."

This was the equivalent of a three-line offside pass because, if that was the case, they should have factored that in during our contract talks. Moments like this illustrated why I always made sure my working agreements stipulated that I had freedom over all editorial content. Furthermore, *Sportstalk* hadn't just been born. We were seven years in with a formula that was working well on game nights and off nights. Evidently too well for Rutherford. It didn't matter that we both had the same mandate of attracting the most listeners. When he saw erosion at his end, he resorted to dirty tactics.

And more sleaziness from 'NW — aka Top Dog — was just around the corner.

There were always many components to the contracts I signed. The most important clauses had to do with time slot, money, length of term, editorial freedom, guest freedom and the right to choose a producer. Also high on my list was the station agreeing to send me to all Vancouver Canucks playoff games. Wherever they went, *Sportstalk* would be there too. This was vital for me, a real perk, and not just because I knew the profile/marquee value would be terrific for the show. But personally, having not experienced the joy of reaching my play-by-play dream, a chance to see these away venues was a treat I wanted.

Being with the Canucks not only helped the sound of the show during any given series but was also something we could refer to and use to offer better context on future shows. For instance, when the Canucks played Calgary in that memorable 1989 seven-game series that culminated with Joel Otto's controversial series-winning OT goal or years later when Pavel Bure did the same to the Flames, it was always great to be able to refer to those historic moments and tell our listeners what it had been like in the building. Also, the most important thing I absolutely had no doubt about was, if the Canucks were going to win the Stanley Cup, *Sportstalk* had to be there. By virtue of being on the road, we were also able to form relationships with many opposing coaches, managers and other media types, which resulted in countless future guest appearances.

Though I would never express it on the air, I was always upset if Vancouver didn't make playoffs, which is exactly what happened in 1990, my first year on CFMI. However, the Canucks were playoff bound the next season and, about three weeks before the post-season started, I put in a call to Rutherford to ask how he wanted me to set up my travel arrangements. When he didn't answer, I left a voicemail. When he didn't call back, I tried again. And again. After my fourth or fifth attempt, Rutherford finally called back to tell me I wasn't going anywhere.

What the hell! How dare they? How dare he? It was in my freakin' deal! It couldn't have been any clearer.

I had no one to turn to inside those halls, and I was steaming mad. Bremner was long gone and unfortunately not replaced by either of his Dan Russell-adoring sons. I hesitated for a couple of days, not sure if I wanted to upset the applecart. But because this had been negotiated, I called Roger Bourbonnais, my lawyer. At first, he tried to calm me down, but even he got a little miffed when Rutherford also stonewalled him. By this time I knew Rutherford loved playing mind games. When he first wanted me to sign, it was his game of keep away. Now his game was to rag the puck, which he knew would drive me crazy. Just two days before the start of the playoffs, he finally called Roger back, this time employing his oft-used sarcastic tone, something I'd endured in the past.

"Well, why don't you and Dan come down to my office tomorrow and the three of us can discuss this," Rutherford told Roger, evidently satisfied that he had ragged the puck long enough to get his way.

On April 3, the day before the Canucks began a first-round series at Los Angeles, Roger met me in the lobby at the New Westminster studio and we walked to Rutherford's office. Rutherford was all business.

"Actually, we're not meeting in my office," he said. With that, he got up from behind the desk and said, "We're going to the boardroom."

When we got there it was clear Rutherford had at least one more game to play, but this one involved props, human and otherwise. After telling Roger the day before that it would be the three of us, he had decided to invite reinforcements. Already seated at the boardroom table when we walked in were 'NW general manager Rod Gunn and CFMI program director Rick Shannon. This was my first experience with CKNW's roughhouse politics — Rutherford style. His play was to gang up and try to intimidate rather than be involved in a reasonable discussion. He told us to take seats and pointed us to the other side of the table — Roger and me on one side and the three 'NW amigos on the other.

Oh, and smack dab in the middle of the boardroom table, serving as a metaphoric table tennis net, was our non-human prop — my employment contract. Thank gawd it was no longer in J.P.'s unlocked car!

Given that neither Roger, nor I for that matter, had ever met Shannon, there was no reason for Rick to be there other than to give Rutherford numbers. In fact, Shannon sat like a bump on a log through the entire meeting, never uttering a word. How could he, though? This was the Doug Rutherford show. It was his chance to flex, intimidate, browbeat and unnerve me while threatening my future all because that pesky *Sportstalk* program was cutting into his CKNW hockey ratings.

"What's your position on this?" Rutherford immediately barked at Roger, the most mild-mannered gentleman I've ever been around.

Roger absorbed the verbal blow then tried to calm things down. He pointed out a couple of elements about the background of the clause, but before he could finish Rutherford cut him short and again we heard: "What's your position on this?" Inside, I was wishing Roger might sarcastically say, "My position was captain for the 1963 Memorial Cup champs," or "standout centre for two Canadian Olympic teams and several world championship teams," but obviously that wasn't relevant. Instead, Roger, not at all intimidated, once again attempted to explain why the clause was in the agreement and why it was important for me to be on the road in the playoffs.

You guessed it! Rutherford interrupted, completing his hat trick with another round of: "What's your position on this?" Only this time, rather than waiting for an answer, he thumped his chest to tell us he'd only be sending one person on the road. And that person would be J. P. McConnell.

To unpack that, Rutherford's plan was to obstruct our show by grounding us while theoretically bolstering 'NW's post-game activity by having McConnell gruff his way through it from Los Angeles. Rutherford childishly kept repeating his one line of questioning until finally Roger told him, "By not letting Dan go, you are in effect breaching that portion of his contract."

"We don't breach contracts at CKNW," said Gunn, finally speaking up.

Gunn then proceeded to calm things down, even though it was only Rutherford who needed to locate the green zone. Gunn spoke for a few moments more before offering a compromise of sorts. He suggested we let the first round go but promised that *Sportstalk* would be on the road in subsequent rounds, as my contract stipulated.

We may not have travelled the next day, but we definitely won the boardroom showdown thanks to Roger's stance that not only forced Gunn to step in and overrule, but also allowed Gunn to perhaps see Rutherford in a different light.

As it turned out, the Canucks didn't advance past the first round that year, but I would have my chance to make a huge playoff impact in the years to come.

Sportstalk struck an emotional chord a few months later, in July of 1991, when Stan Smyl retired as a player. Though only thirty-three, the Steamer's gas tank had clearly run dry, as the former captain was a healthy scratch thirty-four times in his final season, including playoffs.

Smyl, a heart-and-soul guy, came into the studio and received a well-deserved outpouring of gratitude from local fans not just for his time with the Canucks but also as a star for the New Westminster Bruins during their unprecedented four consecutive trips to the Memorial Cup. Caller after caller not only thanked Smyl but expressed heartfelt gratitude for what he had meant to the team and the city. I was always able to look most interviewees in the eye, but I couldn't with Smyl because he was pretty choked up. Later, he told me his eyes were still moist while driving home after that show.

"My only goal was to play in the NHL," he said. "To hear all those fans thanking me that night was extremely special."

Four months later, Smyl became the first Vancouver player to have his jersey retired.

CHAPTER SIXTEEN

The much-travelled contract

Despite not having everyone in our building cheering for us, *Sportstalk* on CFMI just kept picking up steam. Our ratings were as high as they had ever been, the list of network stations had grown to more than forty, and we thoroughly enjoyed the freedom of the format, especially without newsbreaks.

Also, the CFMI vibe and staff were just more fun. This began with Christine Glen, our promotions co-ordinator, and her assistant, Michelle Fry. They were two highly professional and enthusiastic young women who helped the show by setting up unique contests, great prizes and on-location bannering. They also provided guest relations at the Fogg N' Suds remotes, devoted incredible energy to the *Sportstalk* golf tournament and much more.

The third member of that department became Jody Vance. In 1995, she also hosted a Sunday evening CFMI series dedicated to up-and-coming Canadian music talent, which culminated with Canadian music icon Burton Cummings staging a one-man show in the cozy confines of the Arts Club Theatre on Granville Island. I hadn't seen Cummings before, and I'm still embarrassed to admit – because of either laziness, enjoying a Sunday off, or up until then only having a passing interest in Cummings – that I had to be talked into attending by PD Ross Winters, Vance and producer Scott Woodgate. Being seated with the CFMI group right beside Burton's piano was the start of an unforgettable night. We were blown away by his incredible talent and never-ending catalogue of hits. But the real fun began when the show ended and the crowd left. That's when Cummings returned to sit with us for drinks and to share many stories about his career. He then sat at the piano and played a private mini-concert for us — and even led us in a rendition of the theme from *The Brady Bunch*. The liquor and laughs flowed until well into the wee hours.

During this time I also was asked to anchor Sunday sports on the *BCTV News Hour*, which was a big deal given its legacy and through-the-roof ratings. For some reason, Bernie Pascall, BCTV's sports director, also hired former pro footballer Jan Carinci to work Saturdays. It was a disaster, akin to having me dress as a CFL slotback. Carinci and I were let go after a couple of months. Yes, it may have been a case of baby exiting with bath water.

I remained on BCTV doing a regular Fogg N' Suds feature with Brian Burke that aired during Canucks telecasts and was also asked, along with a couple of others, to audition for the role of colour commentator. Three of us each sat beside Jim Robson for one period of a pre-season game against Dallas. Rightfully, it was a former player Darcy Rota who got the TV job. Still, it was another pinch-me moment to even be auditioning with my idol.

One story we at Sportstalk had all to ourselves — not just in the CKNW building but throughout the media — was the unlikely news of the NBA coming to Vancouver. Orca Bay owner Arthur Griffiths had privately funded GM Place and was in desperate need of filling more dates. But he hadn't even thought about the NBA. Instead, his sights were on an Arena Football League (AFL) franchise. When Griffiths started kicking those tires he was told by Jerry Colangelo, the owner of the AFL Arizona Rattlers and NBA Phoenix Suns, that there were multiple Toronto bids for an NBA expansion franchise. Colangelo also was the chairman of the NBA's board of governors.

A couple of years later, just before the Raptors franchise was officially awarded, we started hearing whispers that the NBA was also considering Vancouver. This was as strange as it was exciting. No one had a better feel for the pulse of the local sports fan than me, and I can promise that Vancouver fans weren't clamouring for a team. Still, the thought of getting a second major franchise was huge, which is how I was able to convince management to send me to the NBA governors' meeting in New York during the first week of November 1993. (It didn't hurt that the Canucks would also be there at that time so I could cover them as well.) It appeared our trip was in jeopardy the day before we were to leave when I was told Vancouver wasn't going to be officially on the meeting's agenda. But rather than tell our station management, I decided to go anyway, largely because any excuse to go to New York is worth it.

It turned out to be a tremendously successful gamble.

BCTV's John McKeachie had also convinced his bosses to allow him to go, and once in New York the two of us joined forces to see if we could find out more about what was happening concerning Vancouver. After a couple of phone calls, McKeachie and I headed to the famed Plaza Hotel on the southeast edge of Central Park, where we were invited up to Colangelo's suite for separate interviews with the board chairman.

"Vancouver expressed an interest and they surprised a lot of people. I liken them to that of a dark horse," Colangelo told me. "I think people in the league were impressed at how strong an entry Vancouver turned out to be."

That was absolutely good enough for me — and right from the horse's mouth. We'd gone from Griffiths not being on their agenda to the NBA saying how strong Vancouver turned out to be. I knew we were sitting on something huge and couldn't wait to get to air later that night.

While in New York we did our show from what was then The Museum of Television & Radio — now the Paley Center for Media — in Midtown. In addition to the huge NBA story, we also covered the Canucks playing the Rangers — something we would famously do again later that season.

Brian Burke, who was now working at the NHL office, came down to the museum one night, and famed broadcaster Marv Albert also was a guest that week. NHL commissioner Gary Bettman also came in for a spirited forty-minute interview. When it was over, producer Woodgate escorted Bettman and his assistant down the elevator, and when he came back he said that Bettman kept telling his assistant, "That host really knew his stuff."

Three months later, in February 1994, we took *Sportstalk* to the NBA All-Star Game in Minneapolis, where Griffiths and his group were officially granted a conditional franchise for the (then) princely sum of US$125 million. It didn't seem like all that much later, in November of 1995, until we were in Portland's Rose Garden for the Grizzlies' first game. Vancouver's second major league team was a reality. And, as it happened, it even won its first game. In fact, as Grizzlies aficionados know, they started their history 2-0, marking, without exaggeration, the high point of their six-season existence. Everything went downhill after that, with Vancouver winning only ninety-nine times in its next 458 games, including one stretch where it lost twenty-three straight. There hasn't been a more nondescript franchise among North American teams that lasted five or more years.

Seriously, aside from a rip-roaring fourth-quarter comeback clinic by a peeved Michael Jordan, a handful of visits from Kobe Bryant and Shaquille O'Neal, boisterous jeering of Steve Francis, and journeyman Doug West drinking seventeen Heinekens upon learning he had been traded to the Grizzlies, there weren't any memorable Vancouver basketball moments.

Think about how bad you'd have to be to not have any highlights!

You might wonder why I would want to upset the applecart if I was enjoying my time at CFMI so much. Yet that's what stupid me did by picking an ill-advised, self-inflicted dispute fight with GM Rod Gunn. It should have been obvious to me that Gunn had other priorities. After all, he was overseeing the move of the entire station into two upper floors of the TD Tower at Georgia and Howe and also preparing to have CFOX and CKLG move into that building — all part of a takeover that had been precipitated by a CRTC decision to allow owners to now hold two AM and two FM stations.

So why did I disturb him?

Because after careful consideration, I thought, not unlike a sports GM, he and I might get together and make a trade I strongly believed would help both sides. I proposed swapping him Fridays in exchange for Sundays. First of all, Friday nights had to be prime for a Classic Rock format. Second, the majority of our working-age listeners didn't go to bed with our show on Fridays, they went out with their friends. Third, Friday was usually the quietest sports night of the week while Sunday was the opposite and often featured the conclusion of marquee events like the Super Bowl, Grey Cup, golf majors, etc. Seems logical, right? How could any rock station object?

Like so many of these exhausting battles, management liked what was good for its side, and in this case it was being able to play music on Friday nights ("Gee Dan, thanks for the great idea"). But it didn't care about the consistency of our show. Clearly this could have gone one of two ways: we stay Monday to Friday or we air Sunday to Thursday. Yet, it was uncanny throughout my career how many times issues like that, where you swore there were only two options, suddenly had a Door No. 3.

Like this one.

Gunn came back and said my idea was fine, except — wait for it — they wanted *Sportstalk* to air from 8 p.m. to 10 p.m. on Sundays because CFMI wanted to keep airing old radio plays from ten until midnight. *Fine by me*, I thought. *Status quo it is. We'll stay on Monday to Friday.*

But ... not so fast.

Gunn clearly couldn't have cared less about one of the wins in my win-win scenario. Furthermore, he wouldn't let the 8 p.m. Sunday issue go, which made me kick myself for bringing it up. Just as in earlier years, the last thing I wanted to do was involve my lawyer because it always rubbed CKNW the wrong way. However, just to make sure 10 p.m. till midnight was preserved, I asked Roger Bourbonnais to call Gunn.

Three days later, I was in Kamloops and on my way to Don Hay's charity golf tournament when my car phone rang. Despite

Bourbonnais having talked to him, the Top Dog's top dog, with his bone to pick, still wasn't ready to lay down and play dead.

"Why are you being so stubborn?" he began, before spending another minute explaining why he thought this would be good for the station.

"Because it's a ten till midnight show," I answered.

"Well, I'll be damned if we are going to conduct 'filing cabinet programming'," he responded.

Translation: Who cares what it says in that annoying legal document — a.k.a. my contract — that is now in Rod's filing cabinet? At least it was no longer in J.P.'s car or in some kind of a prop basket near Rutherford's office. Honestly, I have never understood some of these managers. Did they forget or simply not care that contracts aren't signed by only one party? Did they have amnesia around how badly they wanted *Sportstalk* after I chose CKWX?

I know … playing keep away can be a bitch.

And, to be fair, I also know I had a stubborn side that was vehemently protective, sometimes to a fault, if anyone dared to disrupt what I had built. I often felt sorry for broadcasters who didn't have anywhere near the clout I had. They were often walked over and had to comply with management "requests" they knew were ridiculous at times. Or maybe they felt sorry for us all alone on *Sportstalk* Island. The thing is, I came to understand where we stood: this was a business, and when cut to the bone, I was a simply a supplier of evening ratings.

It took me years to figure out, but I concluded the reason we weren't embraced by CKNW was because they didn't develop me. If they could have taken any credit for the birth of *Sportstalk* or its impact in the market, things may have been different. As it turned out, the best arrangement we had together was never written down in any contract: CKNW knew that a solid and occasionally great show would air without fail every night and, in return, I never had to worry about my cheques bouncing.

CHAPTER SEVENTEEN

The 12:20 rule

Have you ever had a really dear friend who encompasses all the traits you would hope for — honest, loyal, caring, trustworthy, good listener, fun — yet can still drive you bonkers?

Meet John McKeachie.

Like tens of thousands of others, I grew up listening to McKeachie's thorough late evening and weekend sportscasts on CKNW and then religiously watched his late-night highlights on BCTV.

Yet it was him who reached out to me during *Sportstalk*'s first year on CJOR. We kept in touch after that, and it wasn't long before our acquaintanceship became a decades-long friendship. I loved his appreciation of the broadcast business, but what really jumped out to me was his huge heart. He genuinely cared about people, about me and about the welfare of *Sportstalk*.

McKeach, though, was as impatient as he was persistent.

When we started dining together after our respective shifts, he was always anxious to confirm our rendezvous by calling at 12:07 a.m., one minute after he and Robert Malcom said goodnight on BCTV, eight minutes after the *Sportstalk* Orchestra ended our show. The problem at our end was that we were still in debrief mode, assessing what did and didn't go right during our show, cleaning up our papers and, most importantly, planning the next day.

McKeach didn't care.

Also, though I'm sure he was just trying to be friendly, John also had a regular habit of calling me mid-morning, often for no apparent reason, and starting with the dumbest question you can ask someone who just woke up to answer the phone.

"Are you up?"

"I fucking am now," would be my usual groggy response, sometimes for real, usually for effect.

I thought the easiest way to put a stop to this would be to ask if he could please wait until 12:20 a.m. and p.m. before calling. My 12:20 rule. So easy to remember. So hard, as I would find out, to adhere to.

Is phone disease condition — a.k.a. PDC — even a thing? Because if ever anyone had it, it was McKeach. First of all, in terms of any phone ringing, he and I were polar opposites. I'm content to let a call go to voicemail knowing the person will leave a message if it was important, whereas John could trip and break a leg diving to answer it live. He told me it was not uncommon at BCTV for him to answer a call from a viewer just before he was supposed to be on the set, talk to the point of almost being late and be fiddling with his microphone and jacket with the red light already on. This frequently occurred and was part of his on-air charm.

"Why do you answer every call?" I used to ask him.

"Because you never know," he would say.

"You never know what?" I'd invariably respond.

Not unlike those who collect rare stamps, coins, hockey cards, etc., McKeachie collected phone numbers. I never met anyone prouder of the list that he saved and constantly updated on his BCTV computer. He printed a new copy every few weeks and always kept it in a bulging back pocket. Because a great contact list is gold in our business, this meant John literally was sitting on a gold mine.

I came to learn that those with PDC make collecting phone numbers a mission, which some people don't like. Such was the case when he uncovered the phone number of former Canucks owner Arthur Griffiths and used it weeks later while trying to confirm a story. Arthur, who answered after 11 p.m., changed his number the next day. I knew where Griffiths was coming from, which is why, after getting awakened one too many times, I had a second phone line installed in my Kitsilano home and only gave my girlfriend, my parents and Scott Woodgate the number. When McKeach caught wind of this second line it triggered his thrill of the chase, but he wasn't able to talk anyone into giving him the number.

Once during an off-night at BCTV, John came to our studio to hang out while waiting for post-show eats. While I was on the air, Woodgate saw him going around to all the desks of the daytime producers and jotting down the private phone number used by each show.

A couple of days later he set out once again to violate the 12:20 rule, only this time he had a new plan. After the show we would usually debrief in the wide-open talk-show producers' area. Not ten minutes after our show, the private *Sportstalk* line rang. Because of the 12:20 rule, we didn't answer. A few seconds later we heard a phone ringing, one we never heard at night, from a desk a few feet away just outside Bill Good's office. When we didn't pick up that one, we heard one from Rafe Mair's area and then from Phillip Till's. Lines we never heard ring were all ringing within a few seconds of each other.

Scott and I knew McKeachie would be frustrated, but we also knew if we gave in he'd repeat this crazy phone blitz every night. Even though Scott and I were done early, we still waited until exactly 12:20 to pick up *Sportstalk*'s private line, which had been ringing for at least two minutes.

"Yo," I cheerfully answered in the same way I usually did.

"Gordie Howe is dead," he started.

"What! No way? Really? When did that happen?" I replied, not knowing that Mr. Hockey was fifteen years from actually dying.

"Well, if you would've picked up your fucking phone you would've found out," he said.

"I didn't see it on the wire service," I told him.

"But if you would've answered your fucking phone ..." he said again before I interrupted.

"It wouldn't have made a difference because we were already off the air."

The logic had clearly eluded him.

One of the reasons McKeach's phone book was so thick was because he may have met every sports-minded person in the province and certainly most golfers who had ever participated in a charity tournament. For as effective as McKeach was on TV and radio, he didn't have an equal when it came to serving as an emcee. Through his incredible command of any banquet room, McKeach was responsible for helping raise more charitable dollars in BC than anyone else.

His favourite was the Andy Moog and Friends tournament in Penticton. He called it the fifth major, which was enough to convince me to want to go. We planned to go for one but ended up broadcasting *Sportstalk* for ten straight years from the Penticton Golf & Country Club, a stone's throw from that city's famous floating river channel.

Most years when we finished our Thursday show, Woodgate and I would jump in the "Players' Lexus" — the nickname given to my vehicle by Lee Powell mocking how motorsport drivers can't just simply call it their car — grab a Martini's pizza, pick up McKeach at BCTV in Burnaby, drive all night and arrive just as the sun was rising above Lake Okanagan. We would sleep for about four hours, then attend a charity event before heading to the golf course for a practice round and to set up our remote broadcast equipment, so we could go to air at 10 p.m.

I've always felt our shows from Penticton were *Sportstalk* gold. Call me crazy, but for starters there was something so enlivening about broadcasting outside in the warm and fragrant July Okanagan night air. Our remote set-up was unique, comprising two golf carts placed in front of makeshift bleachers near the pro shop and just off the putting green. The atmosphere brought out the best in all of Andy's friends. When we signed on, our guests would have consumed just enough beverages to be loose and free-flowing with stories, without sounding drunk.

The lone exception was "Cowboy" Bill Flett, who I had listened to play on KFI for the nickname-filled Los Angeles Kings when I was young. In Penticton, he caused a commotion while I was interviewing two others.

"Chad, you won't believe this," said Woodgate off-air to technical producer Chad Varhaug back in Vancouver. "Bill Flett is standing in front of our broadcast table with his pants pulled down to his cowboy boots."

I finally understood why "Jiggs" McDonald really called him "Cowboy."

During our decade in Penticton our guests included the likes of Dennis Hull, Johnny Bucyk, Paul Kariya, Glenn Anderson, Rogie Vachon, Greg Adams, Tony Tanti, Brendan Morrison, Garry Unger, Pat Quinn, Brian Burke, Ken Hitchcock, Ron Tugnutt, Corey Hirsch, Jim Peplinksi, Ray Ferraro, Darcy Rota, Guy Charron, trainer Larry Ashley, on-ice official Shane Heyer, CFLers Glen Jackson and Rick Klassen, and boxer (now federally appointed judge) Willie deWit.

But the star of the show each year was colourful Darryl Reaugh, who played a handful of NHL games before eventually becoming an outstanding announcer on Dallas Stars' broadcasts. Reaugh's near perfect impersonation of former *Hockey Night in Canada* analyst Howie Meeker left everyone in stitches. Even more so when I paired him up with Dan Drossos, who did a marvelous Danny Gallivan impersonation, and Toronto sportscaster Jim Ralph with his incredible Foster Hewitt impersonation. It was magical hearing Howie, Danny and Foster kibitzing and trying to one-up each other. My only two jobs were to stay out of the way and not pee my pants.

Sportstalk also got in the spirit of hosting charity golf tournaments during the 1990s. Mostly held at Mayfair Lakes in Richmond, these tournaments were great successes. Golfers called in to purchase their spots, and we also secured many sponsors. Over the years we raised money for amyotrophic lateral sclerosis (ALS), the Tim Jardine Trust Fund, and the BC Heart and Stroke Foundation.

Doing our show from the venue made our event stand out from others vying to raise money. Over the years our guests included Dave Barr, Dave Babych, Cliff Ronning, Martin Gelinas, George

McPhee, Brian Burke, Rod Beaton, Steve Tambellini and Brett Hedican, while McKeachie kindly did our auctions.

Charity golf days are long ones. Golfers often show up before lunch, play for several hours and attend lengthy banquets after. In order to shorten the day and keep our audience from leaving, we recorded *Sportstalk* "live to tape" beginning just after 8 p.m. Most years that worked well, but not at the start of our 1996 show when the program didn't record properly at CFMI's end. Our feature guest that night was Jim Robson, and after twenty solid minutes, which included interacting with our audience, producer Woodgate whispered the bad news in my ear. *Oh shit.*

Very sheepishly, we interrupted Robson and then told our audience. The pro that he was, Robson totally understood and agreed to start over. My questions were the same, but we turned it into a fairly amusing bit with Robson sometimes saying, "Well, I'm so glad you asked that" or "I hadn't really thought about that until now." The audience also liked being in on our secret, quietly snickering. A couple even re-asked their questions to Jim with the same vigour as in the first take.

Remotes were usually rewarding but always stressful. Home base was my domain, with a daily routine that consisted of hours-long show prep and writing during the day, the show itself, and post-game eats with McKeach and my crew at Martini's on Broadway. We usually went to Martini's four times a week, though John boasted his record was sixteen straight days, including weekends. Their food was great, their staff respectfully accommodating, and they were open until 2 a.m., often much later for us.

We mostly shot the breeze about the day in sports and shared laughs about other things. The only time we would cringe would be when someone famous died, which invariably would go like this: a little reflection about the person, perhaps about a five-second pause and then McKeach cheekily asking, "Did you have him in your pool?"

Martini's is where we memorized the "McKeachie-isms," his go-to list of phrases. For example:

— Any story he might tell often was a "good news-bad news scenario."

— The "car-accident syndrome" is how he described having to wait too long to learn something important because "the not knowing is the hardest part."

— McKeach was never out until the wee hours, it was always until "a hundred o'clock in the morning." Nor was he out for drinks — always "cocktails" said with fervour.

— The over/under on the use of "vis-à-vis" could easily be placed each night at 5.5, and taking the over was always the safe bet.

— If you shared particularly great news with him, perhaps a new contract or a great ratings book, it was never "congratulations" but, regardless of the month, "Happy New Year".

— Each year as Christmas approached, McKeach proudly proclaimed, "I never start buying gifts until the twenty-fourth because that way you can spend only one day shopping."

During my bachelor years, I spent almost every Christmas Eve at his South Vancouver home where, besides consuming festive drinks, I was asked by John and his wife Sandi to write individual Santa notes for their three young daughters. Always the last to leave, I recall going into the cold night around 2 a.m. and heading back to my Kitsilano home where I would start wrapping gifts for my own family visit the next day. After all, if you wait until December 24 to start wrapping, the most time you can spend on it is one day.

It's true, McKeach was infectious and I loved him.

But only after 12.20 — a.m. or p.m.

CHAPTER EIGHTEEN

Foul ball, called strike, swing and a miss

During the late stages of Jim Robson's radio career, he negotiated a contract that allowed him to ease the travel burden by taking ten games off each season. Naturally, this news piqued my interest and I was quick to throw my hat into the ring to be his replacement. My first call was to program director Doug Rutherford, followed closely by calls to Pat Quinn and Brian Burke to see if I might get some help. I was pleasantly surprised when Rutherford told me I'd get to audition by calling one pre-season game. It was another instance of a conversation you don't forget if only calling one NHL game is a lifelong ambition.

Lee Powell was told he'd get the same opportunity, and it was suggested that we both get ready by practising with a mock game. That was fine by me, but Lee, who had radio play-by-play experience with the Brandon Wheat Kings, didn't much like the idea. As close friends, it was difficult to be pitted against one another, but we told each other there wouldn't be hard feelings either way.

However, the pre-season came … and went … without either one of us getting the audition that Rutherford had promised. Lee smelled a rat. Keep in mind that Rutherford hadn't said you "might" do a game; he told us we would. We were never told why that promise was broken.

As the regular season started, I kept doing mock games and kept talking to the Canucks in an attempt to find out what was going on. But they told me they were also in the dark. One thing that was clear as day, however, was that Lee and I had enough experience — each of us had called about three hundred junior games — to professionally navigate our way through these games. In fact, we could argue that, nerves notwithstanding, calling NHL games (with ideal broadcast locations, replays available, easier access to information, etc.) would be easier than what we were used to. Still, as the Canucks' season marched along, our big question remained unanswered. Would it be Lee Powell or me who would parlay his junior experience into a ten-game shot in the big leagues.

In the last week of November, we learned that Robson's first miss would be a December game in Calgary, and a couple of days later sports director J. P. McConnell called a meeting. The answer was — drum roll, please — good old Door No. 3. McConnell tapped himself to fill in. Unbelievable! We had gone through a three-month charade and they chose neither of us? Honestly, I would've been happy for Lee because I knew he didn't have full time aspirations but would have liked to have been able to say (and for his parents to hear) that he did a few big-league games.

Naturally, J.P. knew we would ask him how this decision was reached, even though we assumed he just wanted to do them. He said Powell had misidentified a couple of players on his audition tape, something that would have been impossible to determine. Powell just rolled his eyes, especially when McConnell played it up as if he was doing the station a favour.

"Seeing through the game is not the same as winning the game," Lee quoted to me from one of his favourite movies, *North Dallas Forty*.

As for me, McConnell said I didn't have the voice, which was just an excuse. Sure, almost no one had J.P.'s voice, but McConnell didn't have hockey play-by-play skills, as we would soon hear. Also, if I didn't have the voice, how was it that I was successfully hosting a show every night on FM, the radio band stereotypically reserved for the richest voices?

Later that day, I ran into Quinn at the rink. He hadn't yet been told the news, and when I told him McConnell was doing the games, the response was: "Like hell he is."

He still did them.

None of this is to suggest J. Paul McConnell wasn't a great broadcaster. He was — and with an on-air presence most could only dream of. He also worked extremely hard in every role he had during his multi-decade career, and was as excellent as he was dedicated in his role as the long-time play-by-play voice of the BC Lions. But I think it's fair to say that while he "lovvvved" football, he only kind of "liked" hockey.

Not surprisingly, once they dropped the puck his feel was suspect and flow choppy, which, come to think of it, would be how I would have sounded had anyone asked me to call a Lions game. There is no substitute for experience when calling an NHL game. Not just because of the speed, which catches every newcomer by surprise, but because it's your job not to be caught unawares. For example, McConnell missed a goaltending change during this game, which led to identifying a wrong netminder for a long stretch. I know, I know … these things happen — when you're calling games in Prince George or Prince Albert. But it's not supposed to happen in the National Hockey League. I'm sure even a seasoned pro such as McConnell would've felt overwhelmed that night, which is maybe why he kept referring to the game as being played in the Corral, rather than the Saddledome, the home of the Flames for nearly a decade by then.

Having said that, McConnell's first game sounded like a cross between Vin Scully, Bob Costas and Al Michaels in comparison to what CKNW allowed to happen years later with John Shorthouse's highly embarrassing 1998 debut. Of course, that shouldn't have surprised anyone given he hadn't called a hockey game in his life. Not a minor hockey game. Not a junior game. Not a minor pro game. None. Shorthouse's rise to the NHL began in the NHL.

The job was gift-wrapped for Shorthouse courtesy of Canucks director of broadcasting Chris Hebb, with whom he had worked three years earlier at CKVU. The only audition tape Shorthouse could provide 'NW program director Tom Plasteras was of him, pre-puberty, calling a Canucks game off TV. Shorthouse knew what had happened. As he told Kirk McKnight for the book *The Voice of Hockey*, "I just happened to be the lucky one who weaseled his way into the job." I have never begrudged Shorty for accepting the gift, and he eventually grew into the position. But that doesn't change the fact that Hebb's decision was an embarrassment to the broadcast profession. In that vein, Shorty's quote in that book was exactly right — Shorthouse was the lucky one; Hebb was the weasel.

At any rate, the disappointment of the ten-game fill-in fiasco was only an appetizer for the real thing, which happened when Robson officially left the radio booth following the 1994 Stanley Cup Final. The job I spent my life dreaming about and working towards was open for the first time since ... ten years before I was born.

Since the job seemingly came open every four decades, all the clichés applied: Time to pull out all the stops. This is crunch time. It's now or never.

First, I did the handicapping. Who was the competition? Topping that list would be Jim Hughson. But not only did he have an even bigger gig — national TV logically would trump local radio — but he had just signed a long-term extension to continue as TSN's lead voice of the NHL and the Toronto Blue Jays. Next on my list was Kelly Moore, my friend in Kamloops, who'd been calling WHL games for nearly twenty years. Powell would have been a candidate, but he still was disillusioned by the fill-in charade, plus he also didn't like travelling. Paul Romanuk, an eastern-based broadcaster, expressed interest and may have been a dark horse. With Hughson out of the mix, I concluded it might well come down to Moore or myself.

After handicapping the field, I lobbied. First, I pled my case with general manager Rod Gunn by sending him a package and following up with calls. I did the same with Quinn and his assistant, George McPhee, who'd taken over from Brian Burke and was a weekly guest on *Sportstalk*. I spent four days talking with Burke at Langara Fishing Lodge, believing he still carried some weight with the Canucks. I even contacted club owner Arthur Griffiths, with whom I had a strong relationship.

But, as I would learn, neither the station nor the hockey team had a business reason to back me. *Sportstalk* was profitable for the station and valuable to the Canucks, who enjoyed the priceless coverage we gave them for years, something that had been punctuated a few weeks earlier with our must-listen extended playoff coverage. Naively I was, as Bob Seger once famously sang, truly running "Against the Wind."

I thought I was a leading candidate because I had a name and strong market credibility, had called many junior games, and deeply knew the entire team's history dating back to opening night in 1970. I put all my cards on the table and even told the Canucks that if I wasn't successful, I wasn't sure I wanted to continue doing *Sportstalk*. It wasn't meant as a bluff.

To be successful, I was banking on two things: Hughson not being available and support from the Canucks. The wait finally ended on July 29 when I received a call from Gunn asking me to meet him at the Vancouver Yacht Club. The combination of me having heard some whispers and listening to my gut told me I wasn't going to get the job. But I didn't know until Gunn told me that it was Door No. 3 — yet again!

Hughson was walking away from his TSN deal to take the Canucks' radio job reportedly for significantly more than what Robson had been earning. But Gunn wasn't there to tell me that. He only had one motive, which became obvious even before we finished our salads. He wanted to find out if the rumours that I had started were true and that I might leave *Sportstalk* if I wasn't chosen. His biggest concern wasn't so much a loss of ratings. As I was told months later by the Canucks — who had to approve who was hired — Gunn had assured the hockey club they wouldn't be losing their platform on *Sportstalk*.

A short time later, in what was clearly a case of glutton meeting punishment, I caught wind that the Winnipeg Jets were looking for a replacement for Curt Keilback, their play-by-play broadcaster. Despite the less than desirable location along with persistent rumours of the Jets relocating, I was willing, at thirty-five and still single, to go to where the work was. After sending the Jets and CJOB, their flagship station, an audition package, a funny thing happened. Although it didn't have a punch line — unless you count a punch to the gut.

I got the job.

It is interesting how during the life of an average adult, he/she will hear tens of millions of words but so few can be remembered verbatim.

"Congratulations, I'm going to be speaking with your new bosses tomorrow," were the eleven unforgettable words spoken to me by the Winnipeg Jets' director of broadcasting.

The Jets had chosen me and they were meeting the next day with Ralph Warrington, CJOB's station manager, to complete the process. CJOB was CKNW's sister station, but I thought that was okay because I had an escape clause that would allow me to walk for an NHL play-by-play opportunity. Once again, what I didn't know then was that the Canucks had been promised that the *Sportstalk* platform would be there for them. Alas, the Jets called two days later to tell me there'd been a "snag with CJOB."

Zero for two.

It was just like years earlier when I lost out on those summer jobs at 100 Mile House and Prince George. Except that back then I certainly couldn't have claimed to have been a victim of my own success.

CHAPTER NINETEEN

On the road again ... and again ... and again

OK, I admit it was a crazy idea. Who in their right mind would host a popular nightly talk show in Canada while commuting to Seattle to broadcast an entire WHL season? For three consecutive years!

The thing is, even after striking out on the Canucks' and Jets' play-by-play jobs, I discovered that my hunger wasn't as much about reaching the NHL as it was to experience the journey of calling one team, with all its ups and downs, for an entire season. My NHL ship had sailed, but I wanted my own team if for no other reason than to rid my system of this fantastical play-by-play dream.

In the summer of 1995, I received a phone call out of the blue from Colin Campbell, the assistant GM for the WHL Seattle Thunderbirds.

"Would you be at all interested in doing play-by-play for our team?" he asked.

I'd never met Colin, but he seemed to know what was going on in my world, starting with acknowledging my unsuccessful pursuit of the Canucks' job. Caught completely off-guard, I told him that of all the scenarios I'd considered for so many years, doing games in Seattle wasn't one of them. I was, however, flattered that someone thought highly enough of my skill set for something other than *Sportstalk*. I asked Colin to give me a few days to investigate whether this was even feasible. One thing was certain: I couldn't take the Seattle job for the money being offered. But would it even be possible to do *Sportstalk* five nights a week on top of seventy-two regular-season and possible playoff games all outside of Vancouver? I played with a bunch of scenarios, starting with surveying the previous season's schedule to figure out if it could even conceivably work.

"Absolutely you can," Bill Wilms told me when I mentioned it to him.

Bill had taken early retirement as a teacher and had ventured into the seasonal golf business while maintaining his status as one of the top amateur golfers for his age group in BC. He pounced on the idea, especially after I floated the suggestion of him doing colour. I wanted Bill not only because we had worked well together for years on community TV games, but also because travelling alone would have been tougher.

I called Campbell back to tell him I'd take the job if I could use Wilms at my own cost. He then arranged my US work visa — Bill didn't have one — and also agreed to pay gas and lodging.

"T-Birds hockey is brought to you in part by the Days Inn Town Center in downtown Seattle, with big clean rooms and comfortable beds. Our home away from home."

I read that twice per game, and it did become our Seattle home, not far from the Key Arena, and not in an ideal part of town. But because the woman at the front desk took a liking to me, I was usually upgraded to a bigger room that provided me a perfect view of the interesting late-night clientele coming and going from The Dog House (restaurant?) located across the street.

To help with travel, I made a deal with Air BC — the out-of-town scoreboard — that gave us unlimited free airline tickets to Prince George (we never drove there), Kamloops and Kelowna (if we chose not to drive), Spokane (via Calgary with a connecting aircraft that looked more like a flying coffin), Seattle (which I only used the first time in order to test my work visa), Portland (never used), plus Calgary and Regina (which were our eastern conference hub headquarters before renting a car and driving to the other stops in that conference).

Before starting for real we did a couple of pre-season practice runs (first time I had seen the name Jarome Iginla) to get a feel for things and also to make sure the equipment was ready to go. I thought we were ready — but I was wrong.

Even though Campbell had agreed I could use Bill, team president Russ Williams — a short, stout man with an even shorter and stouter temper — wanted to continue an arrangement he had with *Seattle Times* writer Bob Finnigan to continue doing colour. Finnigan, a non-broadcaster, apparently fancied being on the radio whenever he could pop in at his own leisure. Campbell had mentioned his name in passing, but he didn't want to risk losing me.

A week earlier, in the spirit of being a team player, I had called Finnigan to tell him I had a colour guy but he was welcome to join us on other parts of the broadcast. His response was icy to say the least. I thought that was the end of it until we arrived for Game 1. After setting up the booth, I went to the coach's office to record the coach's show — "Brought to you by Ally Chevrolet; it pays to remember Ally Chevrolet" — with Don Nachbaur.

When I arrived, Williams was there, waiting to lay into me.

"I want Finnigan to do the colour, and I'm fucking pissed about it," he yelled in front of his coach and just two hours before my Seattle radio debut.

I told Williams I had offered a compromise to Finnigan.

"I already heard," he snarled.

I told Williams I was going to stay with our initial plan or I would just drive back to Vancouver right then. Williams stormed off, and Bill and I called the season opener from the Mercer Arena — our first four home games were the last four they'd play in that old rink that was constructed in 1927 — not knowing if it would be our only Seattle broadcast. Afterwards we climbed down from the booth wondering what was awaiting. When nobody said a word, we drove back.

The next day was Seattle's first road game. It was at Kelowna's Memorial Arena — constructed in 1945 — where the only quiet place

I could record the coach's show was outside. Once again, Williams approached me before I began with Nachbaur.

"I just want to tell you," Williams said, "I heard some of the game last night and you did a real good job."

Finnigan wasn't mentioned again.

One week later, I had to make an uncomfortable entrance into the Kamloops rink, where Colin Day, the Blazers' president, was waiting for me near the rear entrance. I knew exactly what this was about. I had strongly bashed him on *Sportstalk* for firing GM Bob Brown twenty-two days after Brown had guided the Blazers to their third Memorial Cup title in four seasons. It wasn't so much the firing, rather it was Day's asinine quote about it being time for the team to go "in a new direction." That had *Sportstalk* fodder written all over it. The heavyset Day, his arms folded, was blocking the door, glaring at me. I squeezed past him, ignoring his attempt at intimidation. That "new direction" he had mentioned? Not only were there no titles after that, but Day was later forced out after his office manager embezzled nearly a million dollars from the organization.

Meanwhile, the T-Birds had a shake-up a few weeks into the season when GM Bob Tory was replaced by Russ Farwell, who had guided the team years earlier. Farwell had left Seattle to become the Philadelphia Flyers' GM, where he had engineered the 1992 trade for Eric Lindros. Farwell was quiet, polite and always respectful. Nachbaur was more enthusiastic and more personable but also respectful. I liked both men.

Once, in late November during our first season, we decided to meet the T-Birds at their practice facility and jump on their bus for an in-and-out midweek game at Tri-City. So much for what we thought was a good idea. For starters, the "Iron Lung" became more crowded and Farwell made Bill and I sit together in the same row rather than with an empty seat beside us. We drove the four hours to Kennewick and did the game, during which one of their players got hurt. It wasn't serious, but he was taken to hospital. What I hadn't counted on was this: when a player is taken to hospital, the team doesn't leave town without him. The bus got to the hospital parking lot before eleven and waited for nearly three hours before the player was released and we could head back.

I never set foot inside their bus again.

So how did I pull off WHL radio and *Sportstalk* on the same nights? For starters, twenty of the seventy-two games were played on weekends. But that still left us with fifty combo nights. Seattle home games were played at the Key Arena, an NBA building with big league technology, meaning we could use a high-quality ISDN broadcast line for *Sportstalk*, a huge advantage. The quality was so good there were many nights where I never even mentioned we were originating from Seattle. I would never lie, but if my location didn't affect the sound of the show, I also wouldn't make a big deal of it.

Canucks game nights were the biggest challenge, but there were usually only about ten of those conflicts each season and only a handful in the same time zone. I would make sure our listeners knew I was in Seattle on those nights, and Brook Ward joined us in our Vancouver studio where we would do our usual post-game, including calls. Some listeners took great delight in telling me about something interesting that had happened in a game. Often it was their take on a spirited fight, a blown call by the ref or a particularly poor performance by some Canucks player. Remember, this was in the era before laptops or smartphones and before all Canucks games were televised.

My routine for Key Arena games meant I would leave my home in Kitsilano around noon, pick up Wilms in Blaine, Washington, where he left his car in a church parking lot after crossing the border. From there it was off to the IHOP in Bellingham before a leisurely drive towards the Space Needle. People used to wonder how I could handle this commute, yet I usually found the drive relaxing, if not therapeutic. I'd shut off the cell phone in Blaine (expensive roaming charges), put on my favourite CDs (heavy '70s), and before we knew it we were in Everett. Traffic was often snarled for the last half hour, but we'd always arrive around 4:30 p.m., park in the NBA 'Sonics' caged lot and make our way to the booth.

On weekdays we'd have two sets of equipment. Despite Bill's inability to change a light bulb in his own home, I somehow trained him to set up the WHL gear while I was plugging in and testing the CFMI connection. All things being equal, we were set to go.

But all things weren't always equal.

There were some panicky moments when the ISDN wouldn't work, and I'd spend valuable time figuring it out because I had promised myself *Sportstalk* wouldn't be sacrificed just because I wanted to do play-by-play. Thanks to a couple of helpful T-Birds off-ice officials with technical knowledge, these rare fires were quickly extinguished.

Also, from time to time — like when Trevor Linden was traded while I was en route to Seattle — I might spend upwards of an hour pre-taping hastily arranged *Sportstalk* interviews from my booth. Fortunately, games began at seven and usually ended by 9:40, which made it fairly easy because *Sportstalk* didn't start until ten in those days.

Still, we knew delays were going to be inevitable, which is why we learned every trick possible to make sure *Sportstalk* wasn't affected. We became proficient in the art of CTB — Covering Thy Butt — with emergency pre-records done the night before leaving Vancouver. This included a vague show intro in case our WHL game bled into the start of *Sportstalk*, along with undated interviews designed to buy us more time. Truthfully, we had enough material to do an entire show if for some reason we couldn't get to air. I recorded a lot of CTBs knowing there was little chance they'd see the light of day but fully knowing Murphy's Law would rear its head if I didn't.

I brought a portable fax machine (no internet yet) that I set up right beside me in the booth so producer Scott Woodgate could feed me all the NHL recaps and sports news. During play stoppages in the third period, I began ripping the paper from the fax and putting stories in order for *Sportstalk* while being mindful of the real clock, the game clock and, of course, the score. If the game was running late and tied, I'd be worried about overtime. I was happy if either team scored before OT. Conversely, on occasion I had to fake excitement if Seattle scored with their goalie out to tie it in the final minute while inside I was pissed. Amazingly — and without exaggeration — we never had one *Sportstalk* hiccup in the three-plus years I did the games. There were some close calls, but *Sportstalk* always made it to air cleanly and on time.

That's not to say there weren't a couple of times Seattle radio took a back seat. For example, I actually aborted a game in Red Deer during that infamous Canucks season when Mike Keenan was constantly turning over the roster. When the T-Birds were on the road I didn't have the same technical set-up, and I had arranged to do my show ninety minutes away at our sister station, CHQR, in Calgary on that night. With *Sportstalk* starting at 11 p.m. MT, I had planned a half-hour pre-tape to air off the top before doing the rest live. That is until Keenan swapped goalies with Philadelphia, giving up Sean Burke for Garth Snow, moments before the WHL game.

Because I vowed *Sportstalk* wouldn't ever take a back seat, I knew I had to be live off the top. But how? I was calling the game robotically as my mind raced for a solution. The only way I could do it would be to find someone to take over after two periods. During the first intermission I was introduced to Pete Montana, a local broadcaster sitting in the press box who told me he'd called a couple of games in the past.

Good enough.

After giving him the headset, I ran to my car, cursed as it took forever to warm up in -25°C conditions, then drove south, arriving in Calgary with fifteen minutes to spare.

On more than a few occasions I simultaneously ran two broadcasts in two different countries — pulling off that magic trick from the same chair! On nights when the WHL game ended just before 10 p.m., I would talk on KMPS until about fifteen seconds before the CFMI *Sportstalk* intro before music began and then tell our Seattle listeners to stand by for the post-game show. With that, I'd switch headsets, start my stopwatch knowing I had three minutes to begin *Sportstalk*, promote what was upcoming and then send CFMI to a three-minute break. That's when the KMPS post-game show was starting, so I switched headsets again and did a two-and-a-half-minute recap of that game, concluding with something like, "It was a winning night for the T-Birds. Coming up, Bill Wilms will have tonight's three stars. This is the Seattle Thunderbirds' post-game show on KMPS."

Once again, this would time out perfectly with *Sportstalk* starting up again as I switched headsets. I began this segment with a sports recap, making sure I had a voice report or clip to air so I could quickly turn on the Seattle mic and introduce Bill with the three stars. With a longer headset cord, Bill walked a few feet away so we could both broadcast at the same time without our voices bleeding onto the other station. While watching me, Bill ragged the puck until I sent *Sportstalk* to a break, and in those final two minutes I'd chat with Bill about his stars, the next game, sign off KMPS, resume *Sportstalk* and even wonder to myself how the hell we had pulled it off.

The Seattle experience not only improved my play-by-play skills, but after having gone through all of our juggling experiences not much could phase us on *Sportstalk*. Plus, I made valuable contacts along the way — future NHL players and coaches, current NHL scouts, etc. — many of whom would become *Sportstalk* guests.

Calling the games was more fun than getting to them. Kelowna and Kamloops might be fun to drive to for summer vacation, but not so much during hockey season. Though I must've had a guardian angel as we didn't often encounter the worst the Coquihalla had to offer. Yes, it was slippery at times and visibility was a bitch, especially on the connector between Kelowna and Merritt, but we were never significantly delayed, or worse.

One exception was a 1996 game Bill missed (he always missed the worst weather) in Spokane. My friend Steve Snelgrove not only volunteered to do the colour but also drive his snow hardy Jeep. About two hours from Spokane, Snelgrove and I were talking about fishing of all things when we suddenly hit a patch of ice and spun off the road. He held tight through a pair of 360s before jamming it into a lower gear, stomping on the accelerator and returning to the highway. It all happened in a span of less than ten seconds. The moment the Jeep was back on pavement, Snelgrove continued the fishing story as if nothing had happened. He didn't miss a beat.

"What the fuck just happened and why are we not talking about it!?" I loudly interjected.

Snel may have been used to it, but I was shaking for the next hour.

The snow kept accumulating while we were doing the game. Even in the best of conditions, Spokane to Vancouver was my longest drive, about seven hours. That night, after driving in thick snow and zero visibility, we overnighted in Moses Lake and limped home late the next afternoon. Once again I may have been a little grumpy with some callers that night.

The US-based WHL teams are unique insomuch as they tolerate playing Canadian-based clubs but financially live off games against American competition. Moose Jaw at Seattle on a Tuesday would be a ghost town, but Portland at Seattle on a Friday with a return game in Oregon the next night could draw huge numbers. As an example, I called the game with the largest (indoor) WHL crowd ever (19,103) in March of 1997. When the T-Birds and Winterhawks played a home-and-home, it wasn't uncommon for a combined attendance of 25,000, which explains why they played each other sixteen times plus playoffs in one of my three seasons.

I had planned to do one Seattle season but enjoyed it so much I decided to come back for two more. In one of those seasons, 1996-97, the T-Birds made the final but were swept by Lethbridge.

Ironically, it was while doing Seattle when I finally made it to the NHL. Ironic because this time I didn't lobby to get there. George McPhee did, though. The soft-spoken McPhee was the Canucks' VP/director of hockey operations and a weekly *Sportstalk* guest. He wasn't convinced he should dare follow in the radio footsteps of Brian Burke, but I convinced him I'd walk him through the interview and be right there with a follow-up question when it seemed he was struggling for words (which he did, early on). This resulted in such great trust that George soon began providing me with endless information I could use on the show knowing I wouldn't let him down by using something he didn't want on the air. We became friends. I tagged along to a few junior games, which is where he taught me the seven words an NHL scout never hears — "Last minute of play in the third period" — and got to know him and his wife Lea.

In 1996 when the Canucks announced they were going to experiment with pay-per-view, McPhee didn't have to ask if I was interested. In fact, George went to bat for me, and my "Wish Upon a Star" became reality on December 31, 1996. The Canucks were at home to Philadelphia.

Though nervous before the game, I settled in quickly, relying on the mechanics I'd developed in the previous twenty years. However, I did have one recurring bizarre thought as this voice in my head kept telling me that if I suddenly stopped talking it would be the first ever Canucks game with no play-by-play.

I didn't have any idea how many people watched, nor did I care. Truthfully, I was happier when it was over than when I was calling it because completing this one game allowed me to fulfill my lifelong dream. So when the clock struck midnight to usher in 1997, a more satisfying thought entered my mind: *Okay, now I can die a happy man.*

CHAPTER TWENTY

Don't pee on my leg and tell me it's raining

I was perfectly content on CFMI. I loved the format's freedom and all the travel. I mostly enjoyed being an arm's length away from CKNW — a.k.a. "Top Dog" — and all of its agendas. But, as goes the expression, all good things come to an end. For me, that day came in April 1997 when I was called into a meeting and told by CFMI program director Ross Winters (one of my favourites) that the show was leaving FM because upper management wanted it on CKNW.

I wasn't surprised, but my feelings were mixed.

CKNW was the hockey station and still the ultimate Vancouver radio destination, so it made sense management wanted some of our younger demographics. Had it been my decision, I'm not sure which way I would've gone. (Ask me today and I will tell you that CFMI was my absolute favourite *Sportstalk* station.)

Up until 1997, late evenings on CKNW weren't in play. Jack Cullen's *Owl Prowl* had been immovable for decades. Deep in the back of my mind, though, I thought they might move me over after they moved him out. Winters wished me well and said it would be the best thing for the show, though I'm sure he meant best for the company.

After he shook my hand, I walked a few feet away into the office of Tom Plasteras, who had taken over as program director from Doug Rutherford a few years earlier. When Dave Nonis was running the

Canucks, it's doubtful he did anything major without running it past Brian Burke. I believed the same was true at CKNW, with Plasteras needing Rutherford, who was now based in Edmonton but with the company, to approve big items.

I asked Tom when they wanted to make the transition and how we would do it. He suggested we start in May and that we'd begin by simulcasting with CFMI for about a week before going solely on CKNW.

That was fine by me, but I said I wouldn't start without a new contract in place. My current deal was expiring that summer, and it didn't make any sense to start this new chapter without a deal in place. Plasteras agreed, yet nothing happened. In fact, Plasteras's plan to start in May went by the wayside because there hadn't been any contract talks after several weeks. After putting my lawyer, Roger Bourbonnais, off for over a month, Tom finally agreed to meet him. Incidentally, it wasn't like location was logistically inconvenient as Roger's office was also located in the TD Tower, seven floors above Tom's. Plasteras and Bourbonnais went back and forth for a few days, and on May 29 at 4 p.m., Roger called to say they had shaken hands on a deal. I was relieved. The plan now was to start on 'NW the next week.

But Roger called again two hours later.

"There's been a snag," he said. "They want to take back one of your vacation weeks to which they just agreed."

I didn't know whether to laugh or scream.

"Seriously Roger, who do they think they are?" is a cleaner version of what I said.

Roger agreed because he was the one who'd told me it was a done deal. A cautious man, Roger wouldn't get that wrong. Was Rutherford taunting my bench? Or was it general manager Rod Gunn? Both had shaky pasts when it came to my contracts. The more Roger and I talked, the more pissed I got. Both of us agreed this probably had far less to do with vacation than with power. Not only that, but I'm sure Roger negotiated the extra vacation week in lieu of something else.

Roger tried calling back that night but didn't get a response, so I headed to the station. When I arrived in my office there was a big brown envelope sitting on my chair. I guess that answered the earlier question. Rutherford's DNA now seemed all over this. Remember when my contract was sitting in the middle of the boardroom table years earlier? Now the new contract both sides had shaken hands on hours earlier was sitting on my chair because it was — wait for it — off the table.

Seriously, this was the respect I was given.

What a way to get me in the mood to host on their Top Dog station. An hour later I had to enthusiastically greet the audience on the Little Dog and force myself to squeeze every ounce of professionalism out of my body to keep my foul mood from bleeding onto the air. When the show was over, I had no idea what would happen. I only knew that this was now a big (unnecessary) mess all because they went back on their word again.

Roger had his work cut out for him, and when he hadn't heard from CKNW by late Friday morning, he went to their lawyers to show them the paper trail of specifically what CKNW had already agreed to. Then my mild-mannered representative delivered the killer blow: if they took the deal off the table it was his legal opinion that CKNW would be liable for the entire forty-month term of the agreement. Oh, to have been a fly on the wall when 'NW's lawyers relayed that word back to — in alphabetical order — Gunn, Plasteras or Rutherford.

By late afternoon I still hadn't heard anything, so I asked Scott Woodgate to join me at a Kitsilano pub for a beer, something I'd never done before a show. Mind you, at that stage I didn't know if we even had a show. When I got home just after seven, there was a voicemail from Plasteras sheepishly explaining how there had "been a misunderstanding."

A misunderstanding, was it?

I actually felt sorry for Plasteras, who was obviously undermined the previous day only to see his bosses get outsmarted/embarrassed by my lawyer. Now he was being asked to leave this egg-on-all-of-their-faces voicemail. It felt good to win this battle, but what a terrible way to start my official relationship on CKNW.

CHAPTER TWENTY-ONE

Week 666 — The devil's number

I wish I could have helped myself, but my NHL aspirations hadn't been eradicated by doing WHL radio or the Canucks on pay-per-view. Foolishly — and I am the only one to blame — I was guilty once again of listening to my heart and not my brain. The desire to do NHL play-by-play really was my opium. Why couldn't I have realized that it's rare to want to do one specific thing for your entire life, especially when the math says it's practically an impossibility? Yet, like a cat teased by string, I kept chasing.

What I also couldn't forecast was just how stormy things were about to become in the market and for me. And it all started as we began week number 666 — "the devil's number" — in the history of our show. On that day, Monday, July 28, 1997, Canucks GM Pat Quinn, a year after an unsuccessful quest to land Wayne Gretzky, reluctantly caved in to ownership pressure and signed the nearly washed-up Mark Messier. It was the beginning of the end for Quinn in Vancouver and, ultimately, though only temporarily, for *Sportstalk* too.

Sportstalk was with the Canucks when they began that regular season with two games in Tokyo, and we had Trevor Linden on the show just a few minutes after he agonizingly gave up his captaincy to Messier. Prior to this encounter, the lowest I'd ever seen the usually upbeat Linden was in the dressing room following their '94 loss to the New York Rangers. Broadcasting from the top row of an empty

Yayogi Arena a couple of days before the season opener, I can still picture the hurt in Linden's eyes. Considering he had poured his heart and soul into the team, I believe giving up the "C" may have hurt him more than not winning the Cup. It was impossible not to feel his pain.

"I was driving back from Whistler and heard on the radio we signed Mark Messier," Linden recalled years later on our show. "I spent the summer considering why they brought him in, his history and what they were paying him. So I thought the right thing to do was to offer him the 'C.' Mark could've said, 'You know I'm here to support you.' But instead, he decided it was in his best interest to (take it)."

Messier's first two decisions in Vancouver set the tone. His jersey number, 11, had been taken out of commission after Wayne Maki died in 1974, but he refused to change in order to honour Maki. More critically, did Messier really need the "C" to be a leader, because the only thing Messier led Vancouver to during his three seasons were non-playoff spots.

Quinn also made a poor decision in hiring coach Tom Renney, who'd had a good junior career in Kamloops but was the third-best coach out of that program behind Ken Hitchcock and Don Hay.

It was exciting to take our show to Japan and novel to begin broadcasting at 3 p.m. Having the nights free also led to a memorable dinner with Quinn, his wife Sandra, Arthur Griffiths, who still held a small stake in the team, Jim Treliving and George Melville of Boston Pizza fame, producer Scott Woodgate and a couple of others. With saké and Asahi beer flowing freely, Quinn told story after story, spanning all his eras. Beyond the stories, I remember how much Kobe beef he consumed. Quinn, large in presence and size, ate at least eight plates of the world's most expensive beef all by himself.

Though the Canucks split the two games with Anaheim in Japan, the team got off to a terrible start with three wins in its first sixteen games under Renney, which led to a bombshell announcement.

No, it wasn't the coaching one we were expecting.

Exactly two months after our Kobe beef dinner, on November 4, 1997, Pat Quinn was fired. It was shocking news considering he'd built the greatest Vancouver team ever, one that had come an eyelash from a championship three years previous. John McCaw owned the team, but Quinn got his walking papers from new CEO Stephen Bellringer, who had been hired from BC Gas to run the Canucks only two months before.

Being a huge Quinn backer — as most were in BC — I was upset by the decision and couldn't get my head around the fact that the hockey team was being run by an executive from BC Gas Inc. I dubbed him "The Gasman." *Perfect for our show*, I thought, especially with the Canucks fumbling one decision after another in the aftermath of Quinn's firing. From there on, we never called Bellringer by his actual name. The nickname even stuck with the callers during open-phones.

The first call I received the morning Quinn was fired was from a terribly upset Brian Burke. He wanted to come on *Sportstalk* that night so he could "run these guys" — referring to McCaw, his right-hand man Stan McCammon, and Bellringer. Burke, now working in the NHL head office, ripped the Canucks' ownership for firing the man who had given him his start in management. I asked him, on and off the air, if he would be interested in being a candidate to replace Quinn. Burke made it abundantly clear that he was not.

"I am not interested in replacing Pat Quinn," he said on air. "After all he has done for me, I think it would be very bizarre … it would be that bizarre. So I am not interested at all."

Not only was he seemingly on an ownership-bashing mission that night, but for the next few days he kept calling off-air to make sure I was still giving them shit for what they had done to his friend. I didn't need Burke's prompting; the Canucks were in complete disarray, and the *Sportstalk* heat was turned up to high.

Not only did the Canucks keep losing, but they were clueless off-ice. At a news conference in the aftermath of the Quinn firing, I asked Bellringer who was running the team. His answer was that he was the de facto GM.

Sportstalk was all over every new development, including being the first to report that McCaw had gone back to Quinn a few days after the firing to ask him to return as coach. (Shades of Harold Ballard's embarrassing Maple Leafs saga with Roger Neilson in the '70s.) After Quinn turned down that offer, Messier sprang into action, convincing ownership to hire the controversial Mike Keenan to replace Renney as head coach. A few days later, yet another news conference. This one to tell the fans they were going with a three-headed GM monster comprising Gasman, Iron Mike and Tamby — aka Steve Tambellini.

Three GMs? What could possibly go wrong?

For starters, it didn't take long for the infighting to begin between the two dressing room factions — Linden loyalists vs. those putting their money on Messier. Linden, of course, didn't stand a chance. The game was rigged, as became most evident one night in St. Louis where Keenan famously berated Linden in an epic tirade between periods.

There was way more fodder than *Sportstalk* had airtime. Anyone hosting a program like ours knows that when the stuff hits the fan it makes for captivating radio with a phone board full of hopping-mad callers. That's not to say you're hoping the local team does poorly, but there was way more reaction during stormy times.

I presumed Burke would've been happy to hear that. But guess who suddenly had a change of heart? Guess who now wanted the GM's job?

I'd been told by a couple of contacts that Burke, who'd been doling out suspensions on behalf of the NHL for the previous five years, had either grown tired of that job or vice versa, and that he was trying to get back in as a GM. Initially he went after the Atlanta Thrashers job, but when the expansion team drgged its feet Burke set his sights on a return to Vancouver, and he desperately wanted my help to make it happen.

When people ask why I became disillusioned and if it affected *Sportstalk*, perhaps the next few pages will best explain. This is the first time I've told this part of my story.

It started one Friday in early 1998 when Burke called to tell me he was going after the Vancouver job.

"I need your help," he said. "Dano" — he always called me that off-air — "I really need for you to start talking me up. These guys [Orca Bay ownership] listen to you. Your show carries a lot of clout and I need you to go to bat for me."

Ohhh shit, I thought. At least a dozen more thoughts swirled through my head, not the least of which was: *What happened to "I'm not interested in replacing Pat Quinn....not interested at all"?* I thought I knew Burke, but it turned out I didn't know this side of him. Before this call, and before what would happen in the next few months, I'd always considered him a man of his word — loyal to his convictions and to those in his inner circle. He was unyielding in his opinions to a fault; I don't recall him changing his mind on anything. But, suddenly, he was completely reversing course on this issue. The same people who'd fired his friend Pat — the same ones he'd been urging me to run — were still there, and he wanted to climb into bed with them. To me, it made no sense.

Not only did Burke call me that day but several more times over the next month, each time telling me how much clout my show had and how they (Bellringer, McCammon, McCaw) listened to the show. This put me in an extremely tough spot. On one hand, I'd obviously admired Burke's credentials as a long-time regular on our show, not to mention we considered each other friends. On the other hand, his demeanour was brazen. All I could do was follow my heart, and when I did editorialize on the possibility of Burke being hired, I felt he would be a good hire.

Sure enough, Burke landed the job. But despite pressuring me for weeks, he didn't give me the exclusive to break the story on my show. Instead, for reasons I could only assume were designed to curry favour with an old foe, he gave the scoop to — "You can cover his spine with a piece of dental floss" — Tony Gallagher, who had been his long-time enemy and now was allowed to break the story in *The Province*.

Compared to what was coming, the scoop would only be a minor bone of contention.

Not wanting to attract reporters, Burke flew into Seattle on June 21. Once he picked up his rental car, he drove north while talking to me for most of the three-hour duration of his drive. And when he got to Vancouver just after 11 p.m., he asked to stop by my apartment for a beer, where we talked just like old times for another hour or so.

Selfishly, I was more excited about Burke being named president than GM because his hiring coincided with Jim Hughson jumping back to TV, which meant the Canucks' radio job was opening up again. This was a major surprise. After all, Jim Robson had held that position for four decades and now Hughson was leaving after four seasons. So, as per the cat chasing the string — and call this human nature — I felt that the favour Burke had so presumptuously and successfully asked of me might lead him to strongly consider a return favour.

The next morning, June 22, Burke called me two hours before his news conference saying he'd left a bag at my apartment with his dress shoes in it. He wanted me to come early with them, and he invited me to lunch afterward. *Perfect*, I thought. *Finally, a chance to talk about something that was important to me.*

Wrong.

Boy was I wrong.

Big time fucking wrong!

Burke did his usual masterful job on the podium at the news conference and in various scrums. When it was over we walked to Yaletown for a bite. Less than two minutes after we sat down, I heard another of those unforgettable quotes.

"The tone of your show has to change, and it has to change now," he began emphatically just as the first beer arrived.

I was dumbfounded. Still processing the hours I'd spent talking with him the previous night, the numerous lobbying phone calls he'd placed in the previous weeks and the long history we had together, I didn't know what to say.

He continued.

"You've been very hard on the team, and I've told them that would change. I also told Mr. Bellringer [that's what Burke called him] you will no longer be calling him 'Gasman.' I've promised him that would stop immediately."

Oh, you did, did you? I thought.

Now put yourself in my place. This man had just used me for the past few months, strongly urging me to boost and endorse him as the best man for the GM's job — these people listen to you! Your show has clout! Seriously, what kind of an ass would have the audacity to admonish me about the tone of my show and someone's nickname within an hour of being introduced as GM and six months after telling me to run the decision makers?

I learned then that Brian Burke could be exactly that kind of an ass.

I honestly didn't know what to do. Stupid me — and I mean this — I should have in that very moment aborted any thought of the play-by-play opening. But I just couldn't process quickly enough. Either that or my heart wouldn't allow me to. I just couldn't fight back. So, I didn't say much. Nor did I promise him anything. This lunch had become unbearable before any food had arrived at the table. Burke was flexing, and I had managed to tie both hands behind my back.

I did say that over time I would give up the "Gasman" moniker, but not immediately because people would guess Burke made that happen. Smelling a deal, he pounced on that.

"Fine, I'll tell Mr. Bellringer that within a short period of time you'll no longer call him the 'Gasman,' because you need a little time to phase it out."

Too funny. Burke actually admitted he and Bellringer had discussed my clever nickname. Oh, to have been a fly on that wall.

Lunch ended without me bringing up play-by-play, but I called him a couple of days later and said, "I know the radio job is up again, and I'd like to have a meeting with you before it is filled." Burke agreed, but didn't know when he would be free. After a few more days I tried again but still had no luck setting up a meeting. I even tried to go through Dave Nonis to see if he'd help me get a meeting. Finally, on Thursday, July 16, Burke told me to meet him the following Monday at 3 p.m.

However, on that Monday morning, I received a call from Scott Woodgate, who told me John Shorthouse had just gotten the Canucks' play-by-play job.

I thought Woodgate was joking, believing it'd be utterly impossible for someone who'd never broadcast a single game to land an NHL position. Then I quickly pivoted to Burke, the club president, who had signed off on this announcement before his scheduled meeting with me.

I was beyond pissed.

Perhaps I should've given myself time to cool off, but when I got him on the phone the first thing I asked was, "What the fuck happened to our 3 p.m. meeting?"

Without missing a beat and completely ignoring my question, he took this opportunity to lay into me once again.

"I told you the tone of your show must change, and it must change now."

I couldn't believe my ears.

"What the hell are you talking about? You said you'd meet with me about this job, but you signed off on Shorthouse before giving me a chance to be heard. That's fucking bullshit!"

Burke never apologized, but after hearing me fight back in a tone he hadn't heard from me before —and perhaps it dawned on him that I still had a large platform in the marketplace — he tried to shift the blame to CKNW.

At that point I didn't want to hear more. I ended the call but couldn't stop shaking my head. This had gone from Burke insisting publicly he wouldn't apply for the GM's job, to changing his mind, to pressuring me for on-air help, to promising "Gasman" his moniker would go away, to falsely promising me a meeting before filling the play-by-play position.

It was difficult to believe this was the same guy who'd come on our show a couple of years earlier and said, "I consider Dan one of my best friends." That now was past tense. Our relationship had transformed from mutually symbiotic — we used each other — to parasitic. I was to make his life better or suffer the consequences.

So, yes, I felt a huge sense of betrayal. Yes, there was some disillusionment. And maybe some bitterness.

CHAPTER TWENTY-TWO

You can't have "Fuckhead" on your show

Eight days after our heated phone call, Brian Burke and I found ourselves together for the annual Langara Fishing Lodge trip. I so badly wanted to cancel after what Burke had done, but felt it'd be unprofessional not to honour my commitment. Aside from having to uncomfortably interview him on the air, we spoke barely a word to each other during four excruciatingly long days in the Queen Charlottes. I mostly passed the time by playing countless cribbage games with his right-hand man, Dave Nonis, with nothing more than small talk between us.

I didn't speak to Burke for the rest of the summer, but when training camp began in Whistler we butted heads again. On Day 2, right in the middle of a scrimmage, he asked me to meet him in the parking lot. Once outside, Burke complained that I was still calling his boss "Gasman," as if I was in any mood to stop now. Next, he told me he'd heard that Scott Woodgate, now assistant sports director, had arranged for head coach Mike Keenan to be a regular guest on *Sportstalk*.

"I don't want 'Fuckhead' on the show every week," Burke said.

Trying to feign confusion, I replied: "What? Who's 'Fuckhead'?"

"You can't have our fuckhead coach on every week," he repeated, this time a bit louder. "You can have him once a month because I want Davey [Nonis] on two times every month and me once. I want Davey front and centre."

You want interesting? At the same time, Burke was telling the media, "I feel blessed to have Mike Keenan as my coach." Uh, not exactly. Furthermore, who needs a producer when you have Burke booking your guests? Wisely, I didn't tell him to fuck off. I just said, "Let me look into it."

Then I did something much wiser, something that would expose CKNW management for what it was. I put the ball in management's court with a paper trail to which it had to pay attention. I should point out I've always been a thorough note-taker. For example, every one of the nearly eight thousand *Sportstalk* shows was diarized. We tracked every guest, what time they came on, for how long and whether they were in studio, on the phone or pre-recorded. We also tracked the number of calls each guest attracted and how many participated during open-phones.

In addition, I also kept a personal annual calendar in which I logged all my comings and goings, including important meetings, allowing me to recall where I was on any given day. And I kept all the important work files, including correspondence, memos and the recordings I made of key conversations, not just because I had a home studio but because my memory was often overloaded.

Armed with contemporaneous notes and knowing it wasn't me who'd arranged for Keenan's appearances, I contacted program director Tom Plasteras to put the ball into management's court. Do you want Burke to program our show? Do you want him telling me who our guests will be? What should I tell him in response? After speaking with general manager Rod Gunn, Plasteras got back to me on voicemail on September 29, 1998, with this CKNW proxy.

"Rod is in full agreement with myself and yourself that we cannot be making any deals ... that there is much more at stake than, you know, just hockey. So I would feel comfortable, if I were you, going ahead and just saying we're not going to be making any deals — but you're still welcome to be on the program," Plasteras said.

The next day I met Burke for ninety minutes during an uncontentious, yet unproductive lunch at the Fogg N' Suds. Burke was still complaining about the tone of our show until I reminded him that he had said the last Canucks season was like the *Titanic* movie — a complete disaster — on TSN that week.

I then proceeded to tell him what my official position was. I said there could be no strings attached but we were willing to have a weekly Canucks segment.

I repeated that to Burke in writing on November 12, 1998, the day after he debated with me during another testy phone conversation as to whose show it was. I told him it was our show, and he said, "Wrong — this segment is ours, and I will tell you who the guests will be."

After my letter, Burke left me a voicemail.

"Dan [no longer was I 'Dano'], it's Burkie. I got your message. A couple of observations. I don't agree to your invitation. I intend on taking this up with CKNW tomorrow." He went on to say, "I don't think it's your call. Ah, certainly if that is … if they turn to me and say 'It's Dan's call' and you say it's a three-man rotation, then we've got a problem. And I think, Dan, your refusal, or inability, to separate all the issues involved in this is driving this thing right off a cliff, and I resent it. I don't understand, and I can see where this is going, and I resent it. I feel it has compromised our friendship. It has compromised our professional relationship. And uh, I don't get it. So we'll let the proper authorities deal with this tomorrow and we'll go from there."

During a three-way phone conversation that same day with Plasteras and Woodgate, Tom told me, "Brian is going to have to understand that, yes, we are his rights partner, but editorially speaking you don't own the station. And for the two hours Dan is on, he has editorial control, and he has our full backing. He has to understand that we must stand up to this, and the station has never in the past given in on these issues."

Burke didn't understand and continued going up the chain. A few days later, Plasteras was singing a different voicemail tune, telling me on November 16, "I don't think we should push this too far" and that he did not "view this as Burke trying to program the show."

On November 24, I was told by Woodgate that Plasteras had met with (now company president) Doug Rutherford, and after explaining the issues, Rutherford decided to give Burke what he wanted. He told Plasteras who then told Woodgate it will "pay off down the road." Plasteras then instructed Woodgate to tell me "This is what we want."

The next night, November 25, Burke called from Boston. It was nearing midnight there, and he had been celebrating Thanksgiving with his family. Celebrating was the operative word, as I don't believe he was completely sober. When the conversation began I wasn't sure whether he wanted to continue fighting or to make peace. But as he rambled on, it became clear that it was definitely the former. He quickly began to sing his greatest hits:

"I want Davey front and centre."

"The tone of your show must change."

"I don't want 'Fuckhead' on."

Only this time, equipped with the proxy from CKNW management, I said, "Brian, you can't tell me what to do on my show."

Whether it was the booze or the arrogance, the next words out of his mouth blew me away.

"It's not your show," he said.

"What are you talking about?" I replied.

"It's not your show," he repeated.

Not that it mattered but, for clarification, I asked, "Are you referring to the show that airs five nights a week from ten to midnight or the segments in which Canucks personnel happen to appear?"

After a short pause, he repeated himself: "It's not your show."

Before I could think of anything new to say, he dropped his new tune on me, one I would never get out of my head.

"I got someone fired from MSG [Madison Square Garden] Network, and I can get you fired too."

While I don't know anything about that story, in March 2012, David Menzies of *The Huffington Post* wrote: "The real story of Brian

Burke is what a despicable human being this man is when he doesn't get his way or he takes offence to fair criticism." The article went on to say, "Indeed, Burke is a vengeful man, and he has been successful in terminating the employment of at least two journalists because he thought they were being too hard on his sad-sack team."

By then, Burke was in Toronto trying to lift the Maple Leafs from the depths of the NHL. In March 2012, Don Cherry, he of *Coach's Corner* fame, alleged that Burke had tried to get him fired.

"...I say to this — If he wants my job — if he wants to get me fired, like he tried to do — go behind my back with my bosses and try to get me fired," Cherry said on *Hockey Night in Canada*. "Not only that, he went to the governors and said it too. All right? Now I don't care. 'You want to get me off? You want to take me on?' Two years ago you said you were going to do something to me (during) the playoffs....remember that? And I said, 'Oh, Brian Burke, I'm shaking in my boots. I'm shaking right now. Do your best!'"

All I thought, but didn't say, was *Happy Thanksgiving, asshole.*

Continuing to build my paper trail, I told Plasteras and Gunn what had happened, knowing full well they'd soon be hearing from Burke. It seemed I was spending more time covering my butt than I was doing the show. Mind you, the show was still writing itself as the Canucks were on their way to yet another horrible season. The mounting losses were one thing, but it was the asinine threat by Burke to the great Vancouver fan base that became the *Sportstalk* gift that never stopped giving. Burke was part of a news conference at then-GM Place on Jan. 21, 2000, where he commented on a decision by the federal government not to provide a financial bailout package for Canada's NHL teams.

"I want everyone clear on the stakes of the card game we're playing today," Burke said. "To move this team takes one phone call — one phone call — twenty-five cents and a payphone to move this team. That's how hard it is — that's how easy it is. This is high-stakes poker, folks, and it's a lot about the future of this city and our province."

That short piece of audio became the most played clip in the history of our show. Nonis told me one day that Burke hated it. The usually media-savvy Burke should've known better, especially when his team was on its way to a twenty-three-win season.

With 100 percent editorial freedom, any benefit of the doubt for Burke was entirely up to me. For some reason, Burke thought he could threaten my livelihood without considering how that would shape my opinion of his tenure as president and GM.

At about the same time, opinionated CKNW sports personality Neil McRae staged a short-lived battle with Burke, who had complained to management about McRae using audio clips from his weekly 8 p.m. show the following day. The day they sparred I was in my office getting ready for my show. Burke bullied and threatened on the air.

"I think it's about common sense and professionalism, which obviously you're short on and you're determined to air it out now. We will sort this out tomorrow. This is about your ego and your morning ratings. You don't make this decision. This decision will be made by 'NW management," an angry Burke told McRae.

"Having someone tell me what I am going to run or not going to run blows me away, and anybody who's in this business knows where I'm coming from," responded McRae, who was just as angry.

"Well, it didn't trouble your bosses," Burke said, letting McRae know how much pressure was being applied to 'NW management.

During the first commercial break, McRae bolted from his studio to my office to solicit advice. I told him he was doing great and that I wouldn't give in to Burke's tactics. On that night he didn't. It turned out the laugh was on me, though. Two weeks after asking my advice, McRae became bedfellows with Burke. So much for strength in numbers.

Three things I knew:

1. Burke was going to continue coming at me and wouldn't stop until he got his way;

2. *Sportstalk*'s ratings were larger than ever. Our share was a staggering 22.8 in Vancouver, plus we had more than forty network stations; and

3. Despite my detailed paper trail, CKNW wouldn't be backing me because Burke was using the future of the Canucks' broadcast rights as a hammer.

That was illustrated on June 2, 1999, after Gary Mason, then of the *Vancouver Sun*, caught wind of the behind-the-scenes turmoil and wrote about it in a column headlined: "Is something smelly about 'NW moves on *Sportstalk*?"

"Can Brian Burke's dislike of Dan Russell be at the root of an expanded weekend show?

"I smell a rat. It's no secret Canuck management, namely GM Brian Burke, dislikes Dan Russell but more deeply dislikes Russell's show. Burke has complained to 'NW management many times about the 'hostile tone' Russell has taken.

"Burke was especially upset when he wasn't allowed to dictate the rotation of Canuck guests on Russell's show last season. He took the matter up with 'NW management, which solved the problem by giving Burke his own show every Monday night.

"However, it didn't diminish the fury Burke continues to feel towards Russell and his show.

"The combative GM has made no secret of the fact he wouldn't hesitate in taking the lucrative broadcast rights to Canucks games to another station if 'NW insists on allowing Russell to 'continually' criticize the handling of the team and Burke's own performance in particular.

"It would be easier to get rid of the problem. Dan Russell.

"In this town the [*Sportstalk* name] has been synonymous with only one person, it is my understanding that if Russell were to leave 'NW, the station would keep the name and it seems there are those at the station silly enough to believe that it's 'NW that is responsible for *Sportstalk*'s monster ratings and not the host himself. In other words they could get someone else to host *Sportstalk* who would be more palatable to the Canucks.

"These people are wrong and if they are even thinking along these lines they are contemplating a terrible decision.

"Dan Russell is above all an excellent journalist. He asks smart questions. He is knowledgeable. And those are just two of the reasons his show has thrived for 15 years, while sports personality after sports personality who have tried to take him on [have] failed. Miserably.

"It is Russell that's made *Sportstalk*, not any of the four radio stations on which he has done the show. If 'NW decides to cow to the threats of the Canucks and Russell is forced to take his show somewhere else, the station will be the big loser here. Trust me.

"Russell will take his show to another station that'll pay him a bundle and 'NW will try and put some poor schmuck up against him who will fail just like everyone else.

"And five years from now, or six, or seven, after Brian Burke has moved on to another job, 'NW will be begging Russell to come back.

"I know the scenario I lay before you has been discussed by several people at the station. And I know there are those who are expecting Russell to blink, to drop the editorial independence that so defines his show and start towing [sic] the Canucks party line.

"Let's hope that doesn't happen. For the listeners' sake."

Clearly, management was being sloppy. There was still one year left on my contract, but they and/or Burke couldn't keep their mouths shut regarding their master plan. As a result, I decided to flush out Plasteras by extending a rare invitation for him to come on that night and react to Mason's column. Why not? On occasions like that, management should have to go on the air and state its position on the record. Obviously, I knew the invitation was putting him in a no-win position. If he didn't come on, it would be interpreted as the show's demise. If he did accept, he might have to lie. He chose the lesser of two evils by appearing and publicly shooting down Mason's theory, telling our listeners CKNW loved our show and there weren't any plans to fire the host.

By the time the next season began in the Fall of 1999, everyone's patience was wearing thin, as illustrated by this Plasteras memo:

"I've reached an agreement with Orca Bay for the Canuck Update with a 50/50 split between Marc Crawford and Dave Nonis.

"I believe this entire negotiation has been blown out of proportion due to the 'Burke/Russell feud.' As a result it's taken longer than it should've to work out an arrangement any other radio station would kill for.

"If you have any concerns about this, I would appreciate you discussing it with either myself or Doug Rutherford (he has been involved) behind closed doors. I do not want this to become a topic for the program."

Everything had skidded off the rails. CKNW was violating my contract by making arrangements to book guests. Weeks earlier, knowing the station was up to something, I had encouraged Plasteras to program a different Canucks show during a non-*Sportstalk* time slot. I knew that suggestion wouldn't fly with Burke because, while he hated the host, he couldn't get enough of my ratings.

Once again this was likely the crux of everything. I strongly believe that was the reason he didn't want anything to do with me doing play-by-play. Why? Because that would significantly reduce the Canucks' impact on *Sportstalk*. He knew that better than anyone, having first made his name in Vancouver on my show. And now he wanted his "Brian Burke" — a.k.a. Dave Nonis — to take up that mantle.

I reflexively responded to most things at that time with a "They're not going to have their cake and eat it too" mentality. Beyond pissed and clearly seeing the writing was on the wall, I decided not to back down on or off the air.

Meantime, I knew Rutherford was involved with our show again — was he ever not? — and judging by Plasteras's memo he was highly concerned about what I might say about this on air. Also, as Mason mentioned, another battle had ensued behind the scenes after I accidentally found out Rutherford had tried to register the name "Sportstalk."

Roger Bourbonnais, my representative, put me on to a trademark lawyer who got ahead of Rutherford by also applying to register the name on my behalf. (Novel concept, given I'd had the name for fourteen years.) With an apparent conflict before it, the trademark office in Quebec ruled the Sportstalk name wasn't able to be registered/trademarked. This was a clear win assuring me I could keep using the name on another station if they fired me. Sure, they could use it as well, but they wouldn't dare. When Rutherford learned of the ruling, he left me a less-than-friendly voicemail suggesting I shouldn't have done that.

Around that time, Greg Douglas quoted an unnamed source in his *Vancouver Sun* column saying, "Dan became quite difficult. He was giving the impression that he might think he was bigger than the show itself." Exactly right! I was the one who created it, grew it, protected it and had hosted it solo since the beginning.

For his part, Burke did his own lashing out. In April 1999, he told McRae I was no longer his buddy and the "saddest part of my return to Vancouver is my relationship with Dan."

And Douglas, no doubt still feeling betrayed from years earlier when I surprisingly left CKWX after one year, kept piling on in the *Sun*: "It became painfully obvious and tiresome Russell was in a snit. If a caller would defend Burke on the air, a frustrated Russell would quickly cut the caller off."

Okay, now back to you, McRae.

"The guy [Russell] sounds like Kermit the Frog on speed. He's blowing it because his credibility is shot because he's just taking runs at Burke for no reason at all other than he wants to jab him whenever he possibly can. And he's got the same stupid flunkies that phone him every night."

While all of that was nauseating, it was in some ways amusing to watch Burke's obvious "anti-Russell" campaign with his compliant media friends bowing to him. He even got former jockey Tom Wolski, who covered horse racing for *The Province*, to write: "It could only be a plus to have Dan Russell off the air." I can only assume the newspaper's astrologist was busy that day.

Burke's media campaign made it clear to my listeners that something was up, resulting in a deluge of emails.

Dear Dan,

After reading the Gary Mason article I must ask is CKNW management via Brian Burke actually trying to change the tone of your show? If so, that's absolutely pathetic. You've just been echoing the fans' feelings for years. If Burke can't come to grips with this, then he should quit his job. I had the utmost respect for Burke in years past, but his mindset these days has been intolerable. If CKNW discontinues Dan Russel [sic] as *Sportstalk* host I'll no longer listen and also convince many others to follow suit. If they believe that getting rid of Dan Russel [sic] and changing the tone of the show will not hurt your ratings they're dead wrong.

Bruce Randall

———Ⓜ———

Hi Dan!

Burke's comments (on the *Bill Good Show*) about you and *Sportstalk* were absurd. The season has been absolutely horrendous and he just refuses to take responsibility.

Burke's had a brutal season as GM and the team's been a pathetic disgrace.

He'll shift blame to anybody but himself (now it's your turn, Dan).

You have been reporting the facts on the show and in my view have been giving Burke the benefit of the doubt in many instances. For him to be saying that you are biased, have an axe to grind or whatever is a joke.

David G. Bibby

———❦———

Dear Dan:

Love your show but did you hear Neil Macrae [sic] roast you this morning? He hit you big time. He said that the management at CKNW is pissed off with you for badmouthing the Canucks. They seem to forget all the years you boosted them.

Allen O'Grady

———❦———

In response to Mason's article, your commentary regarding the Canucks is shared by many in this area. I don't care which station you're on, I will listen to your show. But the night you start catering to Burke, or management's requests to cater to Burke, will be the night I turn my radio off.

Tom Grainger

———❦———

Juxtaposing all the professional drama I was going through was a huge development in my personal life. The previous year, my friend Mike Davis from Cathay Pacific had taken me to Thailand to possibly create a Golf Trip of a Lifetime. Once in Hua Hin, I became friends with Tony Meechai, a St. Louis native of Thai descent, who was teaching golf at the Springfield Royal Country Club. Not long after, he introduced me to Paula. I went back and forth for the next few months. When I was in Thailand, I was happy. When I returned to the drama, I was unhappy. Now in my late thirties, I had been wondering over the course of several months about my professional and personal futures. The timing of our relationship was perfect, and I have always been keenly aware that we wouldn't have met and raised three children had I been the Canucks' broadcaster.

Paula visited Vancouver in February of 2000. The first hockey game she saw was the infamous one in which Marty McSorley clubbed Donald Brashear over the head, ultimately leading to McSorley's retirement. As Paula watched *Sportstalk* in person that night, it amazed her how almost every caller started with the word "unbelievable." For the next twenty-plus years that was a personal regret because "unbelievable" is usually the first word she utters to describe my lack of proficiency with simple household tasks.

As time ticked down on my contract, my gut told me things would soon get uglier. I knew Burke had gone all the way to the Edmonton-based Rutherford, whose title included head of programming for Corus Radio. We also knew Mason had exposed everyone's hands months earlier — fire Dan or lose the broadcast rights.

One early spring day in 2000, Rutherford, in Vancouver on business, tried to summon me to a meeting. With his dialling finger apparently injured, he had his administrative assistant place the call. The tone of her voicemail put me off when she essentially told me I had to drop everything and meet with Rutherford that day. Because I was so familiar with Rutherford's meeting style and didn't have any interest in being blindsided and/or ganged up on once again, I ignored the voicemail.

Two weeks later, he was back in Vancouver and tried again. This time I returned the call but told his assistant I wasn't available on such short notice. Yes, I was taunting their bench. Amnesia clearly had set in with the management team who had given me specific instructions months earlier as to how to handle Burke's behaviour, which I implemented. I'm sure Rutherford wanted to give me one last chance to conform (i.e., apologize or promise to soften my commentary ... or else). Keep in mind that no one ever claimed I said anything libellous on the air, nor once argued that I was factually wrong. Indeed, to this day I stand by everything I said at that time.

No doubt it was my relentlessness Burke hated the most. But no matter how many times I aired his claim about how easy it would be to relocate or remarked about the Canucks poor play, it didn't make it any less true. I still wear this entire episode as a badge of honour — proud not to have given in on my journalistic/broadcast/ talk-show principles to the people who should have been guarding those principles above all else.

I returned to Thailand during the first week of May. That's when a note was slid under my hotel room door late one evening asking me to call Woodgate. I knew what the note meant. Because we were heading to Bangkok the next day to pick out a ring, I knew I was going to get engaged and fired on the same day. Woodgate kindly wanted to give me the heads up, knowing 'NW hadn't informed me. He also said 'NW had hired *Sports Page* host Don Taylor to replace me. 'NW's excuse for not telling me I was terminated was contained in a note that was sent to Bourbonnais later. It read in part: "... recent attempts to meet with Dan have not been successful."

A couple of days later, Mason updated his *Sun* readers with what had happened in a column headlined: "*Sportstalk*'s Russell a casualty of radio rights."

Mason wrote:

"Last summer I wrote a column suggesting Dan Russell's job was in jeopardy because CKNW was worried about losing its broadcast rights.

"Russell had become a harsh critic of the team ... Burke, not surprisingly, came to despise Russell.

"Behind the scenes it was made clear the Canucks were prepared to take those rights elsewhere if the station insisted on allowing Russell to continue firing his nightly arrows in the direction of

Burke. I suggested the station would sacrifice Russell rather than risk losing the rights.

"The day that column appeared, Tom Plasteras, CKNW's program director and Russell's boss, appeared on *Sportstalk* to shoot down my theory. CKNW loved Dan Russell and loved his show, Plasteras insisted. He assured Russell's listeners there were no plans to fire the popular *Sportstalk* host.

"So much for promises."

CHAPTER TWENTY-THREE

Broadcasting to a sidewalk

My plan was to stay in Thailand all summer in 2000. I was getting married on September 2, so why go home? Except the phone was ringing and someone wanted to keep *Sportstalk* going. In fact, there were a couple of things in the hopper.

I had been hearing about plans for an around-the-clock sports station for some time, but I didn't believe it would be successful in our market. Then again, I never thought CKNW would one day lose the NHL broadcast rights. Paul Carson, formerly of *Sports Page*, was the frontman for investor David Stadnyk in a quest to launch a twenty-four-hour sports station, Team Radio. But despite *Sportstalk* being available, Carson's interest in hiring me was mild at best.

While that was happening, Bob Mackin, the first program director to put me on the air after CJOR's Disco Saturday Night years earlier, was starting an internet livestreaming initiative called My City Radio (MCR). Though internet content was off and running in 2000, livestreaming was rather primitive, primarily because most people didn't have the high-speed connections we have today. Mackin's concept was to offer a talk station targeting Vancouver with local talent like myself, David Berner, Fanny Kiefer and Joe "Shithead" Keithley, guitarist and lead singer for the punk band DOA. MCR's model targeted specific advertising to whichever part of the Lower Mainland someone was logged in from. This was to have been MCR's financial windfall, something terrestrial radio couldn't do. For example, under MCR's plan, when I would take a break, the listener in Richmond would hear a commercial for the Richmond Auto Mall, the North Van listener would hear about a sale at Park Royal and so on. Revolutionary technology back then.

I still had four months left on my contract when CKNW fired me, but that would soon be up. Team Radio was not only lukewarm, but their launch had been delayed, so I instructed Roger Bourbonnais to meet with Mackin. To our surprise, MCR was offering me the same pay I had been getting at 'NW. We took the deal, then I went back to Thailand to get married, returned home by myself, and began presenting *Sportstalk* to an audience of ... maybe no one.

My City Radio's debut was a disaster.

For starters, the station wasn't able to technically deliver the streaming product, which is akin to Domino's not being able to deliver pizza. For the first two months, we didn't have an open-line phone board. That meant that despite being hired to do an open-line show, the only listener contact was through email, and the majority of those were people complaining they couldn't log on. There was also nowhere to prep our show. For the first while, producer Bob Addison and I would meet on the sidewalk before deciding to simply arrive moments before airtime.

Because of the uniqueness of this venture, our first guest was Ted Leonsis of America Online (AOL) fame. This was a great "get" given his tremendous internet expertise, and also because he had recently purchased the NHL's Washington Capitals. One takeaway from the interview was Leonsis cautioning that it was going to take a while before internet radio would take off. He said it should eventually work exactly like your TV. You turn it on, you change the channel, and you instantly get your picture. He said we weren't yet near that.

We were grateful to Mackin for employing us, though in the case of the CJOR grads — Berner, Kiefer and myself — I'm not sure we embraced his vision. It was more like, *What have we gotten ourselves into and how long can they pay us?* Whenever we were together that's all we'd talk about, usually with nervous giggles.

Mackin also helped me on a personal matter, for which I was extremely grateful. Having started the long immigration process for my wife and daughter several months earlier, I anxiously hoped they'd arrive in Canada by Christmas. After I shared that with Mackin, he called his old CJOR friend John Reynolds, now the MP for West Vancouver-Sunshine Coast. Five days later, coincidence or otherwise, they were approved as landed immigrants. The official paperwork arrived on December 7, 2000. I flew to Asia later that night and came back to start my family life one week later.

Unfortunately, financial warning signs were starting to appear. During a hastily arranged meeting on January 12, 2001, Mackin asked me to sign a new version of my contract as part of a complicated MCR restructuring plan. After consulting with Roger, we determined it didn't make any sense to do so. By early spring, cheques weren't arriving on time. Initially, they were a few days late for me, but even later for others. Berner quit in late April, while Kiefer reportedly was being paid in staggered portions. For the next two months each pay period was delayed.

Mackin's son, Bob Jr., was doing everything he could content-wise, working tirelessly on the news side trying to attract attention for MCR. But no matter what he or anyone else did, no one was listening.

How did I know?

One night I offered $50 for the tenth caller. Free money for caller ten. Who could turn that down? No one called.

I lasted until the end of June, and I was right about not being paid my final cheque. I didn't feel badly about that; probably guiltier I had cashed all the others.

I may not have had any listeners, but I had huge readership at the *Vancouver Sun* after sports editor Steve Snelgrove asked me to write three columns per week starting in November 2000. This was my most daunting media challenge, and I constantly agonized about it. Snelgrove was extremely supportive, urging me to write like I talk. But radio words, which immediately disappear, flowed with ease whereas I knew newspaper words remain archived and were much more difficult for me to find.

Only a few months removed from the 'NW firing, Brian Burke issued a warning of sorts in a *Sun* piece authored by Greg Douglas.

"If he picks up where he left off on the radio," Burke told Douglas, "I'll make arrangements to write my own column in *The Province* and go head-to-head with him."

I often thought Burke spent as much time obsessed with controlling public opinion as he did building the hockey club.

My *Vancouver Sun* column lasted ten months, and I was more relieved than disappointed when it ended. At the same time, I gained a whole new appreciation for writers like Archie McDonald, Jim Taylor, Iain MacIntyre and others.

After a long delay, Team Radio was finally about to launch, but the process of getting them to hire me was as ridiculous as the time slot they gave me. Call me crazy, but if you were about to launch a twenty-four-hour sports station and a "franchise show" with a large and loyal built-in audience just happened to be available, wouldn't you jump at it? Despite my credentials, they made *me* jump through hoops.

For starters, frontman Carson didn't seem like a Dan fan. This may have gone back to *Sportstalk's* strong criticism in early 1996 when *Sports Page* committed a major faux pas by erroneously announcing that Canucks coach Rick Ley had been fired. Or perhaps it was because Brian Burke, as Carson told me in June 2000, had called him months before the station signed on to say that if Team Radio was interested in the Canucks broadcast rights "Dan Russell cannot be involved in your radio station."

Overseeing all of the Team Radio hiring was general manager Paul Ski who, for reasons I never understood, insisted on a clandestine meeting on March 26, 2001, at the Pacific Palisades Hotel. I was told to call for him from the lobby phone once I arrived.

"Come up to room 1220," he instructed. "I'll order room service and we can have our meeting here."

This was another first in my world.

When I got there, he gave me the room service menu, we ordered, had some small talk, ate and then moved to the two comfortable sofas located in the middle of his suite. Once settled, Ski — who was packing heat in the form of two fairly thick binders — got down to business.

"You're probably wondering what all this is," he said.

As a matter of fact, I was.

"I want you to know we have compiled a 'scouting report' on Dan Russell, and if you don't mind, I want to ask you for your reaction on some of these items."

On a day full of firsts, I said, "Go ahead, fire away."

It quickly became clear that Carson was his chief scout as the early questions centred on my relationship with others in the media, my attitude, working with others, etc. Ski then moved to the other folder, which had to do with my battle with Burke and my volatile relationship with CKNW, in particular Doug Rutherford. Ski carried on for a while, but as a seasoned talk-show host I felt I did a thorough job explaining every negative thing he mentioned.

About fifteen minutes into this line of questioning, I asked, "Is there anything good about Dan Russell in those files?"

Disarmed by my bluntness, Ski laughed it off, said there was and told me a few things I wanted to hear. But he didn't offer me a job. Instead, he told me to wait for program director John Rea to call, which took ten more days. Rea and I had a good meeting at the White Spot in Kerrisdale, mostly exchanging broadcast ideas. There still wasn't an offer, although he told me he'd get back to me.

It took nearly four more weeks before I was offered a position and — wouldn't you know — it was another of those Door No. 3 scenarios. I wasn't offered my highly-rated late evening slot. Or afternoon drive. Right out of left field they offered breakfast. Ski also asked me to partner with old friend Bill Courage, a big sports fan but most noted for his talented DJ work and voice-overs. Because I'd never had a co-host and knew our egos would clash, I would've preferred not to work with him. I also wanted to preserve our friendship. But that's all they were offering.

We started on May 8, 2001. Words cannot describe how much I hated it — all of it. Everything about it.

I hated going to bed early because I couldn't sleep. I hated waking up early for obvious reasons. I hated driving to work feeling tired. I hated starting at 5:30 a.m. not knowing if I should deliver my most salient observations then or wait until so-called prime time between 7:30 and 8:30 a.m.

Courage was mostly fun, and it was nice to have Lee Powell provide the sports updates. But Bill and I could frustrate each other on air because he was a big fan of the Canucks, and I've never seen my role as that of a fan. I often lectured my listeners over the years, telling them their role was to be fanatical, to fly their car flags and wave pom-poms. My job was to offer opinion and analysis.

Then my contract again became a source of contention. Not because I was making significantly less than I'd been used to at CKNW, but because, despite agreeing to their terms, Team Radio still hadn't asked me to officially sign.

"Paper or not, the contract is feeble," Bourbonnais counselled me at the time, rightly pointing out that the station could terminate me and pay only two months' severance. "Think of it only as a two-month contract," Roger added.

I was only two weeks in and I wasn't happy about anything. The mindlessness of not putting me in the right time slot, their silly scouting report, the constant fatigue caused by getting up early while my body was programmed to stay up late, useless post-show meetings and the overall sub-standard sound of the station.

As for that mysterious unsigned contract?

That was about to bite them square on the ass.

CHAPTER TWENTY-FOUR

Second best news of the day

Ten days after starting the breakfast show on Team Radio, my wife and I went to our doctor and came away with about the best news any couple could get. Paula was pregnant. I was already blessed to be a father. Palita, our oldest, was four when I met Paula, six when she immigrated to Canada and seven when I officially adopted her. Now I was going to experience being a birth father. It was thrilling news for many reasons, most of all because we knew Palita would grow up with at least one sibling.

After leaving the doctor's office in the late morning on May 18, 2001, Paula and I went for a walk on the dyke near our home in Richmond to absorb the news. On the shores of the Fraser River, halfway towards Steveston, my phone rang. The call display — CKNW — was familiar. But who? And more importantly, why? As I have previously mentioned, I often preferred voicemail to answering cold, even more so on this happy day and particularly from that phone number. Highly curious, I quickly retrieved the message.

"Dan, it's Tom Plasteras calling," began the voicemail, which I saved for prosperity. "I understand there's been a lot of mending of fences going on lately, and I was wanting to know if you'd like to mend another one?"

He was referring to the fact that Brian Burke, perhaps feeling guilty for what he'd done to our friendship or concerned that I now had a major *Vancouver Sun* platform, had invited me to Monk

McQueens for what turned out to be a friendly lunch absent of any ill feelings and high on reminiscing.

Before Tom's message ended, several thoughts began swirling through my head. For starters, *WOW! They actually want me back?* I also knew CKNW needed Burke's proxy to make it happen. We'd had a cordial lunch, but I never thought it would lead to this. My replacement, Don Taylor, must have been miserable and/or lonely.

I also knew a favourite adage was back in play: you never make any real money in radio unless it's your phone that rings.

Don Taylor, one of Vancouver's finest ever sports personalities and without equal when it came to showing highlights on TV, had starred with CKVU *Sports Page* for fifteen years before taking my radio slot. It was no secret Taylor loved the *Sports Page* atmosphere, working alongside a closely knit team — people who supported each other and weren't averse to tossing a football around their studio on occasion. None of that existed during the lonely evenings at CKNW. Speaking from experience, you could go weeks without hearing a word, good or bad, from anyone in management. Aside from your producer, one newscaster and the janitor, you were all alone. I enjoyed the solitude. I don't think Don did.

I also wondered if Taylor had carefully considered what it took to solo host every night. Naturally he couldn't ask me, but if he had I would have told him the most relaxing hours of my day were on-air hours. Everything else was a build-up, an all-day grind that started moments after waking up — near the crack of noon! — when I began scanning the news. Following a bowl of cereal and a cup of tea, I would call my producer to pick up on the plan we had tentatively put in place the previous night. From there I'd begin reading and researching while Scott Woodgate, or later Bob Addison or even later Heath Morgan, tracked down potential guests.

By mid- to late-afternoon, I had begun formulating and writing an editorial and/or recording pre-tapes from my home studio. In order to deliver quality guests, I had to be ready to record on short notice. It wasn't uncommon for my producer to be told someone like Steve Yzerman or Brett Hull was available, but I had to do the interview at that moment. I did hundreds of interviews on less than fifteen minutes' notice. In our early years, we recorded everything on reel-to-reel tapes and edited with a razor blade, which, because I was good at it, I really enjoyed. Years later we would record interviews onto a mini-disc, and in later years directly into a computer, which I could edit and send to the station for processing. We learned — yes, the hard way — to always back up our recording with a second machine. It's highly embarrassing to have to call a guest back and explain we had a technical problem and ask to start over. It happened only once, and veteran hockey writer Stan Fischler was most accommodating.

Our master *Sportstalk* guest plan — we called it our grid — was constantly being altered. We planned shows many days in advance, knowing they were always subject to change. The advent of email made booking guests easier but less personal. It allowed us to set "fishing lines" before bed and to wake up to see if there were any bites. Sometimes there weren't. Sometimes we'd go all day unable to lure a guest, our stress level elevating with each passing hour. Other days many lines were hooked and we'd have too many.

During my early years, I'd grab a sandwich around 5 p.m. and be in the station around 6. Those times became later after I got married and there were children. My amusing cousin Grant Wilson would occasionally come by and watch the show. He said the most entertaining part for him was just before we went to air. He dubbed it the "Panic Hour," as he watched Woodgate and I often scramble like maniacs — me trying to finish writing an editorial, Scott frantically gathering audio clips or perhaps finalizing one last guest. We often made it into the studio with seconds to spare.

As for Plasteras's attempt at reconciliation?

Initially, I was torn. Though still plenty pissed at CKNW for not backing me against Burke, I also missed my old time slot and format. Plus, I hated working at Team Radio. Maybe I should've called Plasteras back, but I didn't. Instead I called my lawyer, Roger Bourbonnais, told him what had happened and asked him to call. When Roger got back to me, he confirmed that CKNW not only wanted *Sportstalk* to return but also wanted me to host the Canucks broadcasts.

Then he gave me the best set of instructions I would hear in my entire broadcast career.

"Tom asked for you to make a complete list of what it would take for you to return to CKNW," Bourbonnais said.

We were dumbfounded. We also wondered what Doug Rutherford's reaction was when this was first floated by him.

Without speaking to anyone connected to CKNW, I spent the next two days drawing up my fantasy contract. Yes, it was a highly enjoyable process. Ask anyone in my position to make a "wish list" and it would likely mirror what I included: salary increase, more vacation time, editorial and guest freedom, ten to midnight time slot, right to choose producer, budget for regular guests, paid parking, expense account, cell phone, Canucks tickets, etc. I had one child at home, another on the way and my wife was still getting used to living in Canada, so I excluded playoff travel from my list. All told, however, there were more than twenty items. *Why not?* I thought. *What's the worst they could say?*

"Yes, to all of them," Bourbonnais reported back.

"All of them?" I said in complete shock.

Bourbonnais said Plasteras didn't blink an eye, even when Roger said, "In order for this process to work [because of the sensitivity of the Team Radio contract] we would have to get something signed by tomorrow and then hold the contract in escrow."

Sure enough, on June 1, just three weeks after I had started on Team Radio, the contract with CKNW was signed — completed without me having spoken one word to Plasteras. What a way to mend a fence!

The last order of business was to deal with the silliness of the Team Radio contract, which allowed them to fire me at any time and only have to pay two months' salary. Conversely, I had the option to quit if I gave two months' notice. But remember, Team Radio still hadn't asked me to sign it. So what was my status? Roger's opinion was that the agreement would be binding because I was already working under an "implied deal." That said, we both thought it'd be much cleaner if it was actually signed.

So, in order to get out of Team Radio, I first had to sign with Team Radio.

The next afternoon, June 1, 2001, I phoned program director John Rea to tell him I was coming into town to take Paula and Palita to see Rod Stewart and asked, with fingers crossed, "Can I pop in to get that piece of paperwork handled?"

He replied, "Sure, that'd be fine."

I signed just before 5 p.m. In theory, I could have reached into my pocket and immediately given Rea my letter of resignation, but I waited until June 14. That doesn't mean they were any less angry when I did, especially Mr. "Scouting Report." General manager Paul Ski baselessly claimed I didn't have the right to leave and kept me on the air for about a week before finally removing me on June 22. Perfect, I felt. Now they could cut me a two-month cheque and I'd be on my way.

Well ... not quite.

Once again, Ski claimed I didn't have the right to sign elsewhere and therefore Team Radio didn't have to pay me out. Roger and I disagreed. On June 26, I met with Ski in his office. Knowing the summer was upon us, I was anxious to close this book, grab some vacation and get ready for my CKNW sequel. I wanted the two months' pay to which I was entitled, but when I told him I'd settle for one month he leapt out of his chair to shake my hand.

"Deal!" said Ski, loudly and proudly.

He had just saved his station a few thousand dollars, and I walked away thinking there were lottery winners who weren't nearly that excited. It was great to have that summer off. Palita, Paula, whomever was in her tummy (Anna would arrive four months later) and I went on a driving vacation down the Oregon coast towards Disneyland. I have never felt more vindicated.

My return to CKNW was on September 4, 2001, a Tuesday. Seven days later, terrorism struck the USA. I was awakened by five words from my friend Doug Lum: "Turn on your television — now."

Like most everyone, I was glued to CNN all day. After all airplanes were ordered grounded, my wife and I walked along the dyke directly across from Vancouver International's South Terminal and witnessed dozens and dozens of grounded aircraft awaiting further instructions. Like all those airplanes, *Sportstalk*, which had only been back for seven days, was also grounded and didn't return for a week.

Given everything that had happened in the previous eighteen months and my shiny new five-year agreement, it would only make sense that my second honeymoon at CKNW was going to be long-lasting. Believe it or not, fifty-four days after relaunching, Plasteras told me he was under severe pressure from Corus president John Hayes to cut budget. Among other things, Hayes wanted *Sportstalk* to air from 7 p.m. until midnight. According to Plasteras, Hayes had said, "That's twenty-five hours per week. I'd take that job if it were me."

Uh, not quite.

Plasteras applied enormous pressure on me to change, even soliciting highly popular morning personality Brian "Frosty" Forst to twice call me in an attempt to persuade me. It appeared Plasteras had taken significant grief for my new contract. Not wanting our return to get off to a bad start, I made up family reasons for not being able to switch while shaking my head at the thought that even the top person in the chain didn't seem to understand the concept of a signed agreement, let alone grasp/care how many hours of prep it takes to professionally host.

The process dragged on for ten long months before we finally cut a deal for a little more money, a little more term and a little more show. *Sportstalk* now would air from 9 p.m. to midnight.

CHAPTER TWENTY-FIVE

Our next contestant is Mrs. Pat Russell

"The National Hockey League is on the air!"

Those were the eight goosebump-raising words used to open the first Canucks NHL broadcast on October 9, 1970. And to pay homage to original host Al Davidson, I used those exact words when I got to host thirty-odd years later.

Hosting should have been a thrill, and it would've been had I not hosted *Sportstalk*. I was still honoured to do it, but if anything it was more of an add-on.

When I was impressionably young, the Canucks broadcasts seemed bigger than life. It started with the "Face-off Show" fifteen minutes before puck drop and ended with the oft-lively "Overtime Show," especially the ones originating from Branigan's Restaurant across the street from the Pacific Coliseum. During the intermissions, it was Vancouver's version of the "Hot Stove League" from the middle concourse of the press area. On any given night you might hear Babe Pratt, Bill Good Sr., Hal Sigurdson, Jim Kearney or Tony Gallagher, along with the occasional visit from Joe (Mr. Sony) Cohen, a big sponsor who gave each of Al's guests a Sony Walkman. When J. P. McConnell was hosting, he would occasionally have me on as a guest, and even though I worked at the station he still generously made sure to send me Hamilton Beach gift products — toasters, kettles, etc. — that I kept or gave to my family. By the time I hosted, the gifts had scaled down in actual size as we gave them Cross Ion pens, which were particularly handy for Tom Larscheid to pack on the road.

One part of the broadcast that didn't change for years was the "Power Play Contest," an excellent in-game concept mostly sponsored by Safeway. Starting with a one-hundred-dollar jackpot, a new contestant had a chance to win each time the Canucks had the man advantage. If they didn't score, ten more dollars was added. The contest also served as an instant barometer of the Canucks power play, especially when the jackpot reached into the three-hundred-dollar range. For at least twenty years, the starting jackpot remained at one hundred dollars with no COLA or inflation clause.

One loud night in the Russell house occurred in 1974 when (as always) I was listening in my bedroom to a game against Pittsburgh while keeping my in-game stats. I was writing down a Penguins penalty when I heard Jim Robson say, "Vancouver will have the man advantage, and our next contestant in the 'Safeway Power Play Contest' is Mrs. Pat Russell from Rosecroft in Richmond." I didn't even know Mom had entered. I screamed while scrambling to get a fresh cassette into my machine. I was so loud my family came rushing to my room to find out why the commotion. Suddenly, both parents and both of my siblings were in my bedroom listening to the broadcast with the hopes the Canucks would score.

Robson play-by-play: "Penguins are leading 2-0. Canucks back in their own zone. Dailey to Boudrias. Back to Dailey, coming up the middle. To his own line. On the right to Ververgaert. Into the Pittsburgh zone. Cuts along the blueline. Puts it in front — and Lever is upset! There's going to be a Pittsburgh penalty. Lever hooked in front of the net. Now the Canucks will have a two-man advantage for twenty-nine seconds. Lever was getting into the clear in front, was hooked right in front of the net. Ron Schock, the Pittsburgh captain who's been a great player for this team year in and year out, complains about the call, but the penalty is going to be to Colin Campbell. Hooking will be the infraction and the time is 17:28."

Inside the Russell house, drama built while the Pacific Coliseum organist played and the CKNW 9:30 p.m. time tone sounded. (I miss those!)

Peacock PA: "Pittsburgh penalty to number six, Colin Campbell. Two minutes for hooking. The time: 17:28."

Robson: "So with twenty-nine seconds left in the penalty to Paradise, Campbell goes to the penalty box. The Canucks with a two-man advantage, trailing 2-0, and Mrs. Pat Russell from Richmond — a pretty good chance here to win $180 on the 'Safeway Power Play.'

"Boudrias gets the puck to Lever. Back to DeMarco at the left point. Plays it off the boards. Now to Boudrias, his shot went over top the net. Puck bounces off the glass. Ververgaert failed to get control of it. Apps clears it but not out. DeMarco winding up! He shoots, he scores!"

Crowd cheers, and as it slightly dies down …

"Ab DeMarco scoring against his former teammates and it's now 2-1 for Pittsburgh. DeMarco has scored nine goals this year, seven on the power play."

Davidson, doing colour: "That comes at 17:42, and they give Ab DeMarco a good hand. And the winner of $180 Mrs. Pat Russell of Rosecroft, Richmond, a GE entry with the 'Safeway Power Play.' $180. Congratulations to you, Mrs. Pat Russell."

We cheered loudly for that goal. I still recall my mom getting the CKNW logoed cheque in the mail. Just as importantly, I had unknowingly prepared my first *Sportstalk* clip, as I would play that audio a couple of decades later on the show.

I felt my hosting work was solid enough, but I felt constrained. I knew the difference between a Canucks game broadcast — a partnership between the hockey club and the station — and independent *Sportstalk*. As a result, I usually played everything down the middle, knowing that I had my own show on which to let loose if need be.

Having listened to Tom Larscheid for decades on hockey and football broadcasts, it was a delight to finally work alongside him, despite having been warned he could be a little temperamental. For example, there was the CFL night at BC Place Stadium when he and McConnell came to blows in the booth before a game. Or a night in Detroit when Tom slammed down his headphones and left during the "Overtime Show" after some kind of a squabble with Jim Hughson. This forced Hughson to inform host John McKeachie, who was posing another question for Tom, that Larscheid had "vacated the booth." Not sure why McKeach didn't know what a live mic being slammed down sounded like …

I only had one minor Larscheid incident in the five years I hosted, for which I will charitably take some of the blame. On this particular night, the 1982 Canucks were being saluted with Jim Robson serving as on-ice emcee. What I had no way of knowing was the Canucks hadn't asked Tom to take part despite his booth prominence during the 1982 playoff. In keeping with the '82 theme, I was teeing up a question designed to take Tom down memory lane with a preface that saluted his twenty years in the booth. However, I must have miscalculated because of the five years he missed after leaving to do BC Lions games on CFUN, so I was short on his actual number of years. I inadvertently touched a nerve because Tom gently put down his headset and left the booth while we were on-air, leaving Shorthouse and I to carry the rest of the "Face-off Show." I wasn't offended because Shorthouse later told me off-air what happened. I felt badly for Tom for being slighted by a hockey club that ought to have known better.

Superseding everything in terms of working with Tom was a two-week period in early 2004 when CKNW asked me to fill in for Shorthouse, whose wife was expecting their first child, an event he understandably didn't want to miss. Safe to say this appointment was either approved or suggested by Brian Burke. If the latter, I can only assume it was his way of trying to make up for what had happened a few years earlier. Christina Shorthouse's due date coincided with a two-game trip to Los Angeles and Anaheim. It was good for me that the baby was late because that gave me another two-game trip to Phoenix and San Jose as well as a home game versus San Jose.

It's probably good that no rehash is needed because it's impossible to put into words what it felt like to finally be able to claim, after listening to a couple of thousand Canucks games, that my boyhood wish had become reality. Larscheid couldn't have been kinder or more helpful than he was during those five games. Even though he didn't have to, he walked me through every part of what he thought I needed to know. Most of it I already knew — hell, I memorized the format when I was twelve — but I just let him tell me anyway because I thought it was cool and professional.

Tom asked me sit beside him on the charter even though, as the veteran media member he always had the seat beside him blocked. At thirty-five thousand feet, Tom shared some great stories about his life on the road, and it quickly became clear just how thankful he was to have had the opportunity to travel around the NHL for all those years. He called it "a privilege of a lifetime." For some reason I was relieved he hadn't taken any of it for granted.

Already knowing the next answer, I asked him during our first flight to California — a few minutes after they served us warm chocolate chip cookies and ice-cold milk — if during all those trips to LA he had ever made a quick side trip to Las Vegas.

"Are you *kidding* me?" he said, slowly emphasizing each of the words with that all-so-familiar voice. "Danny, let me tell you what I did many times. Usually we would land in the mid-afternoon for a game the next day. I'd go on the team bus to the hotel, which was just a few blocks from LAX. I'd go upstairs, drop off my suitcase, get changed into casual slacks and a golf shirt, go right back down to the lobby, get on the shuttle back to LAX and grab a quick flight.

"The flights to Vegas left every hour, Danny!" he added excitedly while alternating between pounding on my arm or holding the top of my hand. "I'd land before six and be rolling dice before seven! Craps, blackjack, a little roulette. But mostly craps in those days. I'd play all night and around 9 a.m. fly back to LAX and go right to the morning skate. No one even knew where I'd been! I got my game notes, watched practice, and then it was back to the hotel for a great big giant nap."

Of the five games I did, my favourite was the fourth one in San Jose. The location was great, the game was even better, and I now felt comfortable, which allowed me to display the play-by-play rhythm I knew I had.

I can't stress how cordial Larscheid was the whole time — on planes, check-in at hotel (where he made sure I got my key envelope first), game-day skates (in Phoenix he arranged for Coyotes GM Michael Barnett to give us a full tour of their brand new rink), the media rooms (where he thoughtfully introduced me to everyone, including the press room attendant), and the broadcast booth (where he made sure I was comfortable and stressed how much fun we were going to have).

Lastly, we did a Saturday night home game against Anaheim, and that was it in terms of my NHL play-by-play career, although I was asked to fill in for Tom for a game in Edmonton after his mother passed away. Shorthouse also was fun to travel with and I discovered he, too, liked to play a little blackjack while on the road.

Even though I had travelled years earlier on Air Canuck, I'd forgotten just how NHL charter travel spoiled you. It started with the private pre-board lounge and the breeze through screening before settling into a plane with nothing but business class seats. What I initially didn't know — rookie mistake — was that the food they served before we even fastened our seatbelts was an appetizer and that they'd be feeding us a much larger meal — pro athletes need large portions — during the flight. As we disembarked there was a big basket of candies, chocolate bars and gum at the front of the plane — "trick or treat" — we were expected to help ourselves to, along with bottled water and soft drinks for the hotel.

Our bus was only steps away from the plane, ready to whisk us to the hotel where there was a table just inside the front door with your key waiting in a personalized envelope. No front desk check-in required.

After returning late night from the US, two customs officials came on board and grabbed all the official declaration cards in less than a minute. After deplaning around 2 a.m., I saw an incredible sight — the cars that we had left with the valet a few days earlier at YVR's main terminal had miraculously all been parked a few feet from the plane at the south terminal. They were warmed up and running, headlights on.

Oh, and if you didn't have a car — not a bad idea given there was alcohol available on the flight — the Canucks' media relations official asked a half-hour before landing if you would like a taxi. So in addition to all of the cars, there also was a handful of cabs waiting.

Two months later, I hosted on the infamous night of March 8, 2004, when an incident that took all of ten seconds — from one end of the ice to the other — triggered three incredible events: the end of Steve Moore's hockey life, the neutering of Todd Bertuzzi's career and the torching of the first-place Canucks' legitimate shot at a Stanley Cup. It also created endless weeks of *Sportstalk* fodder. I don't like admitting it was a dream topic, but it was.

Sportstalk reaction began before the game even ended when I received a call from *Denver Post* writer Adrian Dater, a frequent guest who on this night came just shy of demanding airtime. Dater's blood was boiling as he cast blame in many Canuck directions: Bertuzzi, coach Marc Crawford for stirring the pot weeks earlier, Brad May for an alleged bounty. Knowing how good this was sounding on the radio, I kept Dater on.

Some callers, but not all, tried to protect or excuse Bertuzzi. Many others were horrified at what they had witnessed, especially the image of Moore lying motionless and then being stretchered off. On that night there wasn't any way of knowing Bertuzzi would be suspended for the rest of the season, face criminal assault charges and a civil suit, be traded a season later and never again play with the same edge or gusto. What I did know was we better extend the show well past midnight.

Bertuzzi was a polarizing figure on *Sportstalk*. Most fans loved him. The host didn't. And not just because, pre-Moore, his public persona came across as forever grumpy. But the year before the sucker punch, during a playoff series with the Wild, Bertuzzi's cockiness and immaturity bit him in the ass. First, with the Canucks leading the series 3-1, he walked past a line of Minnesota fans waiting to buy Game 6 tickets and said, "You're wasting your time." Not only was there a Game 6 but also a Game 7. After Vancouver took a 2-0 lead in that deciding game, Bertuzzi skated past the Wild bench and screamed for the players to "Get out your golf clubs." One hour later, it was the Canucks who were booking tee times.

But he was hugely popular in Vancouver and was even the subject of a catchy song by "Heavy Eric" Holmquist, a faithful *Sportstalk* listener, local singer songwriter, original Canucks season-ticket holder and Elvis lookalike. We frequently played "It's Called the Tood Bertuzzi," featuring rhyming words like Lenarduzzi, watusi and, for some reason, a goalie name Suzie.

CHAPTER TWENTY-SIX

They walked the *Sportstalk* red carpet

Cut to the barest of bones, *Sportstalk* was about a host, my guests and callers on our phone board. There isn't a show without the latter two.

It doesn't take long for the math to compound. When you consider *Sportstalk* averaged just under four guests per night, the extrapolated number over three decades zooms past twenty-five thousand interviews. If I attended a Canucks game and stopped by every seat to talk to each fan for a few minutes, I still wouldn't come close to the number of interviews I conducted. It's no wonder that interviewing became my best skill. I had more practise than virtually every other broadcaster in Canada and took personal pride in each interview.

I'm thankful to every guest for giving up their time, but also because I found most of them to be honest. Though it was entirely possible they were fibbing, two compliments I often heard were the interview had flown by or it was the most enjoyable interview they'd had. Regular guests were a mainstay on *Sportstalk*, and after our top two — Brian Burke and Rod Beaton — I list Harry Neale, who joined every week for a decade starting in 1991, as our third most popular.

Based in Buffalo, Neale was unique because his instructions were for us to wake him at 2 a.m. ET. Neither he nor his wife Peggy seemed to mind, presumably because they liked the two hundred dollars in grocery money we sent each week. As lead colour commentator for

Hockey Night in Canada and midweek Toronto Maple Leafs games, Neale was a marquee guest. Most Thursdays he would be at home watching the early games, then go to bed and awaken when we called.

"If I'm already awake you know you're gonna have a helluva show," he told me before most seasons.

He wasn't wrong, as there were a few occasions we had to abort early because Harry was slurring and we didn't want him to say something he might wish he hadn't.

Harry started each week: "How are you tonight?"

Producer Bob Addison and I became proficient at assessing his blood alcohol level based on those four words. When we heard them, Bob and I would look at each other, pause, then give a thumbs up or down. Sometimes there was a sideways thumb, which accounted for his first two minutes of grogginess before he suddenly snapped out of that mode and into the witty, wide awake, informative Neale we enjoyed each Saturday on CBC.

I don't know which I liked better — the stories he told or the way he told them. A personal favourite was when he put himself in a conundrum while coaching Gordie Howe in Hartford. One night Neale told his struggling team he was imposing a curfew and bed check. But when Harry got to Mr. Hockey's room, he stopped short of knocking, thinking there was no way in the world he was going to insult his childhood idol, the greatest player of all time, by making sure Howe was in on time. The way he painted the story took some time, but it ended when Harry went to the hotel restaurant for an early breakfast to see Howe already sitting there and looking visibly upset. When Neale asked why, Gordie said, "Because I didn't get a bleepin' wink of sleep all night waiting for you to knock."

Harry, always loyal, never once balked about doing our show, even when his schedule was hectic during the playoffs.

To my knowledge, *Sportstalk* was the first Vancouver radio talk show of any kind that scheduled weekly regular guests. This gave us a head start in building our line-up grid while providing on-air consistency.

Don Hay may be the surprise answer to a great *Sportstalk* trivia question. The winningest WHL coach of all time was our most interviewed guest — more than three hundred appearances — joining us every Monday during the ten years he coached the Vancouver Giants. Before we recorded each week, Hay, always looking for a coaching edge, would specifically ask me about teams and players I had called in one of my Shaw TV games. I always enjoyed my conversations with Hay and learned a lot from him.

"Game time is for the players," he would tell me, "but practice time is my time."

Ron Wilson was a regular for three years while serving as a Canucks assistant in the early '90s. Whenever I called to set up the show, he'd answer by saying, "Is this the radio puke?" Then he would break into an infectious laugh. I was happy for Ron when he became Anaheim's first head coach, especially when he told our listeners, "I was greatly assisted by the confidence I gained by being on *Sportstalk* because the Mighty Ducks told me they place such a high importance on marketing."

Wilson often called me when he came to Vancouver. One night after the expansion Ducks defeated the Canucks at the PNE, he invited me to join him and his coaching staff for a celebratory dinner and drinks at the Cannery Seafood Restaurant.

George McPhee proved you didn't need to be flamboyant to be a great *Sportstalk* guest. He was extremely low key but highly loyal, and he seemed incapable of lying, or even spinning.

Incidentally, it was good luck to be a regular on *Sportstalk*. Burke, McPhee and Dave Nonis all got their first GM jobs and Wilson his first head-coaching job after appearing as a weekly guests. Mind you, Nonis only became a regular when Burke legislated "Davey be front and centre." My heart wasn't much into it, except when I would contentiously grill Nonis as to why his boss was spending so much time worrying about media matters — including battling faraway reporter Larry Brooks of the *New York Post* — when the Canucks weren't improving.

Around 2006, we began "Sunsational," featuring the regular *Vancouver Sun* beat writers who joined us on an alternating basis prior to every Canucks game. This segment was a big hit for several years. The three were Elliott "Hell's Bells" Pap, Iain "Along the Watchtower" MacIntyre and later Brad "Born to Run" Ziemer, who came on after Pap stepped away from the Canucks beat. Yes, all three had to carefully choose their musical intros.

Initially, Ziemer was a little nervous and his answers were short, which didn't bother me. But within a few weeks he found his stride and became one of my all-time favourites. Neither Brad nor Elliott cared if anything they said might tick off the Canucks, Ziemer especially. If he didn't like what they were doing or how they were playing he wasn't shy about saying so, and he would often bring up topics that troubled him without my prompting.

All three were different, and all were excellent for the show. Of the three, MacIntyre was the best writer, something I believe the other two would acknowledge. But Iain's perspective was often different than mine, which I found healthy as it led to some crackling debates during which I always hoped he wouldn't get pissed at me. If he was, he never told me. My MacIntyre segments often felt like a role reversal because years earlier I had been accused of having a default mechanism that slanted towards the Canucks' point of view, while the scribes were often more critical. For example, Iain was steadfastly behind Nonis when he was the GM (undoubtedly a good source) and was upset when he was fired. Mind you, it didn't take long until Iain became just as steadfast with the next GM, Mike Gillis, and his coach, Alain Vigneault. Any talk of Vigneault being on thin ice was met with disgust, and Iain was quick to trot out Alain's great regular-season record while ignoring the playoff elephant in the room, save for one season.

Iain was one of the first in the market to develop a man crush on Henrik and Daniel Sedin, which I often found a little much. I concede Iain was absolutely right about the twins during the regular season, but I was always right about them come playoff time.

One night we had a spirited debate that lasted nearly an hour regarding the Canucks' decision to retire Markus Naslund's sweater number. I thought it was a mistake for the same reason: he was a big regular-season point producer with virtually no playoff success. I thought Naslund belonged in the newly-created "Ring of Honour," but Iain couldn't have disagreed more. Though I pushed hard, MacIntyre absorbed the licks and gave back in kind. Those were my favourite kinds of nights.

Even when I hear one of their theme songs today, I fondly remember "Sunsational" as one of my favourite *Sportstalk* features.

When Squire Barnes from Global TV joined as a regular in 2008, I knew the segment would go over well because of his popularity on the *News Hour*. I'd first met Barnes twenty years earlier when he was covering events for radio station CKO. I recall him as a unique looking character with a poorly-groomed moustache, usually wearing a gold San Francisco 49ers jacket instead of a sports jacket. He struck me as both smart and shy. We weren't overly close through the years, but when we did talk I knew we shared many of the same broadcast beliefs. We had some strong segments when he came on *Sportstalk*. Unfortunately, Squire was also one of the most frustrating people I ever interviewed because he'd constantly interrupt before I could finish the question. It didn't matter that I prided myself on my short questions, Squire was off and running before I could finish. I learned to laugh it off, but it was a weird habit, especially from someone in the business.

Unfortunately, that became the least of our problems as our relationship soured during the 2004-05 NHL work stoppage, a season when all the games were cancelled but *Sportstalk* was not. Three hours a night for an entire season without hockey was an enormous challenge, and I felt Squire, who was a paid guest, should have recognized what I was up against versus the few TV minutes he was obligated to provide. Barnes had no appetite to discuss the never-ending labour fight, and I mostly respected that; none of us liked it. But there were occasionally newsworthy developments that needed to be discussed. Squire couldn't have cared less and made it clear he didn't want to talk about it.

After letting him off the hook in previous weeks, I couldn't on one particular night. I even told him the developments on that day were important, but he still didn't care and kept trying to change the subject, which really pissed me off. *To hell with this*, I thought, before saying something along the lines of, "I guess if you don't want to talk about this we should just end this now?"

"Okay," he said, and I hung up and moved on.

It turned out to be Squire's final appearance on *Sportstalk* and, unfortunately, we haven't spoken since. I have asked myself numerous times what I could have done differently. Had I bitten my tongue I know the same issue would've come up in subsequent weeks. Still, if I could do it again, I would've laughed it off in the hopes of maintaining our friendship.

Our *Sportstalk* "Journey Series" was born out of that same NHL shutdown. I wish I had thought of it earlier as those segments became a personal favourite. Far from original, the hour-long concept had well-known figures walking us through their journeys starting from when they were kids. We amassed a large library of "Journey" guests like Andy Bathgate, Guyle Fielder, Charlie Hodge, Cam Neely, Chris Oddleifson, Danny Gare, Dave Babych, Dave Schultz, Dennis Kearns, Don Murdoch, Ed Chynoweth, Ernie McLean, John Ferguson, Johnny Bucyk, Marcel Dionne, Larry Popein and "Tiger" Williams, to name only some.

All of them seemed eager to reminisce, and they especially enjoyed talking about their childhoods, their parents, siblings and other sports they played. And all of them seemed to have a particular turning point that changed their fortunes.

For example, Cam Neely shared a story about getting cut by the Victoria Cougars at age sixteen and going back to play midget in Maple Ridge with a fun team that mostly played tournaments. One was in Portland where a Winterhawks scout approached him and asked if he would like to come to a practice. Long story short, in a span of just over a year, Neely ended up making the Winterhawks, being selected in the first round of the NHL draft and playing for his hometown team. I asked him if he had ever thought about what might have happened had his midget team not entered that tournament.

"I would probably be a petroleum distributor," Cam deadpanned. "My last job was pumping gas."

My listeners and I learned so much about these guests. One tidbit that stuck with me was Dennis Kearns saying his dad never saw him play until he made junior, and then he left after one period to go home to watch *The Lawrence Welk Show*.

Shortly after his nineteen-year NHL career ended, Ray Ferraro became an unpaid *Sportstalk* regular until he was poached by Team Radio, which offered him significant money for appearing daily. This was before Ray became one of today's great NHL TV colour commentators. Though no longer a guest on my show, I was honoured to be a chosen guest of his when he married Cammi Granato.

Ironically, our best NBA feature came after the Vancouver Grizzlies relocated. Then again, Doug Eberhardt would have been a terrific regular on just about any sport. With his quick wit and timely pop culture references, the personable Eberhardt brought something interesting to our show each time. He also took his role seriously, regularly driving (at his own expense) to Seattle and Portland to see games. He would also travel to other playoff venues, the All-Star Game and the Sydney Olympics. He formed some tremendous relationships along the way with many NBA players and coaches, most notably Mike D'Antoni, setting up some of them as guests and getting others to record special *Sportstalk* intros. Those relationships also led to NBA guest-coaching opportunities for Doug, most often in the Las Vegas summer league.

Eberhardt was often my saviour. Due to my WHL-related travel, it was always comforting to have him in the bank and willing to come on live or pre-recorded at the drop of a dime. For example, if I had a Friday WHL game on the prairies, I might record Doug the day before with mostly generic "week that was" topics. However, to keep things fresh, and frankly to fool our listeners, I would record a handful of questions about games to be played the next day. An hour or so before the segment aired, Doug would call my producer and record updated answers. People might have guessed Eberhardt was on tape, but then again how was he able to talk about a Golden State game that had ended an hour earlier?

Easily my least favourite *Sportstalk* regular was Grizzlies' general manager Stu Jackson. We extended an olive branch for him to join us months before their first season, believing he might wish to introduce himself (and the NBA) to the market. Less than warm and gracious, at least to me, the first thing Jackson asked was, "How much am I going to get paid to come on?"

"Not a penny," I told him, to which he took great exception.

"Even in the NCAA the coaches and managers get paid for coming on the radio," he lectured me.

When I told him this wasn't an NCAA market and that we didn't have a budget for this, he asked if the radio station could pay for the installation of a swimming pool at his house. I told Stu if he didn't want to join us, he didn't have to. I suspect owner Arthur Griffiths stepped in and told him he had to; at least, that's what Jackson's demeanour seemed to indicate when he eventually joined us each week.

Not that I knew much, but I still laugh at the memory of Jackson condescendingly mocking me when I suggested during one of our shows that Vancouver ought to consider taking a flyer on drafting Steve Nash.

The most newsworthy Grizzlies interview I ever had was in Washington, DC on the night of the 1999 draft when Vancouver selected Steve Francis second overall. I was first to interview him and was taken aback when he trashed our city and the idea of playing in a city/province/country with a high tax rate.

"I heard it rains a lot and they take your money," Francis told me after I asked him how it felt to have been drafted by Vancouver.

"Have you heard anything good?" I then asked.

"Not really," was his answer.

Francis never did wear a Grizzlies uniform, and after Jackson (who should've taken my free Nash advice) was eventually fired by Vancouver (300 losses in 378 games) no other NBA team came calling.

The polar opposite of Francis and Jackson was Vancouver's Mr. Soccer.

I felt lucky to have known Bob Lenarduzzi through five different decades, starting with his glory years as a player with the Vancouver Whitecaps in the late 1970s. Our paths crossed numerous times when he was a national team player and Canada's head coach, and also during the 86ers years and the birth of the MLS Whitecaps. Thoughtful, honest and respectful can be clichés, but those were Lenarduzzi's true traits, which came from his tremendous upbringing in East Vancouver.

Our last permanent regular was Kirk McLean when I was on CISL. I knew from covering him as a player that, though quiet, he was always thoughtful. I was pleased he was enthusiastic about doing our show, even driving into Richmond every week to join us in studio. Though constantly asked about "The Save" from April of 1994 off Robert Reichel in Game 7 overtime against Calgary, McLean one night brilliantly walked us through the entire sequence. As he was talking, I was taken as to how proud he was to own the distinction of making — as Tom Larscheid labelled it in real time — "The greatest save in the history of the franchise."

The *Sportstalk* diary is filled with so many big hockey names. Bobby Orr, Gordie Howe and Wayne Gretzky made a combined ten appearances. Listing all the others would take pages, but they included Jean Béliveau, Marcel Dionne, Ken Dryden, Paul Henderson, Phil Esposito, Bernie "Boom Boom" Geoffrion, Mark Messier, Steve Yzerman, Mike Bossy, Joe Sakic, Guy Lafleur, Jarome Iginla, all three Hulls (Bobby, Dennis and Brett) and virtually every well-known name who ever wore Canucks colours.

Coaches like Scotty Bowman, Ken Hitchcock, Mike Keenan, Pat Quinn, Pat Burns, Glen Sather, Mike Babcock, Roger Neilson, Marc Crawford, Bob Johnson and (pick your) Sutter are also in our diary.

From humble beginnings, the show kept growing and growing.

At training camp in Victoria in 1992 with two of the most popular
Vancouver players of all time, Pavel Bure and sidekick Gino Odjick.

Don Cherry in our studio with producer Scott Woodgate in 1991.

A Grapes wannabe? Coaching a 1992 charity game. My team included the Bure brothers, Pavel and Valeri, the Courtnalls, Geoff and Russ, and Cliff Ronning. Yes, we won. *(Bob Kruyt Photography)*

Presenting Dana Murzyn with the Babe Pratt Trophy as the Canucks top defenceman in 1993.

Peak of *Sportstalk* and (so far) Canucks history. We were at every game during the '94 playoffs. Perhaps it was wrong for Woodgate and I to have touched the Stanley Cup just before the series started?

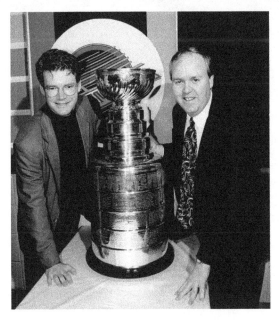

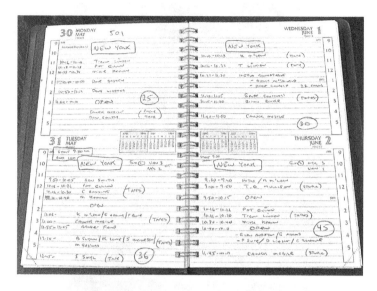

We diarized all of our nearly 8,000 shows, including
these four nights at the start of the '94 Final.

Sportstalk was *the* gathering spot for fans on game nights and off nights. Entertaining
us along the way were the Canuck Mobile boys -- Derek Mah (right, who is now
a BC Provincial Court Judge), Ben Ellison (centre, now a lawyer in Seattle), and
Will Verner (left, now VP Gorman Bros. Lumber Ltd.). *(Colin Price / The Province)*

We often took *Sportstalk* to the Langara Fishing Lodge during the '90s. On this memorable day, I joined the Tyee Club (catching a plus-30-lb salmon), hours before interviewing Harry Sinden, Glen Sather, Pat Quinn and Brian Burke.

We did our show from Vancouver's bench on the night before the Canucks' final regular-season game at the Pacific Coliseum in 1995. Our guests included original season ticket-holder Andrew Castell (right).

In Vancouver's dressing room on May 27, 1995, with Brook Ward (right) and Scott Woodgate following the final NHL game ever played at the PNE. *(Brook Ward)*

With Stan Smyl in 1991 from the Andy Moog and Friends golf tournament in Penticton.

There were loads of laughs each year. John McKeachie (right, holding mannequin from the pro shop) called the Moog tournament the "fifth major."

I called radio play-by-play for all of Seattle's WHL games for three seasons. Our first broadcast in 1995 was from the old Mercer Street Arena with Bill Wilms (left) providing analysis.

Our free and fun CFMI days ended in 1997 when CKNW asked us to broadcast on the official Canucks station.

Mark Messier in Tokyo on the eve of the 1997-98 season, two hours after taking the captain's C from Trevor Linden.

In Tokyo, following two games in 1997 vs. Anaheim. (From L-R) Our Japanese host, George Melville, Pat and Sandra Quinn, yours truly, Arthur Griffiths, Jim Treliving, Scott Woodgate and Dr. Doug Clement.

With Canucks coach Mike Keenan at the PNE in 1998. Months later a certain GM arrived in town and told me he didn't want Keenan on our show.

With Tom Larscheid in 2004 after realizing my dream of doing NHL play-by-play, albeit as a fill-in.

The day before the opening ceremonies in 2010. My Olympic torch run took place on West Boulevard in Kerrisdale, right past where my parents grew up and met. *(VANOC & City of Vancouver Archives)*

NBA great Steve Nash was in my torch group. Afterwards he posed with four-year old son Ben, who clearly didn't know what to make of this two-time MVP, and nine-year old daughter Anna.

I'm proud of my body of work calling WHL games alongside Bill Wilms for Shaw TV from 2004 through 2014.

My favourite building was Portland's Rose Garden. I called many games from there, including the largest WHL (indoor) crowd of over 19,000 fans. In 2014, I somehow ended up on the Jumbotron.

Bernie Pascall presenting me with an award at the BC Hockey Hall of Fame in Penticton in 2014.

Paula and I married twice. Our cultural Thailand wedding in 2000 took place a few months before our Richmond, BC wedding in 2001.

Christmas 2008 with Ben (left), Paula, spaced out St. Nick, Anna and Palita

Gordie Howe with Palita and Anna before a Vancouver Giants game in 2006.

Ben, seven, with Trevor Linden in 2014 at Penticton.

It took thirty years after reaming me out for Phil Esposito to be a guest in 2012. He got a kick out of hearing about my painful maiden interview and I was thrilled to check the Espo box off the *Sportstalk* bucket list. *(Heath Morgan)*

My parents Pat and Ken celebrating their golden anniversary at the Pan Pacific in 2005. They sadly passed away only six days apart in 2013.

After three decades the last call for *Sportstalk* was at CISL radio in 2014. *(CISL)*

All photos from author's collection, unless noted.

Others whose names leap off our diary pages include Pele, George Foreman, Don King, Tommy Lasorda, Vin Scully, Duke Snider, Joe Theismann, John Ziegler, Al Eagleson, Normie Kwong and Bruce McNall.

In November of 1984, less than a month after we debuted on CJOR, I reached out to long-time St. Louis play-by-play broadcaster Dan Kelly, who was in town the night before the Blues faced the Canucks. Kelly was synonymous with calling Bobby Orr's most famous goal, and I hoped he'd say yes. In those days, unless the guest had plans they would usually agree to come on, often accepting our invitation to come in studio. But on this day Kelly was less than enthused.

After a long pause, Kelly asked, "Is there a fee for coming on?"

Gulp! I wasn't expecting that, especially from someone of his ilk. I had to tell him there wasn't, to which he said, "Well, I don't think I can do it." Saddened by the rejection, I called Kelly back a few minutes later and said the radio station had these stylus pens I could give him. For some reason that did the trick. He said if I delivered the pen to him, he'd come on the show.

An hour later I was at the front desk of the Hotel Vancouver dropping off a box of fancy pens. And a few hours after that, Kelly came on *Sportstalk* with his great big famous pipes sounding every bit like the pro he was.

Perhaps Kelly felt a professional broadcaster should not work for free. Regardless, my opinion of him was never quite the same.

During the winter of 1986, Toronto Blue Jays pitcher Dave Stieb came through Vancouver to push his book *Tomorrow I'll Be Perfect*. After he arrived in our limo, Stieb did a great hour. Near the end I mentioned I'd be in Florida for spring training, and he said, "Let's talk again when you get there." The day I got to Dunedin, I waited patiently after their morning workouts, then approached Stieb and reintroduced myself. Before I could even make my request, he blew me off saying, "Not today, bud." As he was walking away, I asked within earshot of two of his teammates why he was willing to come into my studio and push his book when all I wanted now was five minutes. He turned and glared at me for a couple of seconds but kept walking away. Ten minutes later, having no doubt recalled how well he'd been treated while in my domain, Stieb returned and said, "Let's do it now."

Former Boston Bruins playboy Derek Sanderson was in studio for nearly two hours in October of 1987, an interview I label as one of the greatest in *Sportstalk* history. Sanderson spoke about his life as an alcoholic and a drug addict. He was sober by then and dedicating his life to helping people.

Russell: "You had to hawk your Stanley Cup ring?"

Sanderson: "Well, I tried to sell it. I tried to sell it to a guy for an ounce of coke and $1,000."

Russell: "He didn't buy it?"

Sanderson: "The guy only had $800. He said, 'Alright, wait here, I'll be right back.' Well, I looked in my hand. I had the ounce of coke and $800 and I walked away."

Russell: "You have said before it was crazy the money they gave you to jump to the WHA."

Sanderson: "I was only making $50,000 with the Bruins and then some clown comes along and gives you $2,650,000 to play hockey."

Russell: "So it was $2.65 million to go to the WHA?"

Sanderson: "They offered me 2.3 and I said, 'Ahh, well, I don't know.' I was drunk at the time. I was goofing on him. I said, 'I don't know. I own a couple of nightclubs here [Boston]. The fans are good to me. The police are good to me. I have a girlfriend.'

'Well, actually I'm authorized to go as high as $2.65 million,' the man said. He gave me a $350,000 raise in fifteen seconds."

Russell: (laughs).

Sanderson: "So knowing I had him, I said, 'Well, I got to be captain.' And he said, 'Okay.' Then I said, I got to play on the power play, 'cause I never played the PP in Boston.' He said, 'Well, for the money you're getting you'll never be off the ice.' I said, 'Okay' ... then I said, 'Listen, the Bruins traded some friends of mine. I don't want any of my teammates traded without my permission.' He said, 'Okay,' and he's writing this out in paragraphs and initialing each one. Then I said, 'When I first talked to you guys you were the Miami Screaming Eagles.' I said, 'You can't move the franchise without my permission.' He said, 'Okay.' I said, 'You can't sell it either because you guys are pretty stinky.' He said, 'Okay.'

"I basically owned the team. I couldn't believe this. I had no respect for management who did it."

Russell: "You only played — I wonder how many people know this — eight games."

Sanderson: "Some stats are wrong. I only played seven games. I slipped a disc in my back and that was it."

Russell: "Of that $2.65 million, how much did you actually see?"

Sanderson: "A million four, cash. Upfront cash. So I had a ton of money and I made some proper investments. I still hadn't gone goofy at that point. I was still aware of what was going on. I made some good investments and I worked it up to about six million. And then the drinking started. I was in Philadelphia. I didn't know anybody. So I started drinking a lot more, on a constant round-the-clock basis. It was one party after another. And I bought the world a drink. That was it."

Russell: "How long did it take, from the time you had six million and the time you went goofy, to use your term … how long did it take for the money to go?"

Sanderson: "That was 1973. It was all over in '77."

Russell: "So in four years you spent six million."

Sanderson: "Yeah."

Russell: "That's hard to do."

Sanderson: "Not if you stay awake. Cocaine will keep you awake."

Within a week of his appearance I heard from a handful of Vancouver area high school teachers requesting a tape of that segment so that they could play it for their students.

Sometimes we'd present what we called concept shows, and one of my favourites from our early days was called "Bedtime Stories" with Canadian sports legends "Babe" Pratt, Jim Coleman and Annis Stukus. On those nights, I recall so many stories starting but few actually ending before one of them interrupted to begin a new one.

On the twentieth anniversary of the famed 1972 Summit Series, we paired Coleman, a nationally syndicated columnist for decades, with CKNW newsman John McKitrick. Both had been in Russia, Coleman as a journalist, McKitrick as a fan. The two had never met until this night, but their accounts from two decades earlier and the way they played off each other was riveting.

"I was probably the oldest of the media people there, with the possible exception of Foster Hewitt," Coleman said. "And at the end of the game I found myself, a nice dignified old gentleman of sixty-one wearing my sincere three-piece blue suit, standing up on my seat pointing up at Comrade Brezhnev, the head of the Soviet Union. I was giving him exactly the same [finger] salute that Alan Eagleson had given to the crowd about fifteen minutes earlier."

One night Brian Burke was doing his segment while driving home from a game. Suddenly, he stopped whatever answer he was giving and said, "Sorry Dano, I have to break up a fight on the side of the road." Talk about theatre of the mind! I filled time, not knowing how long it'd be until he called back or even if he would. A few minutes later he reappeared, semi-puffing, telling me he got right in the middle of a fist fight. He even told us about the blood on his white shirt (which, incidentally, is the only colour dress shirt I ever saw Brian wear).

Though it was nice to interview big names, I never enjoyed the stress of wondering if they'd show up. Wayne Gretzky, for example, was lined up to come on in mid-March 1988, a couple of weeks before the playoffs. Naturally, I was excited and made the innocent mistake of heavily promoting that he'd be on. CJOR — and I cringe when I remember this — also cut a promo that aired several times that day, saying "The greatest player in the NHL" would be on *Sportstalk* that night. As you have already guessed, when it came time to bring him on, he wasn't there.

Understandably, people like Gretzky weren't overly willing to give us a phone number (McKeachie probably had it!), so we gave him our number and he said he would call at 10:10 p.m. Gretzky simply forgot. He never did call, which taught me many lessons. He should have been promoted as our "scheduled" guest, and we absolutely needed to have the phone number of a team official who could've called Wayne to remind him. This won't surprise anyone who knows Gretzky, but he told me he felt awful about forgetting and made it up to us by appearing two nights before the start of the '88 playoffs, a year the Oilers would win their third Stanley Cup.

Years later I was asked to emcee an event involving Gretzky during the NHL All-Star Game. This half-hour sponsored affair took place on a big stage in the Forum building, next to the Pacific Coliseum, where I conducted an in-house interview (not on air) with questions from the audience. Once over, I went backstage where many of the sponsors had gathered around Gretzky. With my work done, I decided to slip out the other door. Gretzky's vision, the best on the ice, was also excellent backstage because before I could leave he made a beeline across the room to profusely thank me for what he said was "a very professional job." He claimed he was apprehensive before it started, but he said I had made it "so much easier on [him]." It's not every day you get a great compliment from the Great One.

CHAPTER TWENTY-SEVEN

A bombshell and a bull market

March 14, 2006, was a stereotypically drizzly Lower Mainland day, but that didn't prevent me from carrying out my afternoon walking ritual along the top of the dyke in Richmond. I find the walks fresh and therapeutic, and I enjoy the solitude.

But not this time.

Halfway through my walk, I got a call from Jim (JJ) Johnston, my former CFMI program director, who had returned to Vancouver a few years earlier to become the big boss, CKNW's general manager.

"I need to talk to you right away" is how he started. "It's really urgent."

I hurried home without a clue about why he was calling. Scurrying inside, I took off my wet coat and darted upstairs to my home studio. When I called him back, he put me on speakerphone and broke the bombshell news. After thirty-seven years as the official (and only) carrier of Vancouver Canucks NHL games, CKNW had lost the broadcast rights.

I was shocked.

Truthfully, I never thought I would see the day that would happen, although perhaps I shouldn't have been so blind. Yes, the Canucks and CKNW had been synonymous with each other since 1970, and for twenty-five of those years the hockey club and radio station fell under the ownership of the Griffiths family. But the Canucks ownership had changed in recent years, and the radio station now was owned by Corus Entertainment, which had made things much more corporate (i.e., the big decisions were made from Toronto).

Then again, surely CKNW, as the long-time rights holder, must've been smart enough to include a Right to Match in the event a competing offer came down the pike. Right? I was told they did. I also was told that those running Corus elected not to match. Were they too far away to understand just how vital the Canucks were to the station? Or did they believe the value of having the radio rights had already begun what would be a permanent downward trend and therefore were no longer worth pursuing for a steep price? While both answers might have been correct, it's a good bet head office lucked into the second scenario.

Program director Tom Plasteras was conspicuous by his absence; he was with his kids at Disneyland as the station was suffering one of its biggest blows. I've often wondered if the persuasive Plasteras's presence might have made a difference.

One of the Canucks' lawyers who was in the boardroom with Team Radio later told me that when the final touches were being put on the deal he slipped away to the men's room and covertly made one last call to Corus to see if they would match. He was told "No."

That set off a massive celebration at Team Radio, whose brain trust was thrilled and surprised that it had pulled off this feat.

Meantime, it felt like a funeral at CKNW.

As a double whammy, this occurred during a time when Team Radio and Corus-owned AM730 (known as Mojo Radio) were staging a battle for the twenty-four-hour sports marketplace. Predictably, Mojo quickly folded and was turned into an all-traffic station.

After I finished with JJ on his speakerphone, I took a quick shower then hurried downtown for the Canucks pregame show that would begin at 4:30 p.m. In the span of about an hour, we had become a "lame duck" station. Yet we still had sixteen regular-season games remaining plus (perhaps) playoffs before we had to pass the Canucks torch to our competitors.

My mind raced trying to figure out what I was going to tell the hockey listeners that afternoon and then for the next six or so weeks. Knowing CKNW's hockey legacy better than anyone, I quickly determined I would be the best one to close this incredible radio chapter, and I would do so as professionally as possible. As word spread around the city, I knew all ears were going to be on the upcoming "Face-off Show," which meant I had to try and prepare the proper words for our listeners.

I quickly came up with: "This is Dan Russell coming your way from the *Sportstalk* headquarters in downtown Vancouver. Thanks for being with us for NHL hockey on CKNW — the home of the Vancouver Canucks from Day 1. Speaking of which — we have news on that front to tell you this afternoon. And it is not happy news for those of us connected with this heritage radio station. As of this afternoon, we can tell you that the Canucks' radio home is about to change. After broadcasting every game in the history of the club, CKNW will no longer be the rights holder for Vancouver Canucks hockey. You heard right ... CHUM Radio has secured the rights, meaning the games will no longer be on CKNW following the end of this season.

"Our history started on October 9, 1970, when Danny Gallivan called the Canucks first regular-season game. Two days later, the great Jim Robson called their first win. Robson, the Hall of Fame broadcaster, gave way upon retirement to Jim Hughson, who then gave way to John Shorthouse. And for about a quarter-century Tom Larscheid has been providing the colour and analysis.

"This will mark the end of an era in Vancouver radio.

"We're now joined by John Shorthouse alongside Tom Larscheid, from the Gaylord Entertainment Centre in Nashville ..."

I could hear sadness in Larscheid's voice, partly because he wasn't convinced he'd be asked to continue once the switch was made. On the other hand, Shorthouse had already been told by his Orca Bay sugar daddies that he would likely be okay.

We did the remaining sixteen games (the Canucks missed the playoffs), and Bob Addison and I produced a special "extro" featuring many CKNW hockey clips pasted together over Neil Diamond's version of "The Long and Winding Road" for the final broadcast.

Naturally, most people at CKNW were sad. But I wasn't. My stock had risen, and I was the last one standing. *Sportstalk* would be more valuable to CKNW than ever, and I believed management would be forced to embrace it. Also, of all the people I worked for during my career, JJ Johnston was my biggest supporter. He was a fan of the show (even calling during open-phones on occasion) and an ally I could count on.

It only took two days to confirm that.

"Can we meet for dinner before your show tonight?" JJ asked.

In the early evening of March 16, two days after losing the rights, I met Johnston at The Keg on Dunsmuir, believing we were only there to talk about our "new normal" — life without the Canucks. Instead, JJ surprised me by telling me how important I was to CKNW and that he wanted to work on a long-term contract extension.

I was right. My stock had risen.

Plasteras got in on the praise a few days later, glowing about my credibility, which he said, "No one else in the market had." But the biggest compliment he paid me was: "Often when I watch a game I need to tune in your show to either validate what I saw or find out more about what I should have been seeing."

So with JJ initiating a multi-year extension and Plasteras lavishly talking about the show, this was going to be an easy-peasy negotiation, right?

Not exactly.

Truthfully, it would be hard to imagine a renegotiation — especially one initiated from their side — being any more painful in terms of time, language, terms, lawyers and money.

Things started smoothly when my lawyer, Roger Bourbonnais, met with them in the late summer and JJ told him not to think about three years.

"Tell Dan we want to make this a five-year extension."

By November, we had agreed on compensation, which some might think would have been the most difficult issue. However,

Corus headquarters in Toronto insisted that my new deal include the same contract format as everyone else in the company. They required "standardized Corus language," which Roger said was unnecessary legalese and appeared as complete gobbledygook to me. A silly example involved time off: No longer were we to call them "vacation weeks." No sirree. These were now "hiatus weeks."

But clauses like the following, which were not at all part of the language we had used at CKNW for more than fifteen years, were not so silly:

> Name and Likeness — Corus and its assignees and licensees shall be entitled to use and reproduce the Principal's approved name, likeness, photograph and biographical information (the "Materials") in connection with the Services and in connection with all advertising, publicity and promotion of the Services; provided that the Materials shall not be used or reproduced in any manner which implies, represents or portrays the Principal, directly or indirectly, as recommending, using or endorsing any product or service other than the Services or the general business activities of Corus and its assignees and broadcast licensees unless the prior written consent of the Company has been obtained, and provided that Corus receives prior written approval from the Company with respect to all Materials before such Materials are published or made available in any manner to the public.

There were many others, each of similar length and the same legal gibberish, under categories such as, "Results and Proceeds," "Indemnity," "Representation and Warranty," "Continuity/Benefit of Agreement" ... blah, blah, blah.

A week before Christmas, Roger got a voicemail from Tom claiming he "wasn't getting anywhere with my people in terms of changing the [contract] format." He then asked Roger to provide him with a memo as to how we could go forward. Bourbonnais, adamantly opposed to this new language and concerned about my rising legal bill that had already reached nearly three thousand dollars, told Tom, "Sorry, but we're putting the tools down."

I was told that call took less than a minute. Merry Christmas?

In January 2007, still wanting Corus language to be adopted, Tom told Roger that CKNW would pay my legal bill. But that was essentially the only development for that entire year. There didn't seem to be any urgency from either side, as I still had time left on my old deal.

Sensing that I wasn't panicking about my future, Johnston again took me to dinner, this time to Joe Fortes on Thurlow (at least I was eating well) in early January 2008. When we got to the topic of my contract, I mentioned that Plasteras had offered to pick up our legal fees. Johnston said that came from his boss, John Hayes at head office, who wanted us to "Find a way to look at their language." Johnston then tried to pick up on something Plasteras had tried with me a few months earlier, asking about "the role of Roger Bourbonnais in all of this." Johnston wanted to know how much of this decision was coming from Bourbonnais and how much from me.

"Roger represents me and has for twenty years," I responded. "He's never given me bad advice and is largely responsible for where I am today. If Roger recommends not to accept, then I can guarantee you I won't sign."

Johnston said he accepted that but added, "Just as long as Roger tries to keep an open mind about it."

I then reminded Johnston of my history and how I was sent away by CKNW seven years earlier despite consistently huge ratings only to be asked for my "wish list" a year later in order to come back. Then I asked JJ how long he expected to be at CKNW. He told me two to five years. I told him if I knew he'd be there for the rest of his career, this would be much easier.

"I want you to be at CKNW for the rest of your broadcast life," he said.

I believed him.

As he picked up the dinner tab he told me he wanted to move on this now, to get a deal finalized in the next month. He suggested that if the lawyers got bogged down, he and I should talk "with no hard feelings" to resolve any log jams.

The contract wasn't done in the next month, but by April it was close, which is when Corus was surprised to learn the size of my legal bill. A person name Ariane Stren emailed lawyer Michael Watt, who was working with Bourbonnais, to inform him that they "...find it strange that the fees will reach $20K." This was one of those "with no hard feelings" conversations I would need to have with JJ.

"Holy Christ. I've dealt with a lot of lawyers over the years, but no one's charged that kind of dough," Johnston said from the Toronto airport. "Tom said he was willing to pay those guys $8K. I'm not sure what they are doing, but they are putting it to us."

Appeasing him a little, I said perhaps my lawyers could've done a better job communicating the actual number. I then told him I believed the deal was nearly done, and I promised to "cap the legal fees at $16K."

Finally, on May 12, 2008 — twenty-six months after Johnston's suggestion — I signed a five-year extension. It was a deal that gave me the assurance that no matter what happened afterwards, I'd be financially fine. Not filthy rich, but certainly able to put my kids through school and live a comfortable life.

CHAPTER TWENTY-EIGHT

My friend "Mr. Canada"

CKNW's brain trust — namely general manager JJ Johnston and program director Tom Plasteras — were tripping on their lower lips in the months following the loss of the Vancouver Canucks' broadcast rights. While I certainly understood why they were in shock — we all were — there were times they also seemed to be in denial. Case in point: Johnston thought it'd be a good idea for us to program a pregame show prior to all Canucks games, home and away.

Johnston was wrong; it was a bad idea.

Mind you, I was a little biased because this fell to me. It was written in my contract that I was the "host of Canucks hockey," which technically was true because neither my agent Roger Bourbonnais nor I had the presence of mind to make sure the language stipulated that CKNW actually had to be broadcasting Canucks games. What this meant, for example, was if the Canucks were playing a 4 p.m. PT game at Tampa, I had to host an hour-long pregame show beginning at three o'clock. Johnston had told me the goal was to confuse listeners into thinking they were still listening to games on CKNW. He reasoned that even if they were listening to the actual broadcast on Team Radio, a listener who had a BBM ballot might mistakenly, out of habit, write in CKNW instead of Team Radio. (FYI, BBM's written diaries soon after were replaced by "Personal People Meters.")

CKNW allocated a token budget of one hundred dollars per show that I could split between *Vancouver Sun* hockey writer Elliott

Pap and former player Gary Valk. Sometimes I might open the phone lines, but calls were sparse, presumably because the actual Canucks station was fully into its pregame show with many more hands on deck.

An 'NW salesperson also thought it would be a good idea for us to do eight of our pregame shows from the popular but extremely noisy Shark Club — another idea I opposed because I failed to see the purpose of broadcasting from a venue where no one was paying attention. Come to think of it, that summed up the entire concept. Also, how was I supposed to sign off this show?

"Enjoy the game you won't be hearing here."

Or:

"This is your cue to switch over to Team Radio."

I settled with, "We'll review tonight's game this evening on *Sportstalk*. Now stay tuned for more of the *World Today* with Jon McComb."

As much as I rolled my eyes, the pregame show caused havoc for the *World Today*. For example, if the Canucks game began at 5 p.m., McComb would start his show at three, turn it over to me at four, and I would give it back to him at five. The ultimate momentum buster. At some point, station management came to realize it was a bad idea and scrapped it after one season.

What was good for me — liberating, in fact — was to once again be able to freely express opinion without wondering if the Canucks would be calling Plasteras the next day. Regular listeners knew — it's why I was fired in 2000 — I wasn't shy about speaking my mind, but there was always that feeling when I was delivering a sharp-edged editorial that the shit might fly the next day. As a result, there were times when I put on the brakes simply because I didn't have the appetite to put out another fire.

Though Plasteras was good at not telling me about those conversations when we did have the rights, I knew they happened. Credit to him — in fact, I believe diplomacy was his biggest strength. He had a terrific knack of appeasing the hockey team, usually without involving me.

But that was then and this was now. A new era. The "non-rightsholder" era.

That said, *Sportstalk*'s staying power was built on credibility and trust, something I would never consider risking. I even recall giving myself a pep talk when the landscape changed. I reminded myself to never waver from fair commentary and to make sure equal heaps of praise were given when warranted. I knew I would be playing more of a devil's advocate, but I wouldn't go out of my way to be outspoken. As it turned out during this era, the Canucks' puck often found its way into the *Sportstalk* slot; I never had to go out of my way to provide thought-provoking opinion and riveting discussion.

This was not the first time we'd had to reinvent. Even though *Sportstalk* was one continuous program, there were many different phases. In the early days of the mid-'80s, our priorities were to find a niche, earn trust and gain credibility. As a result, my commentary was mostly played down the middle. It may not have been intentional, but I was playing the long game. Had I been overly outspoken — too much, too soon — I don't believe the show would have stood the test of time.

It was only after we had established ourselves as the gathering spot for Canucks fans that I slowly began to provide editorials with a little more bite. Fast forward to this era with the rights elsewhere, and I knew the duty unofficially bestowed upon *Sportstalk* was, in part, to provide counterpoint whenever the Canucks engaged in spin.

One thing that became clear in "non-rightsholder" mode was that I was going to need help. The masses, those who used to call after games to vent or opine, were now using new-found smartphone technology and advancing social media platforms to pass comment. Translation? I couldn't always count on a strong phone response, which I had tried not to take for granted during our first twenty-odd years. Furthermore, not only was the quantity of callers down but so too the quality. By and large, callers during our first two decades significantly contributed more than those in our last years.

When we lost the rights there was neither station guidance nor meetings to discuss strategy or new ideas. Nor was there any added budget to help us combat the loss. It's easy for me to say, but I would have thought the station that no longer had to shell out big money for the rights might have invested a few of those dollars to preserve their late evening ratings, especially on all-important game nights. Instead, as always, I was left to my own devices — without even help from what was left of the CKNW sports department — to try and keep the *Sportstalk* bar as high as possible.

Thank goodness for Stu Walters, a former producer on the Mojo all-sports station who now was providing regular updates on the bridges and tunnels for the all-traffic station. Yearning to still cover sports, Walters would head to Canucks games after his traffic shift, which is when, desperate for any kind of presence from the rink, we asked him to join us. But there was one problem. Walters was highly inexperienced. He knew the game well enough, but he was green on the air. Yet I needed him. I needed someone. We didn't have a budget, and I thought (hoped) I could work with him.

Initially, Walters had to call from the street because terms of Team Radio's rights agreement barred competing radio from transmitting inside the rink. (Pap, on our pregame show, was also shut down and no longer able to join us at 6:10 on home game nights from GM Place. This added to my grumpiness.)

Walters was as eager as he was raw, and I liked that. But I also knew we needed a greater post-game presence. As hard as producer Bob Addison and I tried, we didn't know where to turn, but after several weeks we ran into some good luck. Brook Ward, who was competing against us, was fired by Team Radio just before Christmas even though his show was doing so well they had to pay him a ratings bonus five days later.

"I was number two in the Vancouver market in my time slot behind some guy at CKNW," he said later.

Their loss was our gain, as we suddenly had our game-night solution.

Ward and I first met at CISL in 1981 and became instant friends. This friendship further escalated a few months later when we took a road trip to Los Angeles. Barely into our twenties, we still vividly recall the most minute details about what might not have been a rite of passage, but was nonetheless liberating. In the late evening of February 1, 1982, we loaded up my light brown 1975 Chevrolet Nova, picked up another CISL friend, Dan Nordstrand, and began driving south. Our plan was to take up to three days to get there, but I didn't stop until we reached Burbank twenty hours later. Once within range we were enraptured listening to the exceedingly crowded Los Angeles radio market where just the slightest turn on the dial would land us on another great station. We knew we were listening to some of the greatest broadcasters in the world, and we drank it all in.

Our plan was to see a pair of LA Kings games the following weekend, but because we got there so quickly we were in time for a game the next night. It would be our first in an away NHL venue, and Brook and I absolutely loved it. In those days just going to the NHL's only warm-weather locale was novel, as were many other aspects. In fact, the sheer act of finding Inglewood — how did people get around pre-GPS? — was a proud accomplishment. It was our very own "Miracle on Manchester," even if it was two months before the Kings' actual version.

When we arrived at the parking gate, the lot attendant, wearing a bright orange visor, asked if we would like "preferred parking."

Huh?

Because that option was never available at the PNE we laughed and said sure, prompting him to instantly yell "Preferrrrred!" to another lot attendant (something Brook and I often say when starting a phone conversation to this day).

Once inside we couldn't get over seeing hockey fans wearing shorts and tank tops. And, at a time where you could drink beer only in the non-viewing basement of the Pacific Coliseum, we watched people order beer, spirits and daiquiris to take to their seats.

Just before game time, Brook spotted former *Playboy* Playmate of the Year Terri Welles, who was married to Kings winger Charlie Simmer, part of the famed "Triple Crown" line along with Marcel Dionne and Dave Taylor. Brook struck up the courage to ask Welles for directions to the dressing rooms and later snapped a picture of her.

His trip had already been made.

We took a seat to the right of the press box, which was located in the first five rows of the second level and consisted of makeshift tables and dim desk lamps that enabled each media member to see their notes. I sat speechless with endless memories swirling through my head. I might have stared at the Kings radio broadcasters more than the actual game. The goosebumps were endless, knowing that was where "Jiggs" McDonald, the man I had so often heard through the static via the KFI late night radio skip colourfully called games that featured the likes of Ralph Backstrom, Butch Goring and Ross Lonsberry. "Jiggs" had made the Fabulous Forum seem bigger than life. From only a few feet away I was totally fixated on frequent future *Sportstalk* guest Bob Miller, as he called the action.

Now my trip had also been made.

That night, along with only about 7,700 others, we watched Dionne's Kings lose to Dave Keon's Hartford Whalers. (Don Nachbaur, whom I would interview nearly 250 times as coach before each Seattle Thunderbirds broadcast, had two assists for the Whalers in that game.)

A few days later, it was our main event: the first time seeing a Canucks road game. I still recall how strangely quiet it was when Vancouver scored and also how amusing it was to hear LA fans mockingly chant "Harroooold, Harroooold" every time Harold Snepsts touched the puck. The Canucks lost 5-4 when Taylor scored late, a goal that created lots of noise.

The next night we saw the Montreal Canadiens in their famous red uniforms score five times in the third period for a one-sided victory.

In between, we went to Disneyland, Universal Studios, Knott's Berry Farm, Dodger Stadium and Anaheim Stadium. We even attended two tapings of *The Tonight Show with Johnny Carson*. One guest was an unknown comic named Eddie Murphy, and another was Wayne Rogers of *M*A*S*H*. By Brook's request and using his fake ID, we also visited the Playboy Club before heading north towards San Francisco.

Years earlier, when I was in junior high, I had written a letter to KGO talk-show host Ronn Owens telling him of my radio dreams. He not only wrote me back with great advice, but the large logoed envelope was filled with KGO promotional stickers and literature. Before I left Vancouver on this trip I wrote Owens another letter telling him I would be in the Bay Area and asking if it would be possible to watch his show. He kindly said yes.

Upon arrival, a security guard escorted us to the green room where we sat with a grown-up Jerry Mathers of *Leave It to Beaver* fame. Brook and I spoke with the friendly thirty-three-year-old Beav — including about TV brother Wally and Eddie Haskell — for about fifteen minutes before he went on the air with Owens.

When the show was over, Owens talked with us about radio for quite some time before asking if we had a ride back to our hotel. When we told him we planned to walk to the Bay Area Rapid Transit (BART) stop and ride, he said we couldn't because the neighbourhood was too dangerous. Indeed, only a few years earlier, one of Ronn's colleagues, Jim Dunbar, was shot at three times by a deranged gunman while on the air. Bulletproof glass saved Dunbar from injury or worse, but a KGO ad executive was killed. Afterwards, KGO hosts had to park their cars at an undisclosed lot several blocks away and were escorted to and from the station. So, Owens wasn't letting Brook (who was wearing a shiny LA Dodgers jacket in a city that strongly dislikes that team) and I walk to the BART. He arranged for a taxi to take us back to our hotel.

Later, while cutting back towards the I-5 to Sacramento, the Chevy Nova was clocked going a little too fast near the town of Fairfield. The officer, who was in his highway patrol vehicle hiding behind bushes, told me the fine was $120. Brook and I told the officer the Nova was having spark plug misfiring issues — yes, it was a lie — and that we were testing the acceleration of the vehicle when he clocked me. He said it would still be $120. Not only that, he wanted us to follow him to pay the fine because he didn't think we'd be good for it after we got back to Canada.

I complained, saying, "I really don't think I was going as fast as you said."

"Then fight it in court," he countered.

When I reminded him we were on our way home and couldn't wait a few days for a court appearance, he said, "We can do it right now ... follow me."

With that, the Nova followed the highway patrol. I simulated the spark plugs misfiring by lagging well behind and occasionally hitting the brakes to make it seem like we were having car problems all the way to the local courthouse. Before we went into the courtroom, I asked the officer more than once, "What's the maximum a judge could fine me?" When he wouldn't tell me, I asked, "Isn't this a free country?" That's when he finally told me $120 would be the maximum. So with nothing more to lose I said, "Let's go."

Less than twenty minutes after being pulled over, the three of us were in a courtroom. I was seated at the defendant's table, the officer at the prosecutor's table, with Ward and Nordstrand sitting two rows behind in the otherwise empty courtroom. The judge entered, looking as if he might have been fishing an hour earlier. After the officer began the hearing with his evidence I tried to explain how the old Nova was sputtering, how one of my passangers was a mechanic, and why I was intentially speeding to assess the mechanical condition of my vehicle. It was about then, Ward told me, that Nordstrand, who wasn't a licensed anything, began mumbling about how they were going to put all of us in jail.

But it was a brilliant defence, no? Nope. Guilty as charged. The judge fined me the original amount. As we left the courthouse, I asked Ward and Nordstrand, "Did you think that was fun?" Nordstrand barely talked to us the rest of the trip.

In future years Brook and I went to Hawaii a few times, which is where he picked up the nickname "Mr. Canada" for reasons I'll let him disclose in his own book.

Brook and I only hit one rough patch and we were fortunate it didn't affect our friendship. When I was removed from CKNW (the note under the hotel room door in Thailand), the station asked

Ward to host until Don Taylor and his *Sports Grill* would arrive four months later. I was upset at the radio station, which knew we had a long-standing friendship, and also because Brook said yes to them as quickly as he did. However, he was in a tough spot and probably did the right thing, even if I didn't think so at the time.

I was also involved in a similar story with Jeff Paterson, but this one ended differently. I got to know Paterson, ten years my junior, when we were calling WHL games, me in Seattle and him in Kamloops. We became pretty close — if you define close as travelling together to Boston (for an NHL draft and to see an MLB game at Fenway), New York City (where I invited him to stay at my aunt's Upper West Side apartment across from Central Park) and Washington (for the NBA draft). He also asked me to critique tape of his work and to let him know of any Vancouver radio opportunities.

I was more than happy to do all that, but about a year later, during the time I was fighting CKNW for using *Sportstalk*'s name, format and music for their weekend spin-off program, Paterson was suddenly named host. The only problem was Jeff didn't feel any obligation to tell me; I found out from a third party. Though not obligated to keep me in the loop, I found it disrespectful. When I saw him several weeks later at Canucks camp, I asked him: "Is your dialling finger broken?" I was trying to break the ice while also letting him know I wasn't pleased.

"How about you?" he snarled back. "Is your fucking phone broken?"

Add him to the list. It was the last time we spoke.

On the other hand, Brook, personally and professionally, is a loyal friend for life. He always wanted what was best for our show, which is why I was so happy to have him on after all Canucks games. Ward knew it was healthier if he and I didn't always see eye to eye on Canucks issues. He knew how to perform his role, knew he had to offer something with a little different angle, knew when to push buttons and when to entertain. The only thing he didn't quite learn was that old adage, less is more.

But as he often told me, "That's why people love me, Russ."

That sarcasm also was part of his charm.

"Hey Harry, it's snowing out!" was a Brook clip we lifted and played frequently as a reminder of the night Harry Neale gave him shit after being on hold for over two minutes while Ward went on and on about a rare snowfall. When he finally brought him on, Ward uttered those five words, to which Neale, located in snow-ravaged Buffalo, grumbled: "Yeah, that's the third time you've said that so can we just get on with it?"

This might not sound like a compliment but I enjoyed the commercial breaks with Brook just as much as the show. Not two seconds after I would say, "We'll be back after these messages," Brook would launch into some radio gossip or political story that would not only take up the entire break but might continue through three or four more. He also might pull out a cold hamburger from his sports jacket pocket, one he hadn't eaten before the game, and chomp away.

Stu joined us on home nights and all playoff games. I like to think that the three of us, with very little budget, no advertising and nothing in the way of station support, provided an insightful, thorough, thought-provoking independent show on game nights.

I was proud of that.

I'm even prouder when Ward still tells me, "The most fun time of my life was working on *Sportstalk*."

CHAPTER TWENTY-NINE

Carrying the Olympic torch

The three biggest Vancouver sporting events that took place on my *Sportstalk* watch — in any order you choose — were the Canucks' two trips to the Stanley Cup Final and the 2010 Olympic Winter Games.

Because the selection process is so drawn out — nearly eight years between defeating Pyeongchang, South Korea, and the lighting of the flame — Olympic chatter on *Sportstalk* occurred only occasionally in those pre-event years.

Aside from the few days around being awarded the Games, most of the listener reaction took place on current affairs shows where critics and politicians would debate taxpayer dollars, the Sea to Sky Highway, SkyTrain, the impact on the Downtown Eastside, etc. It took the closing of the 2008 Beijing Games when we saw the International Olympic Committee (IOC) flag handed over to Vancouver before we felt it turning into a sports story. I wouldn't call the interest rabid, but people were beginning to get stoked, albeit slowly.

Even more so when the 2009-10 NHL season began and there was speculation nearly every day, along with plenty of debate on our phone board, about who would make the Canadian hockey team.

Then, just over one hundred days out, the cross-country torch relay, something that turned out to be far more popular than was anticipated, began. My friend Dave Doroghy (he of the 33 rpm rendition of "Freak Out" in the long-gone disco days at CJOR) was part of the Vancouver Organizing Committee (VANOC) team accompanying the torch, and he joined us each Friday to share torch tales from the road. While that got me excited, for some reason it took me counting down the *Sportstalk* clock on New Year's Eve and saying, "It's about to be an Olympic year in Vancouver" to get locked in.

Two days before the opening ceremony and a day before the torch was carried through the streets of Vancouver, I received a phone call I'll never forget from someone whose name I don't know. It came only five minutes before I was about to broadcast a WHL game in Medicine Hat, so I'm not sure why I answered the phone, but I'm glad I did.

"Would you be available to carry the Olympic torch tomorrow?"

In the noisy arena, I couldn't make out the person's name at the other end of the call. I wasn't even sure I had heard right.

"Did you just ask if I can carry the torch tomorrow?" I spoke loudly as the Tigers were stepping onto the ice and because I couldn't believe my ears.

When the caller said I had heard right, I humbly accepted. Suffice to say I had difficulty focussing on the play-by-play that night.

After flying home the next morning, I practised running the designated four-hundred-metre distance a few times on my front street, nerdily carrying a tennis racket as my torch. A couple of hours later, a group of us gathered at the Kitsilano Community Centre where we were told how everything would unfold. We were also given our keepsake Hudson's Bay-designed white track uniforms with the blue and green bursts and our soon-to-be-lit Bombardier-manufactured torches.

Soon I was on a Vancouver 2010 bus along with NBA star Steve Nash, Ed Robertson (the lead singer from Barenaked Ladies) and about twenty-five others. Our police escort helped us cruise south past Little Mountain, and we stopped to let off one torchbearer after the other to complete their runs. Our group was among the last of the twelve thousand torchbearers who carried the flame forty-five thousand kilometres by land, sea and air — the longest domestic torch-relay odyssey in Olympic history.

The noise was incredible each time the door opened. All of us had goosebumps, and with every stop my nerves burned hotter. It would have been unreal to carry the torch on any day, but to be asked to do it on the day before the Olympics in my home city was indescribable.

With the bus now nearly empty, my knees were trembling at the knowledge it would soon be my turn. As fate would have it, my designated route was only a couple of hundred metres from where both of my parents grew up. In fact, they had met each other at a pool hall on the exact same West Boulevard stretch where I would be running — sorry, trotting!

The organizers had this down to an exact science, precise to the minute. My time was to be 4:39 p.m., and it was. When I jumped off the bus, the ovation was even louder than what I'd been hearing inside. The screaming was almost ear-drum piercing. Words cannot describe the overwhelming feeling of patriotism I had when my torch — the curved metre-long winter white torch that weighed 1.6 kilograms — was ignited and I started to run.

Though exhilarating, the feeling also was peculiar. A combination of feeling all alone — because the next four hundred metres of torchbearer history was only up to me — while amongst so many. My emotions alternated between *Wow, this is going fast* and *I sure as hell hope my pants don't fall down.* They hadn't had my size, so I carried the torch with my right hand while holding up my pants with my left.

I felt blessed that my family was there — wife Paula, our children Palita, Anna and Ben, my siblings Cathy and Brian, and their spouses Bob and Julia — to share this unforgettable moment. (My elderly parents may have boycotted in protest of the pool hall no longer being there!)

The next day I took the torch to my kids' school where many students and teachers were thrilled to hold it, all seemingly mesmerized knowing it had carried the official flame. I've often thought if I could bottle one feeling from my life to call upon whenever needed, it would be those exhilarating moments in Kerrisdale the day before the Olympics. I'm eternally thankful for whatever strings Doroghy pulled to make it happen, as it left me with an unforgettable memory.

And a burnt-out torch I still have in my office.

I honestly didn't know what to expect for *Sportstalk* during the Games. CKNW wasn't a rights holder, so our content was going to be whatever we made it. Brook Ward was in studio the night of the opening ceremony — two proud Vancouverites marvelling about the magnitude of the moment but then cringing like everyone else when, embarrassingly, one of the four cauldrons didn't rise inside BC Place, the one thing that could not be messed up under any circumstances.

Minutes later we heard a loud commotion from street level that coincided with what we were being shown on TV. It was a pickup truck going right past our studio with Wayne Gretzky standing in the box holding a lit torch that would ignite the main cauldron in Jack Poole Plaza.

The hokiness of that moment, and all that could've gone wrong with that decision, made us cringe again.

Soon after, Nancy Greene Raine, whose cauldron did rise, joined us from a limo to talk about this historic night. It was an interview I'd arranged days earlier not knowing she would be centre stage. Nancy told me Gretzky was sitting beside her, so I asked if she would pass her phone to him. She was in the process of doing just that when — damn — his phone rang. We were so agonizingly close to getting Gretzky only minutes after he raced from the stadium to a pickup truck to the main cauldron and now to this limo. Or, as one of my TV heroes Maxwell Smart would've said, "Missed him by *that* much."

The IOC guards its broadcast rights ferociously, which is my way of saying sickeningly so. For example, it seemed to take years before a clip of Sidney Crosby's golden goal was made available for viewing. In terms of media access, CKNW was only able to secure two international credentials. But for the largest sporting event in Vancouver history, management didn't believe one should be assigned to someone in our sports department, either Jim Mullin or Stu Walters. I agreed that one of the passes had to go to a news person in case of events such as demonstrations or the tragic death of Georgian luger Nodar Kumaritashvili. CKNW's two accreditations went to Nafeesa Karim, who did an outstanding job, and Marcella Bernardo, who, when we called upon her, acted too much like a fan, something that drove me up the wall. Being the only two who could get behind the ropes, *Sportstalk* used them on an alternating basis.

When Karim appeared, she professionally chronicled the various events she had been to that day. But when Bernardo came on, sometimes after prime hockey games where media sat in club seats, she was giddy with excitement either about her view or having been able to see Crosby up close. Throughout our history I never tolerated callers, let along reporters, saying "we" instead of "they" when referring to our home teams. Bernardo did, and I wasn't impressed.

In spite of the opening night cauldron malfunction and the issue of credentials, it felt big league to have the Olympics in Vancouver, and doing the show was even more fun than I had imagined. Knowing we couldn't possibly compete with TV, we took a casual approach with Ward, Walters and Doug Eberhardt kicking around the day's events. A few times Brook and Stu went down to street level to interview locals and tourists about the spirit in the city. Most agreed the only time Vancouver had experienced a buzz like this was during Expo 86.

We slotted in many phone guests during the two Olympic weeks, including Jim Pattison, who had been the CEO of the Expo 86 Corporation, Arthur Griffiths, Catriona Le May Doan, Sam Sullivan, Jim Robson, Jyrki Lumme, Bruce Allen, Bernie Pascall, John McKeachie, Jim Taylor, Alexander Wolff and Brad Fay, if only to get their impressions on how our city was doing. Vancouver ticket broker Kingsley Bailey, a frequent guest over the years, came on every night to give us a sense of what ticket prices were for the marquee events. It was a great barometer. Incidentally, Heath Morgan took over as our new producer when Bob Addison left our show after twelve years to work on NBC's coverage from Vancouver. I was a little nervous when Bob left, but he made a great call recommending Morgan, who not only proved to be highly capable but utterly unflappable.

I attended women's hockey at UBC, sitting near US Vice-President Joe Biden who was there to support Team USA. I bought tickets to both semi-final games in men's hockey and, for my wife and I, the closing ceremony. We watched the Canadian hockey games from the popular Molson Hockey House and also visited my hometown Richmond Arena and marvelled at how it had been incredibly transformed into Holland's Heineken House.

Brook and I watched Stephen Colbert do his show from Creekside Park, saw Nancy Kerrigan and Alexander Ovechkin at a Science World party, and, while at a great Shaw party, saw Hayley Wickenheiser (Brook spilled a drink on her), Kevin Martin hours after he won gold in men's curling, and 54/40 playing a few feet from us.

The Games were golden in pretty much every way, but I've always been disappointed with how little showing off Vancouver was permitted afterward. Aside from the Richmond Olympic Oval, where a deal was made to allow the rings and the name to stay on the building, and one plaque without rings allowed near Vancouver City Hall, it's nearly impossible to detect any evidence that Vancouver was once a proud host city. Considering what it cost taxpayers to stage the Games, there should be signs on all highways leading into the city and at the airport that read: "Welcome to Vancouver, host city of the 2010 Olympic Winter Games."

CHAPTER THIRTY

Seven hours after Game 7s

Mike Gillis was now the Vancouver general manager in 2008. In six seasons, his two claims to fame would be guiding the Canucks to one Stanley Cup Final while simultaneously helping them become the NHL's most disliked team. Though it often made me unpopular, only *Sportstalk* would dare ask why they had that unflattering distinction.

While the Canucks had tremendous regular-season success, I didn't much like how they won. Admittedly, I also found them difficult to assess because of 4-on-4 overtime and my biggest pet peeve — loser points. It seemed both of those gimmicks were built for them and the incredible puck-controlling Sedin twins. I often wondered what good it was to assess them to any significant extent during the regular season based on a format that wasn't used in the playoffs. I tried to decipher the standings for our listeners, even inventing the *Sportstalk* barometer, where I isolated "outright wins." But season after season it seemed we had to wait until the post-season to really find out what they were made of.

The format wasn't their fault, but they were responsible for their on-ice antics — biting, diving and whining with the main culprits being Alex Burrows, Ryan Kesler and Max Lapierre — which had drawn the ire of fans and teams around the league. Many of my editorials centred around them not playing with near enough honour.

The period from 2007 to 2012 also was the era of the often moody/fickle version of Roberto Luongo, who was still a couple of years away from morphing into the pleasant and self-deprecating "Strombone" (Twitter) version that we enjoyed in the final seasons of his career and beyond. I also came to admire Kevin Bieksa's demeanour in later years, but as a young Canucks player he was a tad cocky. Our off-air nickname for him was Joe Cool. But I was talking to a fan base that didn't care about any of that as long as they won. And win they did, posting four consecutive one-hundred-point seasons. In spite of their high standing, there was no shortage of fodder for someone willing to play devil's advocate.

For example, when Gillis drafted Cody Hodgson tenth overall in 2008 (missing out on Tyler Myers and Erik Karlsson among others), he bragged about being an "out-of-the-box" thinking GM. Hodgson, however, was out of Vancouver after less than one full season. That same year Gillis named Luongo, the starting goaltender, as captain, a development tailor-made for *Sportstalk*. While "house radio" called it unconventional, "non-house radio" called it an unnecessary distraction. Gillis then rewarded him with a massive twelve-year contract extension, a mistake that hampered the Canucks' salary cap for several seasons and saw Luongo leave town long before it expired. Gillis also signed a washed-up Mats Sundin to a two-year contract worth twenty million that year. Sundin didn't make any impact, playing only forty-one games.

Luongo did have some great moments for Vancouver, but he also had some incredible playoff meltdowns, namely against Chicago and Boston. Most bizarre was the night Luongo missed the start of a playoff OT period in Anaheim due to nature calling at the worst possible time. This resulted in priceless pictures of then GM Dave Nonis looking like he needed to join Luongo in the washroom. Dany Sabourin, who played only nine games all season, was trotted out to try and keep Vancouver's season going and he did, stopping five shots in just under four minutes before Luongo returned.

But in the second OT, Luongo, having made fifty-six saves, got caught putting up an arm and screaming at the referee to call a penalty. The problem was that Roberto was looking to his left at the ref just as Scott Niedermayer was letting go a quick shot from the right. It went past Luongo's "referee arm" and in. A goalie with the runs, the GM looking like he needed to barf and Luongo looking the other way when the season-ending shot was taken. It all added up to embarrassingly expensive *Sportstalk* fodder.

The Canucks' 2011 opening-round near meltdown against Chicago, their biggest nemesis of that era, created some of the most intense caller interaction in our show's history. Having knocked Vancouver out of the playoffs each of the previous two seasons, Chicago looked like it might do it again, only this time by erasing an 0-3 series deficit, the cruelest of blows. The series changed on a dime when Raffi Torres threw a punishing and penalized hit on Brent Seabrook that knocked the star Chicago defenceman out of the series. Suddenly the Blackhawks were on a mission — not unlike Boston three rounds later when a similar hit changed the complexion of the final — and their strong dislike of the Canucks suddenly upgraded to hate.

Chicago ran them out in Game 4, beat Vancouver badly in Game 5, won a nail-biting Game 6 in overtime (Luongo was benched) and then, trailing the Canucks 1-0 late in Game 7, scored shorthanded to force heart-stopping overtime. It looked as if Chicago might come all the way back, but Alex Burrows won the game for Vancouver moments after Luongo made a season-saving save on Patrick Sharp from the doorstep.

It was high drama and when the Canucks won the city went crazy. I maintained for many years that had the Canucks blown that series it would've led to significant organizational changes which were put off by a few years because of how deep they ended up going that season. Again, with trust from my audience being my only real currency, it was important to also talk about all the good things that were also happening, which we did but, admittedly, often with the edge of a devil's advocate.

After escaping the Chicago series it was apparent the Canucks could go a long way. It didn't matter if I respected the way they played, I knew they were Stanley Cup material. Sure enough, they handily beat Nashville and San Jose in the next two rounds — with Joe

Cool being the recipient of an insanely crazy bounce off a stanchion followed by a knuckleball shot few saw to win the deciding game in OT against the Sharks.

Now, just as in 1994, we had to wait and see who Vancouver would meet in the final. I've never admitted this before, but I was relieved when Boston beat Tampa 1-0 in Game 7 of the East Final because now I could position this as a "dream *Sportstalk* matchup." My legitimate lifelong love of the Bruins gave me the perfect excuse to not have to automatically lean towards Vancouver. Or, as I told my listeners: "This was a tough one for me ... a no-lose series. On one hand I've liked Boston since before Vancouver entered the NHL, but on the other hand I spent most of my life hoping for the Canucks." It was true, but I can admit now that I definitely wanted Boston to win.

I thought I might have mixed feelings. Maybe I should have been happy for lifelong Canucks fans who'd waited so long. But no sooner would I think that than I surmised there wouldn't be any living with some people connected with the organization if they hoisted the Stanley Cup. Had Pat Quinn's 1994 team been the first Canucks team to win the Cup then I wouldn't have cared. But the thought of Mike Gillis, whose arrogance was already off the charts, being the first GM to guide Vancouver to a title (and the subsequent worshipping that would go along with that forever) was too much to swallow. It was even more difficult than imagining Alex Burrows, Ryan Kesler, Raffi Torres and Max Lapierre — given their less than honourable playing style — lifting the Cup. Next on my list was home radio. If I thought "They slayed the dragon!" was an over-the-top opening-round call from John Shorthouse (which was airing several times per day), then what would his Stanley Cup-winning call — something we would hear for the rest of our lives — sound like? Just like I wanted Quinn to be the first GM to win in Vancouver, I wanted Jim Robson to be first to call one — it would've been spine tingling — even though I knew both were no longer possible.

This leads me to the Canucks fans. The ones who called *Sportstalk* during that playoff year often sounded entitled and felt picked on by opposing teams or the NHL itself. Being uniquely positioned on the front line with fans calling during both Stanley Cup runs, it struck me that winning was more life or death for the 2011 fan base, while the '94 fans had been happy to be along for the great ride.

Another distasteful turn of events during the '11 playoffs was the Canucks targeting one of *Sportstalk*'s long-time sponsors by asking NHL legal counsel to demand Kingsway Honda take down a "Go Canucks Go" sign displayed in a window. The NHL claimed the dealership, managed by my friend Doug Lum, had infringed on copyright. To my knowledge the team, whose official marketing slogan was "We are all Canucks," didn't go after any other company caught up in playoff fever.

Meanwhile, the on-ice fodder was plentiful, starting with Burrows severely breaking a code when he bit Boston's Patrice Bergeron in Game 1. Then in Game 2, Lapierre taunted Bergeron, daring the Bruins forward to bite one of his fingers. Luongo created controversy with his goaltending counterpart Tim Thomas the day after Vancouver's Game 5 win by saying, "I've been pumping his tires ever since the series started and I haven't heard one nice thing he had to say about me." To which Thomas replied, "I didn't realize it was my job to pump his tires. I guess I have to apologize for that."

There were also instances of bad karma during that series as well. Two sources told me the Canucks were trying to sell broadcast rights for their victory parade and that the Aquilini brothers had a premature celebration dinner in Boston the night before Game 3. No team wants to be labelled "most disliked," but the moniker was earned, and the final example that season was captured by *Edmonton Sun* columnist Terry Jones following Game 7.

"It ended," Jones wrote, "with Vancouver owner Francesco Aquilini telling multiple members of the media in the Canucks' dressing room to go fornicate elsewhere."

The thought of a riot in Vancouver in 1994 never crossed my mind, but it sure did in 2011. I told my listeners the night before Game 7 that my gut was telling me there would be trouble, win or lose. There was too much pent-up anger and emotion, an "us-against-the-world" mentality from a large portion of the fan base.

Before the final buzzer sounded there was already unrest in the downtown streets. Before Boston was even presented with the Cup, that unrest had turned into a riot and resulted in multiple injuries, arrests, fires, overturned vehicles and smashed storefronts that led to widespread looting.

Being privately owned, the Canucks didn't have to disclose what most surmised was a huge profit in 2011, but when it came to the two-million-dollar clean-up bill, there was media talk as to what responsibility, as a corporate citizen, they carried. *The Tyee*, an online newspaper, wrote that "not a dime" was offered by the Canucks. Five years later in the *Vancouver Sun*, Francesco Aquilini claimed to have given two hundred thousand dollars to help clean up, and I'll leave it for others to decide if that was a generous amount or just a token sum. The day after the 2011 riot and again five years later, Canucks ownership continued to claim, "Those were not our fans rioting," a bizarre assertion given so much photographic evidence suggesting otherwise.

After Game 7, *Sportstalk* stayed on the air for seven hours. Unlike in '94, I had to manufacture sadness for the Vancouver fans. Truth is, I would've liked nothing more than to see the Canucks win the Stanley Cup … in 1994. When they didn't, I assure you I wasn't faking. I was truly sad for Trevor Linden, Cliff Ronning, Kirk McLean, Dave Babych, Greg Adams, Geoff Courtnall, Jyrki Lumme, Pavel Bure and the rest of Pat Quinn's group of likeable hockey citizens who lost Game 7 in New York City. But that was the only sad scene in what had been an incredible four rounds, all of which *Sportstalk* was part of at home and on the road.

Down 3-1 to Calgary in Round 1, I still remember pre-writing the obit I would have delivered that night had Geoff Courtnall not wired one past Mike Vernon in overtime. (Coincidentally, I was sitting in the same Saddledome press-box seat that night as I had been six years earlier when Wayne Gretzky blasted an identical OT shot past the same Calgary goalie in Game 2 of the Battle of Alberta, when it actually was a legit battle.) The '94 series-winning game over Calgary was the most thrilling Canucks game I ever covered. Tom

Larscheid was right when he called Pavel Bure's series-clinching double-overtime goal "The greatest moment in the history of the franchise."

It remains that today.

When convenient for my show, I was allowed to fly with the Canucks on their private charter, which I did at various times in all four rounds. Due to the 2-3-2 format, we only had one trip to Dallas in Round 2 and one trip to Maple Leaf Gardens in Round 3 as Vancouver finished them both in five games.

With the table set, it was off to the Big Apple and Madison Square Garden to cover arguably the greatest Stanley Cup Final in league history. The NHL had divided media seating into five categories, and I drew the fifth location, high above the net where Greg Adams scored the Game 1 overtime goal. It was there that broadcaster Dave Hodge, sitting a few seats away, informed me that O.J. Simpson was a suspect in the murder of his ex-wife and her boyfriend. And it was there where I had to share the public washroom with loud, mostly impaired Rangers fans. While peacefully using a urinal in a half-packed men's room an hour before the second game, we suddenly heard a heavily accented New York voice from behind one of the stalls loudly announcing the following: "Good evening, ladies and gentlemen, and welcome to the World's Most Famous Arena for Game 2 of the 1994 Stanley Cup Final between the Vancouver Canucks and your NEW ... YORK ... RANGERS! For the Rangers, starting in goal, number thirty-five, Mike RICH ... TER!" Even the acoustics in the washroom sounded big league.

The next washroom trip, in the second intermission, wasn't quite as much fun. This time it was packed as I happened to walk in with a lone Vancouver fan wearing a Sergio Momesso jersey. He was badly outnumbered. The Canucks fan chose to use a urinal while I ducked into a stall. A few moments later the "relieving" Rangers fans, with an easy target amongst them, started singing a song done to the tune of "Camptown Races."

Momesso takes it up the ass,

Doo dah, doo dah.

Momesso takes it up the ass,

Oh a doo dah day!

Thankfully, this fan didn't talk back. I got out of there, wearing my jacket, tie and Vancouver NHL media pass, as quickly as I could.

I will always maintain games 3 and 4, when Vancouver failed to win either home game, was the series turning point. Going back to New York for Game 5, I dug out my Canucks obit from weeks earlier. And when Vancouver blew a 3-0 lead early in the final period, I began updating it. Then, suddenly, in that amazingly remarkable series, the Canucks scored three to make the *New York Post* eat its front-page headline from earlier that day. It showed a picture of the Stanley Cup and a headline that read: "Tonight's the Night!"

Game 6 — the most electric home win in Canucks history — fell on a Saturday, but we still did a special show after that early-start game. Seldom did I ever go to a bar after the show, but that night I got talked into going to the Shark Club. For some reason, Bob Marjanovich, years removed from playing football for the Richmond Raiders and years away from being an established media regular, engaged in what I could only assume was some drunken radio rival tomfoolery by aggressively getting into my face and saying, "You're going down Russell — you're fucking going down." Okay. Nice to meet you, too, Moj. Beer wise, it was one and done for me that night.

Several hours before Game 7 in New York, I bumped into an extra-nervous Sandra Quinn, no doubt "hockey distancing" herself from her husband, Pat. Both of us were lost for words in trying to describe the magnitude of the moment. To pass the time until the 8 p.m. ET start I walked for many hours in the June heat, trying to take it all in. So many scattered thoughts ran through my head. As an adult, I was a professional in the media now. But the boy inside of me, an original Canucks fan, was desperately hoping to witness a Vancouver championship. *How lucky am I, having followed the Canucks since I was a young boy ... since the day they entered the NHL ... and here they are ... and somehow here I am ... in the world's greatest city about to watch them play one game to win the Stanley Cup.*

Once again I was in Press Box 5, and with Vancouver down a goal in the third period, I still remember thinking that, in a playoff filled with timely goals, it was only a matter of when, not if, the Canucks would tie it and then find a way to win. That sentiment seemed to be shared by many New Yorkers. Their team had gone fifty-four years without a title, and during stoppages in play in the final minute I saw fans turn their backs to the game, unable to watch, expecting the worst. Before the game's final faceoff, I even saw two fans on their knees praying.

It was gut-wrenching to walk into the Canucks' dressing room after that 3-2 loss and witness the hurt on their faces, the bruises on their bodies and their hearts on their sleeves. To a man, they were spent. Frozen in my mind is Trevor Linden sitting alone in one corner. Most of his equipment was still on, and his eyes were a strange mix of black from bruises and red from tears, knowing how close he had come to being the first Canucks player to lift the Stanley Cup.

In 1994, the only riot forecasted was in New York, but seeing all the police on horseback for a two-block radius around Madison Square Garden before the game made me think there was little chance of trouble.

We exited after finishing our dressing room interviews and shared an elevator with the long-time Rangers announcer Marv Albert, who was delighted. It was back to the Westwood One radio studios, adjacent to the Ed Sullivan Theatre from where David Letterman did his show every night, to wait for our 1 a.m. ET *Sportstalk* start on CFMI. While putting the finishing touches to my intro and trying to edit a couple of dressing room interviews, I started hearing through my headphones about unrest in downtown Vancouver. When we hit the air minutes later, it had escalated to the point where I found myself hosting riot coverage that I could hear but not see.

It was riveting, if not scary.

We had a team of reporters, mostly from CKNW, on the streets of Vancouver, but also our own Brook Ward as well as Steve Snelgrove, who did a live hit while being hit with tear gas. Our riot coverage lasted three hours, then we talked about the game for the next four hours. We signed off at 8 a.m. ET and walked out of the dark studio into an extremely bright, warm and muggy Manhattan morning. The first thing I heard — so similar to what's depicted in many movies — was a newspaper hawker shouting: "Extra! Extra! Rangers win the Cup ... Rangers win the Cup ... Read all about it."

I had been incredibly focused on riot and game coverage during the previous seven *Sportstalk* hours, and now this was the first time it really hit me — especially the boy in me who had hoped his entire life to see it — that the Canucks did not win the Cup. It was like I was in an emotional tape delay. Now I felt bummed out.

Producer Scott Woodgate and I went back to our hotel, the Grand Hyatt, grabbed our luggage and headed straight to LaGuardia. Our first flight took us to Toronto. Then, while on the Air Canada connecting flight, we finally saw TV coverage of the riot. After spearheading coverage for hours, this was the first time I'd actually seen any footage. It was worse than I initially thought.

Sitting by myself at the back of the plane, I should have been able to sleep, but I suddenly became emotional, nearly overwhelmed, while reflecting on the body of work Woodgate and I had provided through four magical playoff rounds. I took great satisfaction knowing that we had become the biggest gathering spot for Canucks fans on game nights and off nights. I loved extending many of our shows — including seven hours after Game 7 — because I knew the entire province was locked in on the Canucks and tuned in to *Sportstalk*. I have never felt such pride before or since. It was as if everything I had done — starting when I became hooked on radio as a young boy — had come together to provide a worthy service enjoyed by hockey fans around British Columbia.

We fulfilled the function radio is supposed to — we connected.

When I reflected back to the lack of Canucks coverage in 1982, which was the impetus for *Sportstalk*, it nearly brought me to tears. Because, I reasoned, we had successfully filled that glaring void with a program I had created from scratch.

And what did CKNW management think of all this?

True to form, we didn't receive even one email or phone call from anyone to thank us for providing on-air bonus hours or to congratulate us on our two months of unprecedented coverage.

CHAPTER THIRTY-ONE

Archie, Captain Charcoal and Halls of Bernie

When *Sportstalk* first hit the airwaves, the Vancouver sports media landscape included two newspapers (*The Province* and the *Vancouver Sun*), three TV outlets (BCTV, CBC and CKVU) and three radio stations (CKNW, CJOR and CKWX). Those were the biggies. Eight outlets with about fifty combined sports reporters who covered the same events mostly in the same way. Observe, take notes, interview coaches and players, and file. Rinse and repeat.

One of my first media friends was Lowell Ullrich, whom I met when he was on the Vancouver Canadians beat for *The Province* and I was hosting PCL games on radio. "L.U." showed me the ropes the first time I covered MLB spring training in Florida and then convinced me to convince CJOR that I had to stop by Las Vegas on my way back to cover the world middleweight title fight between Marvin Hagler and Thomas Hearns. It was a great call. Visiting big league baseball venues was special but nothing compared to the buzz of covering a Caesar's Palace fight spectacle, which remains near the top of my all-time *Sportstalk* road memories. The anticipation in the minutes before the boxers' entrance was dramatic, the people watching was amazing — especially when I got to shake Muhammad Ali's hand — and the fights were electric.

Staying a few (long Las Vegas) blocks away at the Marina Hotel (now site of the MGM Grand), I recall running (no chance of getting a taxi) back to my hotel room after the fight (a rare draw) where my equipment was set up on the vacant bed. I breathlessly signed on and broadcast *Sportstalk* as if we were in a big studio. Afterwards I played blackjack (a dollar per hand) for the first time, marvelling at how pretty ladies would not stop delivering free drinks and thinking, *Yes, this is definitely an upgrade from broadcasting hockey at the North Van Rec Centre.* When I got home a few days later, I shook my dad's hand, telling him that Ali had shaken it a few days earlier. (Cassius) Clay, as my dad still called him, was his undisputed all-time favourite athlete. I'm thankful boxing was still a big sport in *Sportstalk*'s first decade because I was fortunate to attend many more bouts featuring, among others, Sugar Ray Leonard, Donny Lalonde, Michael Olajide, Frank Tate, Frank Bruno, Evander Holyfield and Mike Tyson.

Each year, Ullrich and I partnered to produce the Canadians' game magazine and media guide. Lowell did so as a ghost, not wanting his newspaper to accuse him of moonlighting. I felt similarly. We called ourselves "walking conflicts of interest," shortened to WCOI. For the hell of it — or perhaps feeling I might one day have a baseball opportunity — Lowell and I would occasionally broadcast mock games on warm summer nights from the roof atop Nat Bailey Stadium, using the call letters WCOI.

I think Lowell might have loved radio as much as his own medium. He never turned down a request to come on *Sportstalk*, frequently appearing in his various roles that followed baseball — Canucks writer, sports editor and his many excellent years covering the BC Lions. That said, L.U. never wanted to be considered a "regular," I believe out of loyalty to his *Province* teammates, some of whom were still (rightfully) sour at Brian Burke's constant *Sportstalk* attacks of their work, many of them unfair.

I was Lowell's best man for his second marriage, arranging his stag on the Nat Bailey infield on a Saturday night when the C's were out of town. I invited all of his media friends for a softball game under the lights. A barbecue was set up down one foul line and the ball club supplied endless ice-cold Molson's products. Instructing Ullrich to first meet me in the clubhouse, I made him put on a C's uniform so he could be introduced running out of the tunnel by Pat Karl, who was upstairs in the public address booth. I also made him wear a hat I made that said: "Marriage — 0 for one."

In those days Ullrich was close with Kent (Cookie) Gilchrist, which led to us becoming friends as well. Gilchrist was on the BC Lions beat when we met, then he later became sports editor. He also enjoyed the curling beat. Perhaps too much? Having never covered curling, I had only heard the legendary stories about the Brier Patch, a booze-filled area where reporters could enjoy themselves after filing. The operative word being "after." Legend has it that there was one time when Gilchrist's story mysteriously appeared the next morning, byline and all, even though it had been written by a friendly/sober competitor. Very sportsmanlike. Gilchrist, who passed away in 2021, was a *Sportstalk* supporter in those days. He and Lowell arranged a banner ad that appeared in their section every day for a few years — the greatest *Sportstalk* advertisement (there weren't many) we ever had. Cookie and I were friends until he became a columnist, which is when Burke began trashing him. Understandably, Gilchrist was probably hoping I'd stick up for him. When I didn't, he began labelling *Sportstalk* as "house radio," which unfortunately ended our friendship.

One of my all-time favourites was Archie McDonald, a BC Sports Hall of Fame inductee, who finished his long career as a *Sun* columnist. We often found ourselves on the road together, most notably in Las Vegas for fights or during Canucks playoff runs. Fair, thorough and mild-mannered, it was always difficult to believe this was the same man who won junior boxing's prestigious Bronze and Emerald Glove titles while growing up near Kingsway and Knight in the early '50s. On the occasion of Vancouver's Michael Olajide Jr. fighting for a world title belt in 1987 (which he lost to Frank Tate), and on Archie's recommendation, I was thrilled to secure an interview with Vancouver-raised Jimmy McLarnin. He had twice won the world welterweight title — in 1933 at Wrigley Field in Los Angeles and in 1934 at Madison Square Garden in New York. He was eighty when he joined us, sixteen years before passing.

Time and again I was blessed to meet people I admired growing up.

Famed columnist Jim Taylor definitely fell into that category. There were times during his numerous *Sportstalk* appearances when I found myself daydreaming about when, as a kid, I would wait at the front door for the *Sun* to be delivered just so I could be first in our house to grab the sports section and read the witty Taylor.

Almost all of the Vancouver sportswriters were enjoyable *Sportstalk* guests at one time or another. Among them were Mike Beamish, Gary Kingston, Gary Mason, James Lawton, Steve Ewen, Arv Olsen, Jim Kearney, Ed Willes, Lyndon Little, Howard Tsumura, Ben Kuzma, Jim Jamieson, Dan Stinson and Jason Botchford.

Okay, perhaps I didn't enjoy interviewing Botchford as much in his later visits, especially after we got into an on-air scrap when he carved Mark Recchi for comments the Bruins forward made a few months after beating the Canucks to win the Cup.

"In twenty-two years, they are the most arrogant and the most hated team I've ever played against," Recchi said, knowing full well his comments would reach his home province.

I happened to agree with Recchi. Botchford did not. What followed was a long back-and-forth exchange that almost immediately got heated. Botchford fiercely and unreasonably backed the home team and I agreed with the assertions of the British Columbia-born player.

That said, just as *Sportstalk* once gave fans a new way to hear about the game, I respected how Jason created The Provies online post, which he tirelessly compiled after each Canucks outing.

Like everyone, I was shocked when Botchford died on April 25, 2019, and even more shocked when the BC Coroners Service found he had died from an accidental overdose of cocaine and fentanyl. Botchford, only forty-eight, left behind a wife and three kids.

Before Tony Gallagher became my competitor, he was a popular guest when I was on CJOR. I'm not sure if he liked the newness of our show or the limo ride to our studios at 8th and Hemlock.

In Las Vegas prior to the Leonard vs. Lalonde super middleweight championship fight, I enjoyed having Tony and Archie on from my

Imperial Palace hotel room before the three of us spent the next few hours next door at the Flamingo Hilton watching the fight. After those two went to bed, I discovered I couldn't lose at blackjack. Unfortunately, that's not saying much because not-so-brave Dan was betting only five and occasionally ten dollars per hand, much to the chagrin of the dealer given the once-in-a-lifetime roll she said I was on. Drunk with chips and alcohol I finally left the table at 8 a.m. and staggered to bed up about seven hundred dollars. A wise punter — translation: one with balls — would've left the same table with at least ten times that amount. I honestly couldn't lose. And the dealer was right — it never happened to me again.

Among my radio cohorts, Lee Powell has been a friend since the mid-'80s. I'd first heard of Lee from our mutual friend Bill Courage (who called him Boog, after the former Baltimore Orioles great) when they worked together at CHNL Kamloops. I bumped into Lee a couple of times on the WHL trail before he joined CKNW where we worked at the Expo studios.

Hardly a day would go by when there wasn't something emanating from management that made us roll our eyes. That's how "drop the keys" was invented, my self-explanatory game where the only action occurred as soon as he got to the part of the story that was complete nonsense. Lee often prefaced his story by saying, "You might want to get your keys out for this one."

Lee also was a locked-in occupant at our Martini's Restaurant table, along with John McKeachie and Scott Woodgate, where our orders seldom varied. McKeach started with a "Midget Greek" (his socially wrong nickname for the smaller version of his favourite salad). Lee would go with a chicken dill salad. Woodgate loved the quesadillas. I'd start with hummus and pita bread. That often would be followed by a large No. 24 (whole wheat pizza with chicken, spinach and feta cheese). Depending on the conversation, our Martini's sessions would end around 2:30 a.m. Most nights we had leftovers because the last thing we wanted to worry about was the next day's lunch.

On-air, you could throw Lee into every situation and he'd sound professional. Among other things, he hosted Grizzlies games, the *Canuck Report*, practices, news conferences, *Prime Time Sports* and sideline coverage on BC Lions broadcasts. He also did desk shifts and filled in for me. The real Boog Powell wasn't known as a utility player. Our Boog was one of the best.

Lee even made me laugh the day he was laid off in 1999. After program director Tom Plasteras and general manager Doug Rutherford finished their well-practised routine straight from the management handbook, Powell was told to go downstairs to collect his exit package from human resources. Once there, the woman in HR asked Lee what his plans were, to which he immediately said, "I hope to become a heavyweight boxing champion or at least fight for the title sometime in the next year or two." With a worried look in her eye, she inquired about his age (then forty-two) and ring experience, to which Lee said he'd "have to train harder." That's why Lee and I always got along. We were smart-asses who humoured each other to better cope with some key-dropping moments.

J. Paul McConnell once sat in for me but didn't like when I tried to tell him about our format.

"May I respectfully suggest," he said, "I've been doing talk shows in this market since before you were born."

Despite our not-so-pleasant early years, the since-retired J.P. has shown me incredible kindness and respect. This is not hyperbole; McConnell might be the biggest admirer of my career within the media. One (perhaps) over-the-top example was when McConnell raved about my numerous Twitter updates from Thailand in 2018 when the world was captivated by the twelve young soccer players and their coach trapped in a cave for nine days. Though I wish our relationship had always been as it is now, I'm immensely grateful we now call each other friends.

For all the years I covered the Canucks at Pacific Coliseum, my press-box seat was located high above the visitors' bench, right on the blueline. And for a few of those years I sat beside former Canucks forward-cum-radio commentator Garry Monahan, who of all people taught me a valuable interviewing lesson. "Mondo" and I would chat constantly, me picking his brain about the game and he often asking if I might have a particular question for him to ask one of his upcoming intermission or post-game guests.

Once, after he really liked a suggestion, I said, "But I'm not sure what kind of answer you'll get." To which he said, "I honestly never care what their answer is. I'm way more concerned about the question." There's a lot of truth to that. Ask the right questions and follow up when needed but let the guest reply as they wish and allow the listener to decide what they think of the answer.

In those days, Monahan also did a lot of radio colour, either when Tom Larscheid left for CFUN or when Tom had CFL conflicts in the fall. Once, while Woodgate and I were with the Canucks in Philadelphia, we convinced Monahan and *Sun* writer Elliott Pap to jump into my rented car for a day trip to Atlantic City. Leaving the Canucks, even on an off-day, was nerve-wracking for the often fidgety Pap in case something happened to a player while we were gone. Not so for Mondo, who likened our trip to the movie *Thelma and Louise*. Somewhere along Route 446 on the outskirts of the gambling town, I pointed out a billboard advertising Diana Ross playing that night at Bally's. After a short discussion we all agreed if I could get tickets we would go. As soon as I parked, I went to the box office and asked for their best seats, not knowing they'd be in a front row U-shaped booth three feet from the stage.

Hours later, with cocktails at our table, there was the original lead singer of The Supremes stopping at our table halfway through her set and holding each of our hands singing "You Can't Hurry Love" while looking deeply into Mondo's eyes.

One media guy who rubbed me the wrong way was Rick Dhaliwal. It wasn't because I didn't particularly like his on-air style — often more shouting than broadcasting — and not because he felt no day was complete without calling BC Lions owner David Braley and/or Vancouver Giants owner Ron Toigo. No, my problems with Dhaliwal stemmed from his attempts to interfere with *Sportstalk* business during his brief time as CKNW's sports director. Even after he was told

Sportstalk didn't fall under his umbrella, Dhaliwal often complained about me to program director Tom Plasteras and also tried to order producer Bob Addison, who I was paying, to do things for him.

Twice — both times while I was in Calgary — Dhaliwal made me especially upset. As was my habit, I always tested my radio equipment before starting a Shaw TV game. To do that, I'd call Dean Clark, the operator in master control, who would say, "Sounds clear, you're good to go," usually in a matter of five seconds. On this day, for whatever reason, we couldn't get the ISDN broadcast line to click in, and Dhaliwal just happened to be hanging near Dean as we tried. It was several hours before *Sportstalk* began and I was in an NHL building from which I'd broadcast countless times, so I wasn't worried. But Dhaliwal was, and he ran to Plasteras to tattle. Then Dhaliwal stepped farther offside by calling Jim Mullin in White Rock to tell him he would have to host *Sportstalk*, which was ridiculous for many reasons. For starters, no one checked with me. I was also certain the technical problem would be fixed, which it was within an hour. I always had a backup plan. And, most of all, Dhaliwal didn't have the authority.

Another time, he overreacted to a development concerning the last of the Griffiths family shares of Orca Bay being transferred to John McCaw. That was a follow-up to the ownership transfer news originally broken by *Sportstalk*. On this night my heavily promoted guest was famed NFL broadcaster Pat Summerall, but that went by the wayside when Dhaliwal went to Plasteras's office to complain about the layout of my show. To my utter disbelief, Plasteras took Dhaliwal's side. Minutes before my Shaw telecast, Plasteras called to express "great concern that Summerall was pre-recorded," as if there'd be any other way to have the seventy-three-year-old, a man who had worked sixteen Super Bowls, do me a favour and stay up until 12:15 a.m. Dallas time to do *Sportstalk*. Plasteras was relentless. He kept saying "Live is always better," which isn't even close to being true.

With my game approaching, I bent. Summerall was scrapped, giving way to a hastily arranged appearance by Elliott Pap, who came on off the top to rehash the ownership story. The subject matter was boring and, to prove a point, I opened the phone lines for reaction. We got only three calls. Two were from kids, the other from serial talk-show caller "Blind Ray" (his label), all wanting to know whether this meant the Canucks would be getting new uniforms.

The next day, I still was pissed about the *Sportstalk* hijacking and got into a yelling match with Plasteras, who again lectured me, someone who had hosted twenty years in a late-night Pacific Time slot, that "Live is always better." After an angry few minutes, I told Plasteras this was such a big issue that it might impact whether I would sign another deal at 'NW. Almost immediately he did an about-face.

"I'll be honest," he said, "we're trying to work at Rick being a better teammate. Even JJ [general manager Johnston] is tired of getting all his emails. I promise to talk to him."

I never thought Dhaliwal was vindicative; only excitable. Often infectiously. And like many, he eventually found his niche. His being one of Vancouver's best in terms of breaking stories.

To say Bernie Pascall — a consummate professional who was distinctly unmemorable — was a dinner-time fixture is an understatement, given he was seen in that BCTV slot for decades.

"And Tony, that's our look at sports."

Those are the only Pascall words I always remember, his sign-off, robotically delivered at the end of the *News Hour* with Tony Parsons. Given all the plum assignments Pascall drew by being a part of the CTV network — the Olympics, Memorial Cup and World Hockey Championships — I should remember more. He also hosted and did play-by-play on Canucks midweek telecasts and Whitecaps regional telecasts. For a time he even hosted *All-Star Wrestling* after Ron Morrier died.

Don't get me wrong, I honestly like Bernie and there actually is one other memorable thing I do recall him saying on a night we sat together at a crowded banquet. Upon returning from the buffet with loaded plates, Bernie leaned real close to me and said, with that same sign-off voice I'd heard every night growing up, "Hey Dan. Tits on the wall."

I nearly choked on my salad while confirming his observation — no, he wasn't wrong. Nor was he trying to insult anyone because no one else was within earshot. But hearing those words in that voice took me aback. In that moment, I remembered that TV people are also normal and, at times, politically incorrect human beings.

I'm not entirely sure what Pascall's enthusiasm is for various halls of fame, but he's fanatical about the topic. In 1994, I was asked to be a voting member for the newly-formed BC Hockey Hall of Fame (BCHHOF) in Penticton, something I took seriously. However, as the years moved on, I didn't like some of the lobbying that took place. Naturally, all the big names were deservingly inducted, like Cyclone Taylor, Pat Quinn, Phil Maloney, John Ferguson, the Griffiths family, Jim Robson, the Vancouver Millionaires, etc. Then one year Bernie, who by then was overseeing our voting committee, supplied a five-page resume on himself. While a case could be made for his induction, I didn't think it should be him making that case. That was a difficult vote to cast and made me wonder if any media should ever be inducted into these kinds of halls unless the hall has a designated media category.

Worse yet, two years later, Bernie successfully lobbied for his friend Grant Kerr to be inducted. Kerr's bio listed him as a long-time Canadian Press sportswriter and someone who coached minor and junior B hockey, joining hundreds of others from the latter category who've done the same. I also found Kerr to be a nice man, but was that a hall-worthy bio? I didn't think so, and it was one of the reasons I stepped down from the voting committee in 2017.

I'm not sure if Pascall lobbied elsewhere, but then again how many people realize he's also in the Canadian Football Hall of Fame, BC Football Hall of Fame, BC Sports Hall of Fame and the Canadian Association of Broadcasters Hall of Fame?

That's a hall of a lot of halls!

In 2014, the BCHHOF created an award of which I was the first recipient. It is the Bernie Pascall Media Award, and it's given to someone in the media "who demonstrates commitment and dedication to the promotion within the game of hockey." I'm still not entirely sure what those words mean and I don't wish to sound ungrateful, but *Sportstalk*'s function wasn't to promote hockey. Incidentally, the plaque they gave me spelled the last name wrong — Bernie's! I felt bad for him because he was embarrassed. Even though I said it was okay, he insisted on sending me a proper one, making me the only Pascal-Pascall recipient.

No matter the particular hall, there always seems to be debate. For example, why isn't Al Davidson, who owned the Vancouver airwaves on all NHL and CFL games, morning sports, commentaries, etc., in the BC Sports Hall? Sure, there was that alleged arson of his boat which prompted Harry Neale to refer to Al as "Captain Charcoal" on "The Overtime Show" one night. Yes, there was that alleged threat to have his son take out Neil McRae. But if you can put those two alleged transgressions aside …

I admit it. I had a soft spot for Big Al, especially after one particular "Spotlight on Sport" commentary in 1988.

"Like to see young persons coming in to this business, the business of sports reporting. Do a great job and progress and you are paid for doing a top job. Usually it's through dedication, hard work and pride of product.

"So many times I tune into radio, TV, read newspapers — overseas and in North America. It's a blessed joy to appreciate the best.

"Larscheid has fun in sport. McKeachie's McKeach — great heart, slow tongue. Fine guy. None better than Jim Robson at play-by-play, and Jimmy works at it.

"We have a great one on the rise here at CJOR 600, and his ratings show he has been accepted by you, the listeners. Dan Russell started a sports talk show and there were a few of those big shots who do little but scoff.

"I didn't. The guy was in love with what he was doing and worked hard at his *Sportstalk* program. Dan would be the first to admit it was a little rough at first. Now Dan Russell has people in sport asking to be on his show.

"Our dean Bill Good Sr. puts it best, I think. He says Dan Russell asks a short, intelligent question, listens to the guest and continues with continuity that makes sense, is entertaining, informative and very listenable. Dan Russell's recent ratings attest to this, good listenership.

"Great to see a fine young man on the rise, who works his pants off and eventually it will pay off with big bucks for Dan Russell because he believes in what he's doing, works hard at it and does it well.

"A tip of the sports cap to OR's Dan Russell, a young sports reporter and broadcaster who I think has a fantastic future. Here's to Dan.

"And that's 'Spotlight on Sport.'"

Hearing that about me from a legend I grew up listening to every day was better than any award. Davidson died in 1991 at age sixty-six. That night, we paid tribute with a full panel of guests before lowering the *Sportstalk* flag to half-mast.

CHAPTER THIRTY-TWO

Our next guest is James Kush of *The Rochester Times*

Balance?

On those few occasions I was on the ice, I can confirm I had frightfully little.

In real life?

About the same until I got married and had kids, which happened exactly halfway through our thirty-year *Sportstalk* tenure.

The show totally consumed me. In addition to keeping up with everything the Canucks (and the rest of the NHL) were up to, I recorded and watched countless hours of other sports, read newspapers until my hands were black from the ink, subscribed to all the big sports magazines and was forever taking notes. We had set the bar high, and I went about meeting or exceeding that every day, seldom relaxing and never saying "good enough" when I knew it could always be better.

Before I discovered a work/life balance I'd wake up near the crack of noon and still be working on the show, in one form or another, until 3 or 4 a.m. But after getting married, those times altered a little. At first it wasn't easy juggling family, *Sportstalk* and Shaw TV play-by-play, but because of my experience and my dedicated producers, the show really didn't miss a beat after I got married.

My priorities changed the instant Paula and Palita came into my life. Home life became more hectic when Anna was born in 2001 and even more chaotic when Ben arrived in 2006. Go figure. Our home got noisier with every subsequent child and, like most families, chock-full of the usual kids' activities: sports, dance, theatre, music, etc. There are seven years between Palita and Anna, and another five between Anna and Ben. When I consider the never-ending homework assistance, parent/teacher meetings, Halloweens, sports days and Christmas concerts, I selfishly admit I wish they were a little closer in age.

Incidentally, though perhaps not a great claim-to-fame, Anna was the first of our children to swear. When she was eighteen months old and wanted — demanded — to hear music on the car radio, she would loudly say, "I want bullshit!" To this day, whenever someone in our family doesn't like something it's not uncommon to hear, "That's just music!"

Speaking of bullshit, I mean music, Ben was the most active and the hardest to get to sleep. The only thing that would do the trick was a continuous loop of Chilliwack's 1978 hit "Baby Blue," the nearly six-minute live version. I often thought I should've sent Bill Henderson a thank you note.

Ben is the athlete I never was — a high-scoring minor hockey forward, an above-average (for his age) point guard in basketball, and a strong fielding shortstop in baseball. Even though Ben was quite young, I am so glad I had him accompany me to many Shaw games late in my career. Wearing his TV uniform — sports jacket, slacks and (clip-on) tie — Ben sat beside me and wore a headset so he could hear his dad. The longer I am retired, the more precious those memories are, and we both remember how kind many WHL players were to offer him tips and encouragement for his own games, especially Matt Dumba, Leon Draisaitl and Josh Morrissey. Years earlier, Palita and Anna watched me work WHL games and *Sportstalk* on occasion. It was enjoyable to bond with them on those nights even though Anna becomes instantly bored hearing about or watching any sporting event.

After I retired, I took Ben to all his games and practices. It was fun to watch him play, but no fun to witness/experience the politics of minor sports, and it made me recall how people occasionally phoned *Sportstalk* to complain about youth sports. But back then, with no skin in the game, I only paid it lip service. Not until Ben played did I comprehend the importance so many parents (especially parent coaches) place on having their child play the highest level of rep sports. It was often as sickening as it was ignorant. Ben played in two large Lower Mainland hockey associations with hundreds of other kids, virtually none of whom will make the NHL. But that didn't stop many parents from pulling out all the stops. Under the category of "Quotes I'll Never Forget," a newly-named rep coach in Langley once told me "Some of the dads are essentially offering me oral sex just to let them be an assistant [thus guaranteeing their kid a spot on that team]."

Like many young families, we enjoyed camping trips with our travel trailer, often to the Okanagan or our favourite, Cape Disappointment, where the Columbia River hits the Pacific Ocean on the border between Washington State and Oregon. We'd start many summers by camping for two weeks before spending the rest of the time in Thailand with Paula's mom. Other years, my mother-in-law came to Canada. Our kids learned early that airports meant either happy hugs or sad hugs.

Given that my wife owned a restaurant when we met, you'd think I would love Thai food. I do, but it didn't always like me. My friends, on the other hand, always appreciated an invite to be treated to her authentic cuisine. That included Mike Davis, the person most responsible for my family life. Though Mike grew up close to me in Richmond, we didn't meet until I was visiting some BCIT friends in Smithers in 1980 where Mike was working as a radio sportscaster. By fluke I met him again on December 24, 1992, while living about a 5-iron away from the Richmond Golf Club. The only shower in my townhouse had broken and wouldn't be fixed until after Christmas so, thinking no one would be at the club this close to Christmas, I decided to sneak in for a shower. Mike had been using the gym and was the only person in the locker area. From then on we were the best of friends and after we both retired, he accompanied me to watch nearly all of Ben's hockey and baseball games, even practices. I often tell Ben if not for my broken shower, he wouldn't have been born.

When Mike died suddenly in 2019, Ben and I were devastated. Here's part of what I said at his Celebration of Life:

> Mike Davis was my friend first, then a friend of *Sportstalk*. He never got that order wrong. He and I travelled to so many places together. I accompanied him for his work, and he for mine. He helped me with Roadtrip of a Lifetime, Canucks training camp, the Andy Moog tournament and much more. As an added bonus, Mike would often serve as my one-man "security detail" during remotes. We worked hard. We golfed hard. And sometimes we 19th holed hard. Mike was the one who first took me to Asia, first to Hong Kong, where I instantly was enthralled, and later to Thailand where I met my wife.

> Mike and I were lucky. We went to many places on someone else's dime, meaning we both submitted many expense reports. Both of us were creative, but Mike was damn good. After one Asian trip, his report totalled about $2,400. When the Cathay Pacific accountant checked it over, he noticed a $45 submission for hats in amongst the restaurant, transportation and hotel receipts.

> The accountant asked Mike, "What is this?"

> Mike said, "Those are hats. I was away during my dad's birthday and I bought him two hats."

> The bean-counter reprimanded him, saying, "You can't do that! Gifts for family don't constitute a business expense. You have to do it again."

Though not happy, Mike resubmitted his report, but once again the amount was $2,400. A short time later the accountant came back to Mike's desk and said, "Your report still says $2,400." Before Mike could respond, the accountant then said, "But I can't find the hats ... where are the hats?"

Without missing a beat, Mike said, "You find them!"

We once ran into pro golfer John Daly in our hotel lobby in Kelowna, and the three of us talked for quite some time. Mike, an avid golfer, didn't have any interest in how Daly was able to hit the ball longer than anyone on the PGA Tour or his having won a major title. No, Mike and John Daly spent at least ten minutes engaged in a debate about M&M's vs. Smarties. When they were done, it wasn't clear who had the sweeter tooth.

Mike loved all the *Sportstalk* trips, but our Las Vegas boxing junkets were his favourites, especially in 1996 when I covered the infamous Holyfield/Tyson fight in which Tyson was disqualified for biting one of Holyfield's ears. We were broadcasting from a local radio station near the Strip the previous night when our last guest of the night failed to show up. That happens to every show, but it's more challenging when you're on location, especially if you don't have anyone else to talk to. Sensing my semi-panic during a commercial break, Mike sprang into action.

"Welcome back to *Sportstalk* on this the night before Mike Tyson's much anticipated bout with Evander Holyfield. We're joined now, from the media centre down the road at the MGM Grand, by James Kush, who covers boxing for *The Rochester Times*."

We talked for nearly fifteen minutes about the fight, and it was a great conversation. It's doubtful any of my listeners knew there was no such thing as *The Rochester Times* and that James Kush actually was Mike Davis. It was the only time we ever faked a *Sportstalk* interview.

The night of the "bite fight" was scary because the chaos didn't just occur inside the ropes. In certain sections of the MGM Grand Garden Arena, fans were throwing punches at each other after Tyson was disqualified. The really scary part was trying to exit the arena through extremely narrow hallways strategically designed to flow directly into the main casino. With so much anger caused by the way the fight ended, there was no shortage of yelling, pushing and shoving in that tight hallway. Once through, those restless fans charged through the casino knocking over some gaming tables. Fortunately, we were already mingling with thousands of others on the Strip when shots were fired in the casino.

When my wife's and daughter's official immigration papers finally arrived in December 2000, the three of us flew from Thailand to Canada. We arrived at our new Richmond home which my family had decorated with welcome signs and balloons in my absence. There was a heavy snowfall on their first day in Richmond. Though my wife had seen snow the year before in Whistler, I won't ever forget the joy on Palita's face — and the chattering of her non-climatized teeth — the first time she saw and felt it.

Paula and I were married in September 2000 in Asia and again in March 2001 in Richmond. I was grateful that my siblings, Cathy and Brian, along with my nephew Scott and niece Tracy made the journey to Asia to witness the cultural uniqueness of a Thai wedding.

If one takes after their parents, I got my sense of humour from my father, Ken, and my organizational skills from my mother, Pat. Considering it was my dad's love of radio that inspired me, it might seem strange that he only saw me broadcast once and only because we were nearby during our *Sportstalk* golf tournament in Richmond. I tried to get him to come and watch other shows, but he always went to bed early, listening to the radio — always to News 1130, and not his son.

My mom and I usually set late Sunday evenings aside for a weekly phone catch-up. She was always keenly interested in the latest CKNW politics but equally worried I might do something to tick off management.

"Don't cut off your nose to spite your face," was something she often (though gently) drilled into me.

Yes, mothers always know best, and she was giving me good advice ... even if I didn't always take it to heart.

CHAPTER THIRTY-THREE

The A Team

When I gave up broadcasting the Seattle Thunderbirds in the mid-nineties, I thought I was done with play-by-play. It was out of my system, and I was content, especially in light of the changes in my personal life. But then, out of the blue, I received a phone call from Glen Dufresne in the fall of 2004. I had met him a few years earlier when he was the voice of the Prince George Cougars, but he had left radio to take a sales and corporate job with the Shaw TV office in Kelowna.

"We want to reunite The A Team," he said.

I had no idea what he was talking about. He explained that Shaw Community TV, led by programming supervisor Russ Greaves, had formed a partnership with the WHL and wanted to reunite what he thought had been the best broadcast team in the league — me working alongside Bill Wilms. I was thankful they thought of us but wasn't particularly thrilled, mostly because I often heard grandiose proposals that didn't lead to anything.

This one did.

Initially, Shaw and Greaves proposed a few regular-season games plus playoffs for 2004-05 before expanding their WHL relationship in future years. That's when something miraculous happened. Timing being everything, the '05 WHL playoffs occurred during an NHL work stoppage, and our first series, Vancouver vs. Kelowna, included the Easter long weekend. But besides *Sportstalk* promoting these games, we were of the opinion that few people knew they were on TV.

It turns out we had no idea how many people were starving to see high-calibre hockey. The first two games in the Okanagan were really good. Vancouver won Game 1 on a late goal by Mark Fistric; the Rockets took Game 2 on an overtime goal by Brent Howarth. As word of mouth spread, interest took off. Before Game 3 in Vancouver, all the talk shows (including both twenty-four-hour sports stations that, without the NHL, were desperate to fill time) featured lots of discussion about the games in Kelowna. Prior to the series starting, the Giants, then playing in Pacific Coliseum, had pre-sold four thousand tickets for their home games. But as a result of our TV coverage, the *Sportstalk* promotion and the rest of the media taking our cue, there were nearly thirteen thousand fans at Game 3 and a shade under fourteen thousand for Game 4.

Tied at two games each (with both Kelowna wins in OT), the Rockets took Game 5 at home, setting the stage for an even larger Game 6 crowd — 16,183, a sellout — with many fans purchasing from scalpers. It turned out to be the series-closing game with the Rockets winning 3-2.

Tens of thousands more watched on TV. In fact, on the same day Pope John Paul II died, the WHL on Shaw Community TV was the most-viewed show in Vancouver — something unheard of. This exceeded everyone's expectations.

It felt as if this was going to be great, and it was — for six weeks.

That's how long it took me to get ticked at Shaw after they assigned the league championship series to Alberta-based broadcaster Mark Stiles despite everything I'd done to promote their games. When I called Ed Chynoweth, the chairman of the WHL's board of governors, he got upset.

"Leave it with me," he said.

He arranged a compromise where I would do the games from the west and Stiles the ones in the east.

By the next season, I was the lead announcer and would be for the next decade. The timing was good because I got to call Vancouver's first WHL title in 2006. The Giants won that series in what was known as the "Crushed Can" in Moose Jaw, Saskatchewan — a bizarre building in which you only could see the first four rows of fans on the other side from the broadcast booth. Being unable to see the entire arena created a semi-claustrophobic feeling prompting me to remark during one telecast: "It's the only rink you can comfortably bring both your wife and your girlfriend."

Audiences grew even larger the next season when Vancouver met Medicine Hat in the championship final, which was when Canucks fans were introduced to their team's future head coach, Willie Desjardins, complete with his iconic clipboard and unique facial tics. Though both clubs were guaranteed berths in the Memorial Cup tournament, which Vancouver would host, they still staged an incredible series, especially the four games played in the Medicine Hat Arena. It was capped off with an epic Game 7, which was won in the fog in the second OT period on a goal by the Tigers' Brennan Bosch. More than four hundred thousand people watched the game.

Other Shaw highlights included broadcasting three straight finals (2012-14) between Portland and Edmonton with those two evenly matched clubs playing twenty of a possible twenty-one games. Each team won ten games, but Edmonton won two titles. Tyson Barrie's OT goal, set up by Jamie Benn and scored against Martin Jones in Game 6 of Kelowna's win over Calgary in 2009, was also memorable.

So, too, was the 2011 title that brought tears to the eyes of Kootenay Ice owner and general manager Jeff Chynoweth when he lifted the Ed Chynoweth Cup three years after the trophy's namesake, his father, had died of cancer. I felt lucky to have known Ed, the most important man in WHL history. He was the one who transformed it from a league with many high school dropouts — "Young man, do you want to be a hockey player or a student?" was something many talented players heard in the '70s and '80s — to one that emphasized education.

Juggling Shaw and *Sportstalk* was made easier because of my previous experience doing Seattle games. Once again we pre-taped enough material to take us until midnight, knowing there was only a snowball's chance we would ever need it.

That snowball was tossed at us on April 10, 2009, because of what was then the second-longest game in WHL history. The Spokane Chiefs beat host Vancouver 3-2 in Game 5 of their second-round series on Blake Gal's goal in the fourth OT period, ending the game at 12:45 a.m. It was such a long night that *Sportstalk* emptied its chamber of emergency pre-records, I dismantled our remote gear after the third overtime and producer Bob Addison even had time to drive from our downtown studio to the PNE to watch the last half hour of the game from our booth. Incidentally, the last three games of that series each reached OT, with the Giants winning the last two — Evander Kane won Game 6 in the second overtime, and Nick Ross scored Game 7's only goal less than two minutes into the extra period.

In addition to the enjoyment of calling these games, it was a real privilege to see so many future NHLers and to convey so much about them to our *Sportstalk* listeners. Including my New Westminster and Seattle days, I'm blown away whenever I peruse old prep sheets knowing I had the privilege to broadcast games involving these players before they became household names: Jarome Iginla, Joe Sakic, Wendel Clark, Cam Neely, Ray Ferraro, Cliff Ronning, Mike Modano, Trevor Linden, Rob Brown, Mark Recchi, Patrick Marleau, Ryan Nugent-Hopkins, Shea Weber, Jordan Eberle, Theo Fleury, Griffin, Max and Sam Reinhart, Luke and Brayden Schenn, Tyler Myers, Matt Dumba, Shea Weber, Ryan Johansen, Carey Price, Cody Eakin, Craig Berube, Dan Hodgson, Jamie Benn, Brendan Gallagher, Milan Lucic, Marian Hossa, Pat Falloon, Olaf Kolzig, Stu Barnes, Bill Ranford, Oliver Bjorkstrand, Leon Draisaitl, Tyson Barrie, Tyler Ennis, Martin Jones, Gilbert Brule, Robin Bawa and Evander Kane.

And I got to know coaches like Ernie McLean, Don Hay, Ken Hitchcock, Ken Hodge, Paddy Ginnell, Mike Babcock, Brent Peterson, Don Nachbaur, Travis Green, Marc Habscheid, Mike

Johnston, Willie Desjardins, Kelly McCrimmon, Ryan Huska, Tom Renney and Dave Lowry, just to name a few.

I also got to know up-and-coming officials like Rob Schick, Mick McGeough, Brad Watson, Tom Kowal, Steve Kozari, Trevor Hanson, Brad Lazarowich, Shane Heyer and Jay Scharrers.

My relationship with Wilms took on many layers over many decades. He was part father figure, motivator, broadcast partner, occasional golf teacher and more. Sometimes, though, we had our difficulties. I know deep down he appreciated me — and I will never forget how much he supported me when I was in my early teens — but there were times when I felt our friendship needed to be convenient to him.

For example, I was the one who was willing to walk away from Seattle on opening night when the Thunderbirds owner didn't want Wilms. Then, in 1998, I was the one who got Bill into the booth when Sportsnet TV, which had just signed on, had never heard of him. But the next year he didn't take a stand when I was squeezed out and they kept him.

"What do you want me to do, Dan?" he asked using a pleading voice that suggested he had no other choice.

What I wanted was the same loyalty I had afforded him. I'm not saying he made a poor career decision, as he got to do a Memorial Cup which no doubt helped him get the Giants colour job when they entered the WHL. But I did feel it was a poor friendship decision and for the next few years we drifted apart. But when Dufresne said he wanted to reunite The A Team, we were back together and would be for the next eleven years.

Most years we did between forty and forty-five games. I loved driving to the BC games because I liked getting home the same night. Besides, by this stage, I could've driven the Coquihalla Highway blindfolded. I always drove, which said more about my control-freak nature than Bill's driving ability. Thankfully, he never argued over my musical tastes. Wilms enjoyed my favourites — J. D. Souther, Elton John, Burton Cummings (live recording from Arts Club), and

Bob Seger — and wanted the music cranked as loud as possible so he could hear every note.

Anytime we climbed into the car after a game, especially in Kamloops, Kelowna or Alberta, the first thing he'd yell was "Give me max heat!" knowing full well the engine still had to warm up. Drive thrus were a must. Bill was right — they made the trip go by quicker. And I was right about always ordering a "backup burger," something Bill often regretted.

Wilms liked to push my buttons and see how far he could go. Once during a driving rainstorm, he mocked me about an innocent thing I had gotten wrong on the telecast, prompting me to feign anger, stop the car at the summit of the Coquihalla, roll down his window and yell "Get out!" Bill laughed his head off for a few seconds then, freezing and soaked, pleaded with me to close the window, which I did after he promised to stop bugging me.

Bill always wanted to sleep on our way home, often asking me as his seat was reclining to "Please tell me a *Sportstalk* story about your favourite guest," or some topic like that. It took me awhile to catch on because he'd invariably fall asleep a minute or so into the story. All he wanted was a personalized version of what my listeners got every night — my voice to fall asleep to. After catching on, I retaliated. Within a half hour he would awaken, complaining that his rear end was burning hot from the seat warmer I'd set on high. I would always chirp, "Is that max heat enough for you?"

One of the drawbacks to juggling radio with TV was that I never felt the same camaraderie with the Shaw crew because most nights I went right from doing the game into *Sportstalk*, and by the time I finished everyone was long gone. So much of the fun is being able to bond with the crew afterwards, to talk about the telecast and the game. I did get some of those nights, but not as many as I wanted.

I really liked our producer, Dave Roberts, who I grew closer to when he came to Thailand with me in 2008. Having Roberts in my ear during games was comforting. He knew me, knew my style, supported my calls, and made me laugh or laughed at me. For example, one night when Sam Reinhart shot wide for an easy empty-net goal that would've sealed the Shaw money pool for me, Roberts said in my headset, "Dan, I don't think I've ever heard an announcer sound that pissed at any player not scoring." Or my favourite, when a team got an insurmountable lead, no matter what stage of the game, Dave would slowly whisper in my ear: "Ohhh-vver!" My son still says that to me whenever we are watching the end of some games. The Alberta-based Roberts had previously been on my side of the microphone, and though he didn't grow up with *Sportstalk*, he appreciated my broadcast skills and ability to tie everything together.

Grant Wilkins, a quiet and shy man, was brought in to oversee things long after the show was already humming. He had grown up listening to *Sportstalk*, and he was elated after I had him on one night to talk about upcoming playoff coverage.

"I can check that off my bucket list," he told me with a huge grin.

Meantime, the attitude of the WHL brass started to change. In our first few seasons they couldn't thank us enough for giving them the greatest exposure the league had ever had. Coverage that included inaugural games for the Chilliwack and Edmonton franchises, two games from a new rink in Seattle, an experimental game in Winnipeg, more than forty regular-season games from every venue, four rounds of playoffs, and even a U17 tournament featuring many future WHL and NHL players that we did one season from Port Alberni.

Then familiarity suddenly met contempt. Ron Robison, the WHL commissioner, started interfering and became less appreciative of the coverage. As an example, one night after I talked about a player having been with five previous teams, Wilkins told me Robison didn't want me mentioning how many teams a player has been with because "It's not good for recruiting."

"Then don't trade him so much," was my cheeky response.

Robison, usually through long-time VP Rick Doerksen — a prince of a man with an encyclopedic knowledge of the league's history — also wanted Bill and I to take the league's side on controversial issues, calls and suspensions. Wilms was usually quick to make sure his bread stayed buttered, but *Sportstalk* Dan, who was used to calling it as it was, not so much.

I often took a *Sportstalk* vacation day when we had a game in Calgary after discovering I could leave the booth before host Andy Neal signed off, rush to my rental car, scoot to the airport and be back in Richmond listening to the end of *Sportstalk* (guest hosted) before midnight. Most times, however, I stayed alone in an empty arena hoping the Zamboni guy wouldn't do what I knew he would, which was bring out his noisy ice shaver to painstakingly edge the corners. The racket, which sounded like a lawnmower, often bled into *Sportstalk*.

In Edmonton, they let beer league teams play an hour after our telecast. That was bad enough, but it got worse when they thought a more authentic NHL rink experience should also include the national anthem, a PA announcer and the loud horn whenever Hudson's Pub (or whatever they were called) scored.

If we couldn't do *Sportstalk* from the press box, our locations would vary. For example, in Cranbrook, it was from general manager Jeff Chynoweth's office; in Kamloops, it was the lunchroom in the Blazers office; the Medicine Hat Arena ticket office; the Kelowna Rockets photocopy room; and in Saskatoon from the Blades sales department.

Packing up equipment and walking out of rinks sometimes after 1 a.m. and into frigid temperatures, desperately trying to warm the car, hoping to find somewhere (other than 7-Eleven) to eat, getting back to hotels so late, and sleeping (more like napping) for a few hours until an early flight back all took its toll. One night in late January 2015 I finally came to my senses. I had just worked a game in Medicine Hat on a treacherously cold and snowy night. For single games there, I would usually fly to Calgary, drop my bags at an airport hotel, drive three-plus hours to Medicine Hat, then drive back right after the game for a nap and catch an early flight to Vancouver. But on this stormy night in southeast Alberta, Bob Ridley, the long-time Tigers broadcaster and their original bus driver, warned me that the Trans-Canada Highway might be closing.

Stubborn and holding a plane ticket for early the next morning, I thanked him but said I'd chance it. Ridley was wrong about them closing the highway, but they should have. Adding to my stupidity was driving alone as Wilms wasn't assigned to that game. It only took a few kilometres before I was in near white-out conditions. Visibility was terrible as I crawled westbound. I kept both hands firmly on the steering wheel, thinking that if I somehow veered off into one of the fields, they might not find me until the snow melted in the spring.

"What the fuck am I doing?" I said to myself. "I'm forty-five years old. I have three kids at home. This is absurd."

Adding to my thought process was the cold shoulder I was receiving from the WHL brass since I decided to give up *Sportstalk*, which they selfishly viewed as a loss of the free province-wide advertising to which they had become accustomed. *Why am I literally putting my life on the line for them?* I kept asking myself during what would be a slippery six-hour drive back to Calgary. By the time I reached the Sandman Airport Hotel I had decided this would be my final season.

Another thing I had grown tired of was Calgary-based broadcaster Peter Loubardias's nauseating and years-long quest to oust me from the booth. It had started when Sportsnet fired him from doing NHL and CHL games.

"The new [bosses] don't think you're very good at calling hockey," was how Loubardias explained what he had been told about his firing to the *Calgary Journal*. Subjectively speaking, the Sportsnet suits were right.

Before the 2015 WHL championship series ended, things became highly uncomfortable. Judging by how everyone was treating me, I sensed Loubardias had finally succeeded. The day before what would be the final game, I was told my son wouldn't be allowed in the booth. As we were already in Kelowna and Ben had sat with me on numerous occasions, I didn't know what they expected me to do with him. I ignored their request because I figured that, after calling more than eight hundred games games, my son should be with me for what could be my last. I knew this edict had come from Robison and by extension Bruce Hamilton, the WHL's chairman of the board, both of whom were frequently on *Sportstalk* to promote their league. It angered me because it was one thing for them to discard me because I wasn't of use to them any longer, but it was classless to have them invoke my eight year old to rattle my cage.

While sitting in the hotel lobby two days earlier in Brandon, Bill had confided in me that while working a game with Peter earlier in the season, Loubardias had told him, "You know Dan isn't the only one who has done a lot of great broadcasting in this league." I rolled my eyes and knew full well Wilms didn't steer that conversation in the way he should have (i.e., suggest that Peter not stab me in the back). Instead, when I reminded Bill of the endless *Sportstalk* coverage I had generously given the WHL for years, his response may had been accurate, but it was offensive.

"That was then and this is now," he said.

That summer I was curious as to how Bill would play things given what had happened to our relationship in 1999 when he chose booth over Dan. He didn't reach out to me after the WHL asked him to work with Loubardias. He also didn't admonish the WHL or Shaw for not having the decency to tell me that Loubardias was in and I was out. You read that correctly — no one from the WHL or Shaw ever bothered to contact me to tell me that they were going in a different direction.

But ... some things in life simply aren't cut and dried or black and white. Bill, a friend since 1974, is an excellent family man, a man of God, a terrific colour commentator, and a fun person to be with on the golf course, at the rink or even at the Coquihalla Summit – with or without max heat.

CHAPTER THIRTY-FOUR

A fortnight from hell

All of us face heartbreak in our lives, and I am no different. But I faced a double whammy during a two-week span in May 2013 while Edmonton and Portland were meeting in the WHL final. It was the second of three straight championship final meetings for the teams, and it was my fortnight from hell.

Two years earlier, my father, Ken, had been diagnosed with lung cancer. He had done fairly well in the interim before taking a sudden turn for the worse just as the series started. Though he had been bedridden for about two weeks, it wasn't until the day of Game 1, while I was in Portland, when he was taken into emergency. The next day, prior to Game 2, he was moved into palliative care.

After Game 2, I drove back with Stu Walters in the passenger seat. I confided that my dad wasn't doing well, but we didn't talk much about it. Still, I was glad to have the company, but unsure if I was going to see Dad again. After dropping off Stu, I arrived at Richmond General just before 4 a.m. to sit beside Dad, who was sedated. With two days between games, I was able to join my family and again sit with him on May 5 and 6. Early on the morning of May 7, I checked on him again and, with his condition unchanged, flew to Edmonton to work games 3 and 4.

Truthfully, once the puck dropped, doing the games was therapeutic as it took my mind off my father's condition for about three hours. Before the games I was quiet, and I sat by myself away from the Shaw crew (who didn't know anything about what I was going through) listening to some of Dad's favourite music. With my presence not required for post-game, I quickly exited Northlands Coliseum, flagged down a taxi and went back to my hotel to check in with my wife, sister and other family members. I had braced myself to hear of his passing, but he was hanging on. Maybe I shouldn't have been surprised. After all, he often bragged to all three of his kids about having climbed every telephone pole between Vancouver and Squamish when he was a young man working with BC Tel, the company he had been with all of his working life. Every telephone pole? We were kids, and we believed him. And now I couldn't believe he was still alive after Game 4 — Portland had won three of them.

I caught the first flight out of Edmonton the next morning, May 9, and went straight from YVR to RGH, arriving at his bedside by 8 a.m. He was still unresponsive and unchanged. After an hour, exhausted from little sleep the previous few days, I went home, just ten minutes away, for a nap. Just after eleven, Paula woke me to tell me my father had passed. We rushed back to the hospital to join the rest of my family in his room. We sat for about an hour, reminiscing and saying our goodbyes.

My mom, who had been his main caregiver for the previous two years, looked exhausted as she touched Dad's forehead for the last time. The previous day, my sister Cathy and brother-in-law Bob were so concerned about her that they took her down two floors to the emergency room to get checked out and to make sure she got some rest. That night I wrote Dad's obit, did some TV prep and got ready for a flight to Portland the next morning.

I got to the airport early and found myself on the same flight as Craig Hannon, an integral Shaw crew member whose specialty was providing replays. I'd known Craig for a few years and felt compelled to tell him my dad had died but asked him to keep it between us. Hannon was the shoulder I needed, especially when he pulled out his decrepit wallet, which he said had belonged to his dad who had died a few years earlier. Craig offered me great comfort that morning, and I remain grateful.

I didn't want to tell anyone about my father's passing because it felt like the hardest part was over. I desperately wanted to finish the series in tribute to Dad, and I also knew Ron Robison, the WHL commissioner, would have taken any excuse to slide Peter Loubardias into my chair.

After the flight, Craig and I shared a taxi to the Crowne Plaza near the rink where I thought I could grab another much-needed nap. However, just after 2 p.m., I was awakened by the vibration of my cell phone. It was Bob, my brother-in-law, calling because my sister was too distraught to talk.

"I'm afraid I have some more bad news," he said.

"What? The bad news was yesterday," I replied groggily.

"The doctors just told your mom she has a rapid form of leukemia and are saying she has between three and six months to live."

The silence at my end lasted so long that Bob had to ask if I was still there. I just couldn't process what I was hearing. We had absolutely no idea my mom was sick. In fact, her regular bloodwork done a few weeks earlier had come back fine. I was floored. When I got Cathy on the line, we talked for about twenty minutes, neither one of us making sense of the devastating news.

I could've called Shaw and bailed, but my instincts told me to forge ahead. So I walked to the rink to call Game 5 — the night after Dad died and two hours after learning Mom might have three months to live — hoping beyond hope that Portland would finish the series.

So what happened?

Naturally, the Winterhawks outshot the Oil Kings 50-31. Naturally, the game went to overtime. Honestly, I poured my heart into that telecast — I really did — and felt I had an exceptionally strong game, even managing to sound happy when Edmonton's Michael St. Croix scored to end the game.

Instead of taking a pre-arranged drive back to Vancouver, I rushed back to the hotel to call my wife. We started talking about Mom at 11 p.m. and didn't stop until the sun came up.

After a couple of hours' sleep I joined the two teams, league officials and the Shaw crew on the charter to Edmonton. It was an off-day in the series and, all alone, for reasons I am still not sure of, I decided to go to the Bob Seger concert that night at Northlands.

The next day, May 12, was Mother's Day. I began the telecast by saluting the players' moms along with their billet moms. Then, for the first time, I sent a special shout-out to my mom, who was watching.

This time Portland put Edmonton away with a stress-free 5-1 win. After broadcasting the trophy presentation, I quickly exited the booth, hopped in my rental car and roared down Wayne Gretzky Drive towards the airport. Back in Richmond around 9 p.m., I spent the rest of the evening with Mom. Cathy had taken her home the previous evening, and we all tried to lift her spirits with talk of plans we might make over the next few months. It didn't work. Mom looked more exhausted than we had ever seen her and barely made it up the stairs to Cathy's guest room. Mom was so tired and cold that Cathy and Bob took her back to RGH early the next day. When Paula and I got there, Mom looked resigned to her fate.

On May 14, they moved her to another portion of the hospital and then the next day into the same palliative care unit where Dad had just died. That afternoon, my kids and her other grandchildren Scott and Tracy, along with her only sister, Colleen, came for a balcony visit on what was a beautiful mid-May afternoon. My mother, wrapped in two thick blankets and in a wheelchair, took it all in. Not long after we sang "Over the Rainbow" severe exhaustion forced her back to bed.

By this point, everyone knew.

Once she was settled, in what was probably the most gut-wrenching moment of my life, I took each of our three kids — Palita, Anna and Ben — back into her room individually so they could hug Gramma one last time.

As the sun was setting that evening, Paula and I, Cathy and Bob, my brother Brian and his wife Julia sat with Mom, who was still alert. We remembered stories from our childhood, talked a little about Dad, played her favourite music and let her know much she meant to us. A couple of hours later, and only six days after Dad had died in the room next door, my mother, Patricia (Law) Russell, the matriarch of our family, peacefully passed away.

We sat with her for at least an hour, crying, holding her hands, hugging each other and not wanting to leave. After we departed, I told Cathy and Brian I needed to go back for just a few more seconds. I didn't tell them why, but as her youngest, the one who had spent the least amount of time with her, I felt the need to be the last to say goodbye.

Two weeks later, we had a double Celebration of Life. No one associated with the Shaw crew attended. Tom Plasteras was the only one from CKNW management to attend and pay his respects. In a classy gesture, Tom, knowing I was a lame duck host now in mourning, told me to come back to *Sportstalk* whenever I felt ready. I chose June 10.

Three weeks later, we went to Thailand, where my parents had never been — until then. Paula, her mom and our kids scattered some of my parents' ashes in the Gulf of Thailand, just steps from where we had been married years earlier in Cha-am.

CHAPTER THIRTY-FIVE

Pauser and co.

Every Monday, starting on October 22, 1984 (our second week on the air), *Sportstalk* began with:

(Theme music plays.)

Cue Dan ...

"Pleasant good evening, welcome to the Monday night edition of *Sportstalk*. Tonight we start week number [such and such] in the long history of this show, Canada's longest-running sports talk program."

The part alluding to our long history and Canada were added much later, as we modestly limited the claim to our country when in truth we didn't know of another radio sports talk show anywhere with a longer run. One show, one host, thirty years. Longevity made possible because of audience loyalty. At least one full generation of Vancouver sports fans grew up with our show.

It still surprises me how often my voice is recognized while shopping, at a bank or just out and about with my family. It's happened enough to make me wonder how *real* celebrities cope with constantly being identified. By nature, I am often shy, more nervous speaking in front of a room of fifty than I was talking to twenty thousand people on radio or on television with at least ten times more. Most people who stop me are generally kind. If female, the listener invariably takes great delight to tell me, as if she was the only one who had thought of this, "I go to bed with you every night."

Others will say: "I listen to your show every night, but have never called."

Still others ask: "How do you put up with some of the callers?"

Like an orchestra conductor, I'd like to think that handling calls, dancing through our phone board, changing the pace, assessing how much time a caller should be afforded and how much rope others should get, offering point-counterpoint, sometimes debating, on occasion offering empathy, and sometimes laughing were *Sportstalk* strengths.

I don't mean this as a negative, but to a talk-show host, callers are — though integral — props. That said, I enjoyed what most of them offered, especially during our first two decades when we could rely on a full board to keep the dialogue quickly moving. "*Sportstalk*, go ahead," is how I greeted every caller, and according to our *Sportstalk* diaries I said those words more than 150,000 times during our thirty-year run.

In our early years, some callers became as famous as our guests. Like "The Poet" (Art Senft), who listened every night during his shift as a night watchman and would scratch out poems that fit the sporting news of the time. I'm not saying the poems were great, but some were endearing.

There also was "Trucker Dan," who died in his big rig outside Merritt sometime in the early 2000s. He called often and blew his big horn, something our listeners enjoyed. I was told he had pulled off to the side of the highway, perhaps listening to our show, when he passed away.

The "Predictor" (John Connors) was a once-a-week caller who would, as the name suggests, make predictions on upcoming big games. He was often wrong.

"Ranger Smith" regularly called to gloat about his favourite team; fortunately, that was pre-1994.

Joe Babb called every Monday to offer his "Craig Coxe Update" — complete with his own unique intro using mouth-made sound effects — reviewing the Canucks enforcer's fights, especially his famous slugfests with Bob Probert.

We didn't refer to our callers by their first names, as other shows do, because I knew there was a certain mindset among listeners that only the same few people phoned into shows, and, indeed, research has shown that up to 95 percent of the audience would never consider calling. I never wanted to say every night, "Next up is Hartley in Richmond," someone who would call every night if we let him, because it made the show sound small.

A group of shift workers at the Duke Point Sawmill on Vancouver Island listened every night and called regularly during breaks. They once offered to send me a Duke Point ball cap. After I excitedly told my listeners I'd received it, I suddenly became flooded with hats from other listeners and the companies for which they worked. The hats just kept coming, nearly five hundred over the next several months, filling up one room in my Richmond townhouse. Finally, after realizing this wasn't going to end anytime soon, I asked my listeners to please stop, and I donated all the ones I received to charity, except for the original Duke Point hat.

Three university students — Derek Mah, Ben Ellison and Will Verner — became a huge hit during the 1994 playoffs by creating the Canuckmobile. They took a 1977 two-tone pale brown AMC Matador and decked it out with logos and player portraits, including Kirk McLean, Trevor Linden and Pavel Bure. They even painted "ELIBOMKCUNAC" on the front hood so, similar to ambulances, drivers ahead of them knew what was in their rearview mirror. After the Canucks forced Game 7 in Round 1, and after the boys completed their second-year UBC exams, they drove the Matador to Calgary, arriving at the Saddledome three hours before game time.

"While sitting outside the arena, we saw the Canucks bus come by," Mah fondly recalled years later. "A few days later on *Sportstalk*, Canucks assistant coach Glen Hanlon talked about how before Game 7 the team saw a bunch of kids with a car painted in Canucks colours. Hanlon went on to say, at that point, the team felt the city of Vancouver was behind them."

Afterwards, the Canuckmobile boys went to the back of the Saddledome and waited for the players. One by one, led by Cliff

Ronning, most of the Canucks autographed the car using a big sharpie. Five minutes after the bus had pulled away with the Canuckmobile following, the bus suddenly stopped. That's when Pat Quinn jumped off, walked back and also signed the car. I can only imagine what kind of cheer his players must've given him when he climbed back onto the bus. From then on, *Sportstalk* featured a nightly check-in with the Canuckmobile, greatly adding to the joyous coverage we were already providing to euphoric fans across British Columbia.

The Canuckmobile didn't go to Dallas for Round 2 but was back on the road for Round 3. Complete with sponsorships the boys had secured (partly due to *Sportstalk* exposure), they headed for Toronto for what they thought, in a 2-3-2 format, would be Game 6 and possibly Game 7. Mah says the Canuckmobile was somewhere near Winnipeg when they heard CKNW's Game 5 broadcast being simulcast on CJOB.

"The Canucks came back to tie and then we heard the overtime winner by Greg Adams," Man recalled. "We could not wait to get on the air for our nightly interview with Dan Russell on *Sportstalk*. Our scheduled time was approaching but the cell phone service was on and off. With only about five minutes before the end of show, I pulled into a gas station to use the payphone. Luckily, *Sportstalk* had been extended that night so I got on. But Dan wanted to hear from Will as well. I asked the gas station attendant if he would go to the car and wake him up, but he was not allowed to leave the cash register. Instead, Dan suggested the attendant loudly page Will on the speakers located by the pumps. Will woke up and came on."

After the Canucks beat Toronto late that night, the now famous Matador hung a right and headed for New York. A few days later, while walking down Fifth Avenue, I could barely believe my eyes. It was the Canuckmobile and it was causing a big commotion, even by New York standards, with their continuous honking and yelling, drawing jeers and multiple middle fingers from the local faithful.

"The Faxman" (Andrew Castell) listened every night and was often a valuable *Sportstalk* weapon. He was given that handle because he was our first listener to use the newly invented fax machine to send us information, most notably from his collection that includes every official scoresheet in Canucks history. Still known as "Faxman" long after people stopped using that technology, Castell also has every hockey media guide known to humankind plus the greatest individual collection of hockey memorabilia in BC.

This brings us to "The Pauser" (Paul Lafleur), a *Sportstalk* creation who, without debate, is the most-popular caller in the history of Vancouver talk radio. He and I made great radio together, both instinctively knowing our roles. "The Pauser" was the shit disturber and I was the pawn master. He was so popular that even Don Taylor, who had briefly taken over my CKNW timeslot, once invited "The Pauser" as a guest and asked him how he got his nickname.

"I used to call in when the show first started," he answered. "When I first came on, Dan was totally back on his heels. My critique of the Canucks' management was so stinging, so biting and so brilliant that Dan wasn't sure if he should let me go on because he knew he'd have to answer to Quinn and company. So he would rush me. And the more he rushed me, the more dead air I gave him."

That was pretty much it, except for the Quinn part.

But his pacing was more brilliant than many seasoned broadcasters. He would speak rapidly, slow down, build up again, then suddenly jam on the brakes just as his sentence was about to end. I remember finally saying to him, "Quit pausing. You're nothing but a pauser."

And it stuck.

Most people think he drove me crazy. Sometimes he would, but I mostly used him to drive the ratings. I would even promo that "The Pauser" was on hold. Who else does that? Who promos an actual caller, then holds the audience for up to twenty minutes before putting him on? I used to hear from listeners who said they sat in their driveways waiting to hear him while wondering what their neighbours thought about a lone occupant sitting in the dark in their car.

Once on, Lafleur could entertain, aggravate or both. He was always prepared, filled with what he thought were cutting edge ideas and opinions. Deep down, as a Vancouverite, he wanted the Canucks to do well but only if they did things his way.

Lafleur also menacingly began showing up at the Canucks' training camp sites from which we were broadcasting. One night in Parksville after the players had returned from a pre-season game down the road in Cowichan, a few of them began heading up to their rooms. But before the elevator could close, "The Pauser" stuck his hand into the opening, causing the doors to reopen. That allowed him to say to (future Canucks general manager) Jim Benning, loud enough for the entire lobby to hear, "You're a fringe player."

Not a bad player. Fringe!

While training at Victoria's Memorial Arena, "The Pauser" cornered Quinn in one of the nooks and crannies near the dressing room and started telling the Canucks' super-boss how to run his team. I watched that exchange closely, not entirely certain Quinn wasn't going to drill him.

Later that same night we tried not to allow the disruptive Lafleur anywhere near our live broadcast location in the lobby of Harbour Towers. Unable to disrupt from inside, "The Pauser" jockeyed his way into a small garden outside the window right beside our remote setup. After loudly knocking on the glass to get our attention, he then turned around, dropped his pants and, with cheeks touching the window, showed us a full "Pauser" moon.

"The Pauser" argued, berated and agitated better than anyone, while mixing in self-deprecating humour. I'd like to think I brought out the best in him, but maybe it was the opposite.

Dan: "Pauser, I was told by an impeccable source at UBC that you, Mr. Pauser, went to the UBC radio station and lobbied to get your own ten-to-midnight show to go head-to-head against *Sportstalk*. Can you confirm or deny this?

Pauser: "As a matter of fact I said, 'Listen, I've been cut off one too many times. Pure unadulterated fascist censorship. I don't like it, and as a matter of fact I think it's time that Dan and I duel on the airwaves ... and as a matter of fact [now chuckling] I still haven't heard back from them."

Dan: "So you believe I quashed that because I knew if we had to go head-to-head, *Sportstalk* would be in trouble?"

Pauser: "I think you should beat me to the punch and bring me on as a co-host one day a week. My segment would be 'Ask the Pauser.' I can do [Jyrki] Lumme in thirty seconds."

Both: (Long pause ... then simultaneous bursts of laughter.)

"The Pauser" also took great delight in bragging to our listeners about how *Sportstalk* made him a star and that he often ate for free at certain east side restaurants because the owners loved him.

My only legitimate problem with Lafleur was when he would get carried away off the air. He would swear at our producers — once calling Bob Addison a "fucking Nazi" — when they wouldn't put him on right away. That also became on-air fodder, with me warning him that if he continued, I'd put him in the *Sportstalk* penalty box. Eventually he had to be penalized. His first offence cost him a month and later escalated to a year, prompting callers to occasionally inquire as to when he would be released.

After he died at sixty in 2009, his *Vancouver Sun* obit included: "Known as 'The Pauser,' Paul will also be remembered by many old friends and hockey fans. *Sportstalk* will never be the same. Always entertaining, informative and a pleasure to hear. Who's going to keep Brian Burke, the Canucks and Dan Russell in line now?"

The answer was: no one. At least, never in the same way.

CHAPTER THIRTY-SIX

Fired ... but still on the air

Officially, the death of *Sportstalk* on CKNW occurred in August 2013. Unofficially, I knew fourteen months earlier when I went on vacation and management wouldn't allow me to approve my guest host, as stipulated in my contract.

David Pratt had been let go from Team 1040 a few months earlier. Before that, he was fired as a *Province* columnist. Now out of work, he began bragging to anyone within earshot that CKNW would soon be giving him the afternoon drive slot. Though I doubt that was ever seriously considered, 'NW did give him a show that he mostly pre-recorded and aired just before *Sportstalk*. Further watering down the sports airwaves was one thing, but I hated it when program director Tom Plasteras, without my approval, named Pratt as my summer guest host.

The tea leaves were clear, especially when Plasteras wouldn't return my calls on the matter. By then, Plasteras was avoiding me at every turn, including our monthly Marpole White Spot lunch he had initiated as a way to insure we stayed close while working opposite hours.

I finally pinned him down a couple of days before my vacation. He knew I wasn't pleased but agreed I could send him the parameters I expected Pratt to conform to regarding what was still my show.

Plasteras approved my twelve-point format memo, and we sent it to Pratt and his producer Dave Sheldon. The memo was laughed off as Pratt changed the format, regular features and some theme music while trying to duplicate his old Team 1040 format. When I contacted Plasteras a few days after Pratt began, he told me he was "working on it." I knew that was bullshit. When nothing changed, I tried calling again, but he ignored me.

There were fourteen months left in the contract extension former general manager JJ (Jim) Johnston had signed me to in 2008, and Plasteras now was showing me there wouldn't be another one. The guest-host snub made that clear, but the die was cast when Corus moved Johnston to oversee Ontario stations in Cornwall and Peterborough, among other communities.

Brad Phillips, the new GM, had arrived in November. Prior to that, he had been at Astral Radio, and before that at City TV at a time when many employees were laid off. Most at CKNW thought he was brought in to do the same. In the weeks after Phillips arrived, he set up individual meetings with every employee and asked me to meet on February 6, 2013. I decided to take advantage of his (alleged) getting-to-know-me meeting by feeling him out regarding my future, specifically by drawing his attention to an important clause in our contract.

"Should *Sportstalk* still be on the air on January 1, 2013, then Corus will enter into negotiations with *Sportstalk* with a view to reaching a new agreement for the period starting after the contract expires on August 31. Should no negotiations take place by March 1, then *Sportstalk* is free to negotiate with any other party."

Given we were in that window, I asked Phillips if he was aware of this clause. He claimed not to have looked at it, which was implausible given he had called this meeting. I also told him I hadn't heard a word from Plasteras on this topic. I informed Phillips that if I didn't receive any communication by March 15, I would consider that as CKNW not wanting *Sportstalk* beyond August 31 and would make plans accordingly.

Even though he spent most of that meeting deflecting the talk away from *Sportstalk*, there was one topic Phillips was keenly interested in that I found most unusual. He quizzed me for almost ten minutes about how I felt Plasteras was doing as program director. *Using part of this meeting to dig up dirt on my immediate supervisor? How unbecoming*, I thought.

The next week — a day before leaving with my family for a driving vacation to California — I met with Plasteras to reiterate that I wasn't going to twist in the wind, as had happened previously. Before leaving town, I got a message from Plasteras saying Phillips would meet with me a couple of days after I returned. On the drive back from California, I kept joking with my family, "We have to hurry up and get home so I can get fired."

While driving in to meet Phillips on March 6, Plasteras called to let me know he would also be joining us. *Great*, I thought, *another two-against-one job*. I had learned over the years to take copious notes at these meetings, so after a moment or two of small talk, Plasteras said they had "decided not to renew the contract." That's all he said, and he waited a few seconds for my response.

"Cool," I said. Then I asked a one-word question: "Reasons?"

That obvious question seemed to rattle him. Plasteras nervously stumbled through some explanation about block programming, the CKNW format being news talk and my show no longer fitting that format. He then said they wouldn't be replacing *Sportstalk* with another sports show. To this point, Phillips had remained mute. That ended when I asked him to elaborate on his reasons.

"You asked us to meet with you, and we made the decision," he said.

"Because this writing had been on the wall for a long time," I replied.

Plasteras jumped in to deny that, saying they had just made the decision, a claim I met with laughter.

"Before I went to California you said Brad would meet me two days afterwards, so of course you guys already knew," I said.

They both said the decision had nothing to do with ratings or performance, but Phillips did say, "We do pay you a lot of money."

About a minute later, he felt compelled to tell me how hard this was on them, to which I replied that was only because I had forced their hand. That's when Phillips said CKNW would "honour the contract," which made me think, *As opposed to what?*

As I was getting up to leave, Phillips stopped me as he wanted to discuss what was next. *He's asking me that?* It turns out this was his most important topic: how to position the announcement so CKNW wouldn't look bad. I asked if they were going to buy me out. Phillips quickly said no.

"You'll keep me on air until the end of August?" I asked knowing most stations would never dare take that chance. "Or am I going to find out in June that you will pull the plug then?"

Phillips answer was, "If your performance declines, which I don't expect it to, then we would do something."

Next, Phillips asked how we should craft the wording of an announcement.

"Just tell the truth ... it's happened before," I said, wondering why he was even asking.

Phillips then launched into a diatribe that included how "people in your position often care about how things are worded." He sounded like an experienced hatchet man might. He then tried selling me on caring about how this would look for me if it was announced as a firing.

And then it clicked!

The only thing he cared about was 'NW not coming off as heartless pricks to my audience and the staff. Phillips knew the station would look better if this was positioned as "Dan Russell's decision." I was getting worn down, so told him that it should just reflect the truth. Undaunted, he decided both sides should "work on the wording and timing of the announcement." The meeting ended without a handshake or even a goodbye. As I was nearest the door, I just got up and walked away.

Afterwards, I often kicked myself for not warning Plasteras that Phillips had been quizzing me about his performance the previous month. I wish I'd had the balls to say, "Heads up, Tom, you may be next."

The next few days were highly unusual. After being fired on a Wednesday, I chose to work that night when they said I didn't have to. I did the same on the Thursday, took a day off to do a WHL game in Kamloops on Friday, then was back on the following Monday, remaining quiet the entire time while waiting for CKNW to announce it.

The crafting of the announcement dragged on for days before they finally sent me a draft that read: "We would like to let everyone know that Dan Russell has advised us that after much deliberation he will be leaving CKNW when our current agreement expires on August 31, 2013."

Had they not heard a word I said?

I sent back a note rejecting that and telling Plasteras, "Honesty always being my best policy I see no reason not to stick 100% to the truth." I said if they didn't, I would.

A final memo was crafted after more back and forth. It read: "We would like to let everyone know that we have advised Dan Russell we will not be renewing his agreement which expires later this year. We are and have been very proud to carry *SportsTalk* [sic] on CKNW over the years and thank Dan for his significant contribution to the station's success."

Upon the advice of my co-counsel Michael Watt, who was concerned about what CKNW wanted to do with the rest of my contract, I sent Plasteras a copy of the editorial I planned to read once my firing was announced. That same morning, March 12, I flew to Edmonton and, while setting up my remote equipment before the WHL game, Watt called to say I was suspended, meaning I wasn't allowed to host *Sportstalk* that night. Phillips didn't like my editorial that said:

> So here we are in the same spot that we found ourselves
> in about a decade ago as CKNW has decided not to
> renew the *Sportstalk* agreement when it expires later
> this year.

Just as was the case in 2000, we saw this coming a mile away. Certain events, which I won't go into now but will address in the future, occurred starting last June that made it very clear that CKNW was going to go away from *Sportstalk*.

And by the way, that is 100% their prerogative — it's their station, they've been kind enough over the years to let me occupy a time slot on their station, all things do come to an end as we know, and that's the case here. I will continue with my show as per my agreement, and after that *Sportstalk* will no longer be with CKNW.

I believe most people learn to read the people they are working for and believe me, in my case, it's never been a hard read.

I not only saw this coming, but I also initiated two meetings in the past few weeks to confirm my suspicion, and after letting CKNW know that I wasn't going to twist in the wind, I was told last Wednesday of their decision.

The explanation I was given was that *Sportstalk* no longer fit the format and/or branding of the radio station.

As for the future of *Sportstalk*? Perhaps the show has run its course?

Right now, I don't know if that's the case or not. I only know that it has on CKNW after the current agreement expires.

If it's completely over, then it's been a twenty-nine-year run that we're proud of and predict won't be duplicated by many.

Or perhaps *Sportstalk* will be reinvented one final time, as already I've had different options presented to me. One never knows the future, but I'm looking forward to turning the page.

Until then I hope listeners will stay with us on CKNW until it's finished.

I believe most everyone would consider that to be fair. Phillips did not. After returning from Edmonton the next day, I was summoned to yet another meeting. Knowing it would be another two-on-one job, I requested that my counsel be allowed to join us. Phillips wouldn't allow it. Believing that to be unfair, Watt and I prepared these questions to ask Phillips and Plasteras.

— Can you tell me what I've done wrong during this process in terms of honouring my obligation?

— What is your problem with my editorial?

— What is your expectation as to what happens on the air when this is announced, in terms of callers and guests?

Plasteras began the meeting by speaking for several minutes. His points included:

"Both parties want to fulfill your obligation ... initially we were starting to work on messaging but then saw your editorial ... we spent a good deal of time discussing it and we are not comfortable with that editorial, or really any editorial about your status ... we think it's an internal matter. We don't see it as fodder for the program and so we don't consent to doing something like that.

"Further to that, we don't think there should be any comment by yourself on the show or publicly about your contract status while you are under contract to the company.

"Just as you expect us to have your cheques on time, we expect you to comply with what's in your contract ... and there are confidentiality clauses ... we don't want negativity about Corus and its management ... and what we need from you is an indication as to whether or not you are going to be able to do that."

Watt warned me beforehand that CKNW might attempt to find grounds to fire me, which would force me to file suit in order to get paid out. My instructions, above all else, were to protect my contract. However, I did want to know how they believed this could be handled on a live talk show. Not having any experience hosting my kind of program, Plasteras and Phillips could only offer weak suggestions like having my producer screen callers closer or suggesting that if the subject of the firing came up, I would say "No comment."

Once again, Phillips came back to the announcement.

Russell: "So today is almost over. I don't think it can be released today. I haven't seen the wording on it yet, so ..."

Plasteras: "Well ..."

(Plasteras stops talking. Phillips mouths words towards Plasteras. More pausing.)

Phillips: "Maybe do you want to step out for a second and just talk about this and come back?"

Plasteras: "Sure."

Phillips: "That might be the appropriate thing to do. Would you mind if we do that, Dan?"

Russell: "Pardon?"

Phillips: "You mind if we step out? No, we will step out. You stay here. I just want to talk with Tom about something if you don't mind."

Wait a minute, another new rule? First, they outnumbered me. Then they banned my lawyer. Now, as if the game isn't slanted enough for them, they also get to use a timeout? While they were gone, I re-read the wording of the announcement while reminding myself to protect the contract.

They came back five minutes later.

Phillips: "Sorry, Dan. Sorry about that. We would like to make that announcement as soon as possible."

I'm certain their timeout really wasn't about messaging but rather their having not expected my co-operation. When I agreed to their edicts I believe that messed up any plan they may have had of citing a breach, which would have led them to remove me from the air and into potential litigation.

Why do I believe that? Because Plasteras started in once again ...

Plasteras: "So ... you are giving us your word ... and that you don't have a problem with what we have outlined in terms of our expectation going forward, which we will provide you?"

Phillips: "You understand this is a matter between you and us?"

Russell: "No problem."

Phillips then essentially confirmed what his plan had been by saying, "Umm. We do acknowledge that you have done your show professionally since [firing]. We do acknowledge that. We do need to say to you though that, um, we now advise you, as management of the radio station, that we would consider any disclosure or commentary on this can be a breach of your contract. You understand that?"

Russell: "Commentary by me or a caller?"

Phillips: "Well ..."

Plasteras: "Both."

Still not entirely convinced, or perhaps buying himself more time to look for any kind of a breach, Phillips kept my suspension in place that night.

The following day (and this was legitimate) I came down with laryngitis, keeping me off air until March 20. When I returned, in the name of protecting the contract, I shelved the editorial.

Had it been left to Plasteras, I believe they would have paid me out, which is exactly what he had done one morning ten years earlier when he suddenly went on air and said, "I'm here to inform you that CKNW has ended its relationship with *The Rafe Mair Show*." Plasteras was also there when I was removed in May of 2000, four months before that contract ended. He knew it was always better to remove a fired talk-show host and pay them out. But Phillips, who hated me having the clout to force the issue, made me keep working. In time he would pay for his bullheadedness.

Then, with six weeks left in my contract, came perhaps the most bizarre happening in the history of my career — something directly related to Phillips digging for Plasteras dirt, asking questions and feverishly scribbling notes in our February meeting. It was Plasteras's turn to be on the other side. In what may have been a radio first, the man who officially fired me in March was himself fired four months later. While I was still in the building!

However, the similarities ended there.

Unlike my prolonged CKNW death, this was a quick hit with Phillips (or an associate) summoning an unsuspecting Plasteras to the boardroom to be terminated. Plasteras wasn't even allowed back upstairs to collect his belongings. Security escorted Plasteras, who had served there for more than two decades, to the elevator and out of the TD Tower.

Even though I back-end loaded seven of my remaining ten weeks as vacation time, Phillips still wanted his pound of flesh. He was determined to make me work until the bitter end. Then, months after saying if I didn't act in accordance with their wishes they'd consider it a breach of contract and thereby inferring I might not get fully paid out, Phillips got sloppy and was beaten at his own game. Because what if CKNW had paid me out before my contract ended?

It was standard for Corus to pay via direct deposit twice a month, but for their own accounting reasons payday didn't necessarily fall on the middle and last day of the month. Sometimes, as it was in August 2013, money could be deposited several days earlier. I'm sure Phillips was unaware that I had been paid every dollar owing from the contract. He would find out soon when, rather than call in sick the rest of the week, I chose to get a few things off my chest.

"Pleasant good evening, welcome to the Wednesday night edition of *Sportstalk* on CKNW and the *Sportstalk* radio network."

No, I wasn't going to wait until Friday because I knew we had more listeners earlier in the week. Plus I wanted the element of surprise.

"First things first ... as you can tell, my access [key] card worked again! I am saying that tongue-in-cheek, but I have seen stranger things happen. You kick around this business for a while and you see everything. The last words I was given by management months ago, specifically PD Tom Plasteras, who no longer works here, and GM Brad Phillips, the one who made the decision, was *Sportstalk* doesn't fit the branding of what they want CKNW to be."

My comments lasted several minutes and covered a few topics. I also said I was sincerely thankful for the platform I had on a station that had once been a sports powerhouse. I told our listeners that *Sportstalk* would continue on another station because I didn't want it killed off by someone who thought CKNW listeners didn't care about sports. Later, I took a run at morning host Bill Good — nicknamed by some of us as "Company Man" — who, two days earlier, had ass-kissingly defended management on air for the *Sportstalk* decision by using their exact words: "It no longer fits the branding."

The next day, yet another phone call. But rather than step up himself, Phillips tasked interim program director Ian Koenigsfest to try and get more assurance from fully-paid Dan.

"Otherwise," Ian said, "we will take you off the air."

I told Koenigsfest that the next two nights were pre-planned, so nothing was going to happen. Nor did it.

Our sign-off on August 30, 2013, was a much bigger deal than just marking the end of *Sportstalk* on that station. As was the case twenty-five years earlier when I was the last voice to be heard on former talk powerhouse CJOR, our sign-off marked the end to what had been a decades-long CKNW sports legacy. Davidson, Cox, Robson, McKeachie, McConnell, Larscheid, Hughson, Hodge, McRae, Barnet, Powell, Canucks, Lions, Grizzlies — all gone before me. *Sportstalk* with Dan Russell — not unlike Mary Richards at WJM-TV — was the last one to turn out the lights.

CHAPTER THIRTY-SEVEN

Week no. 1,508 — last call

I felt blessed to have caught the last big radio wave — especially at CJOR, CKWX, CFMI and CKNW — when, pre-streaming, you could marvel at its extraordinary impact. Even though I don't believe terrestrial radio will die completely — at least not until all vehicles are self-driving — the glory days continue to fade farther away (especially in advertising revenue) with each passing year.

Believing I had earned the right not to have anyone else dictate the end of *Sportstalk*, and because our CKNW ratings remained strong, I signed with CISL 650, but with an entirely different model. I purchased my airtime, sold the advertising, paid all expenses and kept what was left over. In the first few months I made more money than I had at CKNW, but I was frustrated at not being able to find a sales manager. Doug Lum, a good friend and long-time sponsor, helped put my business plan together and with his many contacts was the driving force behind our first wave of sponsors when we hit the CISL airwaves on September 29, 2013. Before taking its final breath, CISL was subletting most of its airtime. It wasn't illegal, but it certainly wasn't in the spirit of what a licensed broadcaster should be doing.

On CISL, we were introduced by John Ashbridge, a lovely man with a beautiful voice who had served as a terrific public address announcer for the Canucks and Giants, something that had started as a side job away from his successful CKNW news and management career. Ashbridge, who, sadly, passed in 2018, was CKNW's network co-ordinator until 2005 and was unquestionably the most organized manager I'd seen, with various files and papers meticulously piled on his desk, each held in place with an NHL hockey puck/paperweight.

Thankfully, Heath Morgan came along to take care of all the technical and production stress. Lee Powell eased some of my burden by professionally co-hosting, and my sister Cathy looked after accounting. Unfortunately, from a continuity standpoint, not being able to bring over Brook Ward for Canucks game nights stung.

Just as I had gained an entire new appreciation for writers when I became a *Vancouver Sun* columnist, I now have an even bigger appreciation for those who successfully attract and renew sponsors, especially in this age of multi-platforms. But with so much rejection, I came to wonder how they could find that job enjoyable. Do they have different DNA than the average human? I spent all my daytime hours selling, which meant I was often exhausted when I got to the studio. When some of our clients elected not to renew, I could read the writing on the wall. Every month our show finished in the black and paid its bills, but I knew the profits would decline, and I had no interest in losing money just to keep the "Good Ship *Sportstalk*" afloat.

I couldn't blame the sponsors. The show had failed to hit a home run in the ratings. CISL was lowly ranked, its signal had dark spots in key parts of the Lower Mainland, the market was oversaturated, and I was overtired. In many ways, I was in a catch-22. Without sponsors there wouldn't be a show. But the grind of securing and servicing them meant there wasn't enough creative juice time.

Feeding into that, and causing me to become guilty of flogging a dead horse, was that sixteen of the Canucks' first forty-five games that season went to overtime, which rewards losing. I hated it, mostly because it sucked in gullible fans. No other credible sport offers loser points or removes players from the playing surface when the score is tied, yet that goes out the window when they begin the process of determining the Stanley Cup winner.

Was I the only hockey purist in North America?

Did no one else care:

— That teams could face each other six times in a regular season with each able to claim a winning record in the series?

— The format caused some of the most boring hockey ever during the last ten minutes of a third period when the teams tied and were locking things down for fear of losing their loser point?

— That in an east-west overtime game, nothing bad occurred in the standings if the puck went in your net, except the game stopping?

— That an entire generation has no idea what a true "four-pointer" means and how excitingly hyped they once were late in a season during a tight playoff race?

— That a team can clinch a playoff spot by losing?

— How silly it looks when there are penalties in overtime and the manpower on the ice is all over the map?

— How dumb it is to hear broadcasters say, for example, the Jets have points in eight straight games when many of them couldv'e been losses?

— That the standings were pure when they had only three columns: wins, losses and ties?

Perhaps I was showing my age. I come from an era where some games were just screaming to finish tied and no one complained.

On the contrary, if, for example, the 1975 Canucks scored late at Philadelphia to get one point out of the Spectrum, it was a huge deal at school with my friends the next day. Not one of them said, "Gee, don't you think they should've kept playing?"

I wish I could have stopped calling it "Circus Time" because I agreed with those who felt it sounded like a broken record. But try as I might, I couldn't normalize it. It was like a mental block.

Though symbolic, that wasn't the reason I decided to end things. Overall, I just felt my listeners needed a break from me and I needed a break from having to constantly formulate opinion. In what was a lovely gesture, Stan Smyl requested to come on our penultimate show to tell our listeners what *Sportstalk* had meant to him and the marketplace. I told Smyl there was only one thing on *Sportstalk* that I always wanted to say but was never able to: "Tonight we come your way on a night when the Vancouver Canucks have won the Stanley Cup."

After 1,508 weeks, *Sportstalk*'s last hurrah came on May 1, 2014, ending on the same date and in the same studio where I had launched my on-air career thirty-four years earlier as CISL's first ever voice.

CHAPTER THIRTY-EIGHT

Sportstalk's secret sauce

During *Sportstalk*'s three-decade run, the media landscape totally changed. It was hard for anyone's voice to be heard — with radio, TV and print the only outlets when we started in 1984. But by 2013 anyone could have their voice heard. Andy Warhol's vision of everyone having their fifteen minutes of fame was even more possible. Put another way, I'm glad I caught at least the tail-end of a semi-golden age of radio. And I will forever be proud of having been the first in Vancouver to make sports talk radio a success.

What was *Sportstalk*'s secret sauce? Why did we enjoy such longevity? What separated us from the others? Aside from being in the right place at the right time, there were a handful of essential ingredients. Here are the most important ones:

UNDERSTANDING THE CRAFT

I'm a professional broadcaster who just happened to be talking about sports. Not the other way around. I used those skills to identify, capture, inform, provoke, entertain, and build and hold an audience. Then I relied on listeners' loyalty to spread the *Sportstalk* gospel. To accomplish this, *Sportstalk* had to be compelling enough to keep listeners through quarter hours and give them a reason to sit through commercials even when they were dead tired and had to get up for work the next day.

Pure broadcasters know how to do this.

Developing and understanding my role took time, and I had to evolve. But when I fully grasped this role, I knew it (unevenly) alternated between opinionist, interviewer, conversationalist and entertainer. Some people misidentified me as a sports expert and, while I did keep up with most things, my main interest was to improve as a broadcaster. I seldom cheered for a team; I always cheered for the show. The expertise I built was because I got to ask endless questions of some of the greatest sports figures — especially hockey players, coaches, managers and scouts — and a lot of what I heard rubbed off on me. Whether consciously or not, I knew I first needed to build my credibility before I could be taken seriously as an editorialist. As time went on, I was able to take many of the things I learned from guests (on and off the air) to help formulate what I hoped were thought-provoking opinions.

I never considered myself the star of *Sportstalk* — the guests and callers were. My skill was bringing out the best in them. In my early CJOR years (1984-89), I often referred to myself as a traffic cop in charge of keeping things moving.

BEING CONSISTENTLY INCONSISTENT

I was a stickler for format consistency — same theme music throughout, same words off the top of each hour, scoreboard slotted in same spot, Rod Beaton on Tuesday, Brian Burke on Wednesday, Harry Neale on Thursday, etc. — because it gave our listeners a comfort zone. But in and around all of that, our listeners often didn't know what they would hear next.

I might start with an editorial but only if I had something strong to say. Some hosts begin every show with an editorial, which, to me, is a surefire indicator they sometimes share opinion only out of obligation.

From time to time we would mix things up with something we called "concept shows." For example, a couple of days before the final NHL regular-season game at the Pacific Coliseum in April 1995, I decided the perfect place to broadcast from would be the Canucks players' bench. It was an off-night and the rink was quiet but, at 10 p.m., Jim Robson, who was never heard from ice level, joined us. As did Pat Quinn, a player *at* the bench on opening night in 1970 and *behind* it in the 1994 Stanley Cup Final. Captains Stan Smyl ('82) and Trevor Linden ('94) were also there. Harry Neale, one of the architects of the 1982 Stanley Cup Final team, joined us from Buffalo. We also brought in Ron Shute, the original and long-time Canucks stick boy who had been at that bench more than any other person. Lee Powell and Steve Snelgrove also came down, as did original season ticket holder Andrew "Faxman" Castell.

It was great theatre of the mind. I knew my listeners could clearly envision us standing there and were undoubtedly soaking in the great memories. After the show, Scott Woodgate, Snelgrove, Powell, Castell and I played shinny on NHL ice until 1 a.m. It was hard not to remember so many of my boyhood memories, both listening to and attending many games in the building, which outside of my home and school was one I'd been in more than any other.

A great concept caller night was when I asked listeners to share their stories of going to their first NHL games. You couldn't buy a phone line that night as listeners were eager to tell us how old they were, where they sat, who took them, which team they watched play the Canucks, who won, etc. Like a first kiss, I guess you never forget your first NHL game.

"You Be the Star" was another successful concept whereby callers shared their personal greatest moments of sports glory no matter how old they were at the time. What amazed me the most was how people vividly remembered their star moments, sometimes from two decades or more earlier, in minute detail.

Our Christmas show was consistent, playing many of the same features we'd catalogued. That included a radio play — *PING* — once done in studio by Local Anxiety, featuring Mark Leiren-Young. It told the story of a rabid Canucks fan who woke up in 1997 after slipping into a coma just before the 1994 final. Of course, he discovered Vancouver not only had lost to the Rangers but that Mark

Messier now was captain of the Canucks, Trevor Linden had been traded and Pat Quinn had been fired. Every year we had numerous requests to play it.

STARTING STRONG

Getting each show off to a great start was of utmost importance, which is why the first couple of minutes each night were scripted, along with most of the editorials I delivered. I knew if we fumbled the ball in the first two minutes, it would stay in my head and the rest of the show was destined to be or feel sloppy.

Early on, producer Scott Woodgate and I often lived by the famous six P's — proper preparation preventing piss-poor performance — to insure we started well. Also, unless our upcoming guest had marquee value, I often wouldn't promote their name but rather sell our listeners on the topic we were about to cover. My philosophy was to never give the listener a chance to pass on a segment before they started hearing it just because they hadn't heard of the guest. More times than not I felt I could hook someone if I could manage to hold them through the commercial break.

TIME SLOT

I always considered it tremendously advantageous to be heard after the hustle and bustle of a typical listener's day. Their work was finished, they had eaten dinner, put kids to bed and their phones were quiet. In other words, I got them during the calmest time of their day, which gave me the golden opportunity to engage them when they weren't distracted.

I confidently believe, given my interviewing and open-line skills, I could've been successful hosting a current affairs show in the same late-evening time slot. Candidly, I was hoping, especially with aging talk-show hosts set to retire, that CKNW might consider me for a non-sports show. There are plenty of examples of sports people who made that transition: Bill Good, Bob Costas, Bryant Gumbel, Keith Olbermann and Steve Raible, just to name a few.

TRUSTING YOUR PRODUCER

Almost nothing was more important than the host-producer relationship. I feel fortunate to have had only four of them during our long run, which meant plenty of time to forge great chemistry with each.

John Martin (1985-88), Scott Woodgate (1988-98), Bob Addison (1998-2010) and Heath Morgan (2010-14) were talented, tireless and truly loyal — each determined to make every show the best it could be.

Martin was a tenacious bulldog with his scattered ideas. Sometimes too tenacious and sometimes too scattered, which is why I nicknamed him "Gurr-head." But his heart was always in the right place.

Woodgate was a triple-threat — strong at tracking guests, a master at knowing which callers to insert at the right time and a great ear for the production of the show.

Addison's research prep was outstanding. He had great sports knowledge, knew exactly when to jump on the air to give the show a boost and refused to go home until the next day was set.

Not only was Morgan incredibly organized, but I never had to ask him twice for anything. In many ways, he was a hybrid of the other three but completely unflappable. Never once did I see him panic or even raise his voice.

"Provide an environment for me to do my best work" was how I always described their job description. That meant the obvious tasks such as organizing guests, research, gathering audio clips and screening calls. It also meant adhering to all my silly idiosyncrasies, such as having the studio temperature set at David Letterman-like cold, bright lighting to keep us awake, blue pens only, computers always in the same position, a fresh chair (switched from the host of the preceding show), proper headphones, scoreboard consistently laid out, no guests of any sort in their control room booth and no yawning. I wasn't kidding. Even though the show was on late, the last thing I wanted was to look through the glass and see my producer yawning because, in my mind, that translated to … a boring show. Addison became quite adept at turning around to stifle them or leaving the room in order to have a good yawn.

My producers each understood the high bar we had set and the size of the audience we needed to please. We didn't always achieve what we wanted, but it sure felt satisfying when we did. But even on those nights that glow of satisfaction usually lasted only a few minutes until reality set in — as in, "What are we doing tomorrow night?"

Every night my producer and I would rate the show, and we were harder on ourselves than any Russian figure skating judge would have been. We scored many between 7 and 7.5. Seldom did we give ourselves anything higher than a 9, except perhaps in 1994. The only great thing about having a bad score was that there was always a chance to hit refresh the next night.

GOING ON LOCATION

Taking *Sportstalk* on the road as often as we did was great for our listeners. Over the years, many told me they felt a small part of themselves was with us during these often exciting trips. For example, I was able to brag to our audience that I shook President Ronald Reagan's hand when we took *Sportstalk* to Los Angeles for Wayne Gretzky's first Stanley Cup Final with the Kings in 1993. Not to be outdone, Woodgate bragged about turning around and accidentally running into Goldie Hawn's boobs in a packed throng outside the Kings' dressing room. We had been in Edmonton for the dramatics the first time Gretzky returned wearing a Kings uniform in October 1988, and again in February 1989 when the city got to cheer him (named game MVP) as part of the Western Conference team in the All-Star Game.

In 1999, Addison and I went to Florida to cover the NHL All-Star Game and the Super Bowl. First, we overnighted in Toronto and, despite landing late, I wanted to show Addison Maple Leaf Gardens, as he had never been. Arriving at the back door around 11 p.m., we walked in an unlocked door and soon were met by a security guard. After I politely explained who we were and the show we did, he graciously gave us the green light to roam around. We did just that for about an hour. I was happy to be back inside but more thrilled to provide Addison with that memory. An hour later, we were talking about our self-tour when we began our show at 1 a.m. ET from Canadian Press in downtown Toronto.

Once in Florida, our first assignment was to have been the All-Star Game at Tampa. But we weren't able to watch it because Brian Burke had finally gotten around to firing Mike Keenan, replacing him with Marc Crawford, moments before puck drop. So we spent the entire game working that story for a unique late Sunday afternoon *Sportstalk* special on CKNW.

After we signed off at 9 p.m. ET, Addison and I drove five hours from Tampa to Miami for a week of shows from Super Bowl XXXIII, plus, as timing would have it, we also covered Pavel Bure's first Florida home game versus Montreal. The number one purpose that night was to hear Bure talk about playing in front of non-Vancouver home fans for the first time in his NHL career. Unfortunately, Addison got stuck in an elevator for nearly a half hour on his way to the dressing room and missed Bure. It was a bad break, especially after we later learned it was only one flight of stairs.

The media hall at the Super Bowl is always a sight to behold, especially the area from where an orgy of sports talk shows originate back to various home markets around North America. While frantically busy and noisy in the middle of the day, we mostly had the place to ourselves when we were on from midnight to 3 a.m.

Media is treated like gold that week, with endless food, soft drinks, beer, computer work stations, comfortable lounge areas, giant TVs, etc. In Miami, there also was a ping-pong table where I (a one-time Richmond Jr. champion) decided to only play another media member if it was for one dollar per game. Many challenged, but yours truly went undefeated.

However, that wasn't our biggest Super Bowl money maker. I'm not certain how, but Woodgate and I found ourselves holding an extra pair of tickets, in addition to our media passes, for the 1998 game in San Diego between Green Bay and Denver. I tasked Woodgate with unloading them and then watched him scan through the ticket-broker ads in a newspaper. After calling one of them he told me we had to head to a street corner two blocks from our hotel and wait for a specific make and model car. When it approached, a brown envelope containing cash was held outside the passenger side window as Woodgate handed over the tickets. Whoever was in that car zoomed off. The transaction took about ten seconds, and Woodgate and I split the $1,500. Incidentally, the only two Super Bowls we went to were both won by John Elway's Broncos, a team that couldn't win the big game until *Sportstalk* showed up.

When it came to Grey Cup games, other than the ones played in Vancouver, the only other one we broadcast from was in 1988 when Winnipeg beat BC 22-21 in Ottawa. They held on when Matt Dunigan's apparent game-winning touchdown throw to Jan Carinci with two minutes left was tipped at the line of scrimmage by Michael Gray.

We also squeezed in one trip to the NCAA Final Four in Seattle, which I should have remembered only because of Michigan's OT title game win over Seton Hall. Instead, I mostly recall an incredible stroke of domestic luck. Prior to leaving early Saturday morning, I put a load of clothes in the dryer and hit start. Returning home seventy hours later, the machine was still trying to dry my clothes. I will never know how there wasn't a fire. To this day I think about that every time I check a dryer's lint trap.

ENGAGE AND ENTERTAIN

We tried to do many little things to keep our listeners engaged, like our unique way of updating the NHL standings starting each

January. We would go through the top eight in the west, playing a corny five-second clip after I read each team's point total. We always concluded with the team the Canucks would meet if the playoffs started the next day or which golf course they would be playing if they weren't in the top eight.

Once, after the Vancouver Grizzlies put out a news release exaggerating how their new Richmond practice facility, located at No. 6 Road and Steveston Highway, was only ten minutes from the airport, we decided to put that claim to the test. We solicited Snelgrove to drive to the facility, call us and wait for instructions. Once there, we asked Snelgrove to tell our listeners what kind of car he was driving and that we would time his drive from the facility to YVR. By his own admission his car wasn't going to turn heads.

"I was driving a piece of shit Toyota I'd paid five hundred dollars for," he later recalled.

Apparently, it was easy to identify because as he was driving along Grant McConachie Way and talking to us on the air, an RCMP car pulled up behind with lights flashing. The two constables had been listening to the show and realized what was happening. They detained Snelgrove long enough that we never did get an official time to argue against the Grizzlies' claim.

Each night we concluded by having the top sports star of that night playing with the *Sportstalk* Orchestra.

For many years during open-phones I would randomly blow the Fogg N' Suds horn for our "Caller of the Night." By themselves they weren't that big a deal, but again they offered consistency for our regular listeners.

One particular night just before midnight, a late-to-the-party caller named Trevor wanted me to catch him up on something we had previously discussed, so I asked him why he wasn't tuned in earlier. He said he was "talking to a girl." I asked him if he was interested in her. He confirmed it. I then asked if she was interested in him.

"I wasn't sure, but she knows I listen to *Sportstalk* every night, and I think she's listening right now," he said.

After asking her name, I did a shout-out to her saying, "Sharon, if you are interested in Trevor please call because we might have a gift for you guys."

With less than two minutes until our sign-off, Sharon called. After she said Trevor was a nice guy, I blew the Fogg horn, set them up for a dinner date and thought nothing more of it ... until four years later when Trevor called with a belated thank you. He said he owed me a dinner because he and Sharon had gotten married a few months earlier.

EPILOGUE

I have been humbled by comments from listeners over the years, but it was extra cool to hear from guests who had once been listeners. For example, Cliff Ronning, Joe Sakic, Milan Lucic and Mark Recchi were among many who told me they were listeners while playing minor or junior hockey in the area. Brendan Morrison told me he called the show at age thirteen with a question for that night's guest — who happened to be Wayne Gretzky. In the mid-nineties, Jarome Iginla once spotted me from one end of the Kamloops arena, briskly walked to see me at the other end, extended his hand and said, "Mr. Russell, I listen to your show all the time and really respect what you do."

Rare as it was, one night after a show in the early nineties I was talked into going across the street to the bar at the Georgia Hotel where only a few folks were still scattered around the lounge. We were so busy talking that I wasn't really paying attention to the entertainment. But when the young singer took his break, he asked if he could join us for a few minutes because he wanted me to know he was a regular listener who enjoyed *Sportstalk*. Many years later, he called in and displayed his great sense of humour.

"Hi Dan, it's Michael Bublé. Of course, I want to congratulate you on your twenty-fifth anniversary, but more than that I want to say thank you for the singing lessons. Those many hours and tireless nights helping me define my voice. The breathing exercises were huge for me, and a lot of people don't know this, but also the dancing lessons were good too. Honestly, sincerely, what a joy to listen to for these years. Thank you very much for being great for all of us."

Before I started this project, there were only a few times I missed not having the show: most notably the night Pat Quinn died, when Henrik and Daniel Sedin retired, when a Canadian team won the NBA championship, or in the aftermath of all the sports being cancelled at the start of the COVID-19 pandemic. I actually wasn't sure I wanted to start this in case I didn't like what I heard, but this project has caused me to go back and listen to old recordings for the first time since ending the show. Though I'm not claiming *Sportstalk* was the end-all, in listening back I have determined it was better than I had thought.

My biggest regret?

Not having time to enjoy it enough while it was happening because there always was another show to plan.

Acknowledgments

There are many people I want to thank, but there is one person I want to thank a lot. Gregg Drinnan, former sports editor for the *Regina Leader-Post* and the *Kamloops Daily News*, who I got to know in the 1990s during my WHL travels, became my trusted sounding board as soon as I became serious about completing this project. His fresh eyes were the first to see each chapter. His decades of writing experience — including co-authoring *Sudden Death: The Incredible Saga of the 1986 Swift Current Broncos*, and his popular Taking Note website — was a godsend in terms of initial edits and suggestions. But it was his encouragement, professionalism and trustworthiness through every step of this process that kept me most motivated.

Huge thanks to my three long-time producers, Scott Woodgate, Bob Addison and Heath Morgan. They were the unsung heroes of *Sportstalk*, and they worked tirelessly to keep the bar high.

I'm forever indebted to Roger Bourbonnais, who was introduced to me by Pat Quinn and Brian Burke in 1990, for keeping me calm while providing the soundest of advice. Without him, *Sportstalk* never would have lasted three decades.

Special thanks to Roy Kendal, Lee Powell, Brook Ward and Steve Snelgrove for jogging my memory with many *Sportstalk* facts and recollections.

Additionally, I want to thank Bob Alexander, my research assistant, for his tremendous help in gathering and isolating many entries from our *Sportstalk* diaries and assorted archives.

Also, a bigger than huge thanks to Cathy Russell, who inspirationally helped me in more ways than I could ever describe, but specifically (and tirelessly) with photos, interior design, and our website.

Thanks to Tellwell Publishing and their professional team who guided me through every step of this process, including editor Darin Steinkey, a loyal *Sportstalk* listener and (like yours truly) a lover of both radio and sports.

Lastly, I will always be thankful to the thousands of guests and callers who came on the show ... but I'm most humbled and eternally grateful to all those who faithfully listened each night and dutifully followed me around the radio dial. I wish they could all play with the *Sportstalk* Orchestra!

CPSIA information can be obtained
at www.ICGtesting.com
Printed in the USA
LVHW050010030622
720385LV00002B/144